Regional Development in Australia

T0330931

In Australia, regions are not just geographic locations, they are also cultural ideas. Being regional means being located outside the nation's capital cities and in the periphery of its centres of power and influence. Regional development in Australia is thus significantly different from its European or American counterparts. However, surprisingly little has been written about the unique dynamics of development in Australia's regions; this book has been written to fill that gap.

In recent decades the Australian government has made repeated policy efforts to achieve sustainable development in its non-metropolitan areas. Over the same period, those who live and work outside the nation's capital cities have come to identify as regional Australians. This book takes an anthropological approach to understanding the particularities of regional development in Australia. It draws upon rich, on-the-ground observations of towns, industries, universities, development organisations, and communities across different settings to provide an in-depth understanding of the subject.

This book will be of interest to researchers and practitioners concerned with regional development and policy.

Robyn Eversole is Director of the Institute for Regional Development, University of Tasmania, Australia. She is an anthropologist of development and the author of several books including *Knowledge Partnering for Community Development*. She is originally from West Virginia, USA.

'In *Regional Development in Australia* Robyn Eversole demonstrates her profound capacity to challenge our established – and too often unquestioned – understanding of what it means to live and work outside the nation's capitals. This elegantly written book sheds new light on the social and economic processes shaping regional Australia and throws up new possibilities for its future development. *Regional Development in Australia* is a book of potentially enormous benefit for researchers, policy makers, economic development practitioners and all those who study how non metropolitan places grow or decline.' — *Andrew Beer, Dean, Research and Innovation, University of South Australia Business School, Australia*

'Robyn Eversole presents a valuable and original analysis of the state of Regional Australia that goes beyond identifying problems to propose realistic solutions.' — *Professor John Tomaney, Bartlett School of Planning, University College London and Fellow of the Regional Australia Institute, UK*

'This book is both a reflective and provocative contribution to the study of regional development in Australia. [...] Robyn Eversole brings her lived experience of regional Australia to this book and her analysis of the experience of 'doing' regional development is empathetic, perceptive and well informed. This books celebrates the complexities of non-metropolitan Australia and the many people who are dedicated to its viability and sustainability. It is not however shy of articulating the often city-centric decisions and policies which clearly do not understand the particular nuances of regional Australia and which so often undermine the potential opportunities of this highly productive but also challenging environment.' — *Professor Fiona Haslam McKenzie, Co-Director, Centre for Regional Development, The University of Western Australia, Australia*

'Eversole has a perceptive grasp of the contemporary issues and challenges for widening conceptions of regional development in Australia.' — *Professor Andy Pike, Director, Centre for Urban and Regional Development Studies (CURDS), UK*

'In this *tour de force* Robyn Eversole brings great insight into the challenges facing regional Australia. Her anthropological perspective shines a light on aspects of life in regional Australia overlooked by the dominant regional science paradigms of geography and economics. It is a must read for metropolitan-based policy-makers concerned with the future of regional Australia. Notwithstanding the continuing 'institutional gap' Eversole reveals between local and central institutions we are left with an optimistic view of the capability of regional Australians to address the challenges they face.' — *Dr John Martin, Emeritus Professor, La Trobe University, Australia*

'Robyn Eversole provides an insightful analysis of the Australian regional development situation, melding her theoretical knowledge with significant practical experience in regions around Australia. The reasons for our lack of progress in many regions are exposed, as are the ways in which our outdated assumptions about the state of play in many places clouds our judgement about how to best enable a brighter future outside our major cities. The book serves as an essential brief for anyone seeking to make an impact in their region or in regional policy.' — *Jack Archer, CEO, Regional Australia Institute, Australia*

'Robyn Everesole has produced a succinct but deeply insightful review of key aspects of regional development in Australia. The predominance of an anthropological rather than economic perspective on regional processes and experience is a refreshing contrast to many other Australian commentaries. Her account is highly personal yet comprehensive in the other sources on which draws, and the onsights which she presents to complement her own. This is a very useful resource not only for students of regional development in large developed countries, but also for researchers and policy makers who will find thaf she offers many thought-provoking insights.' — *Professor Bruce Wilson, Director of the European Union Centre, RMIT University, Australia*

Routledge advances in regional economics, science and policy

Regional Development in Australia

Being regional

Robyn Eversole

Routledge
Taylor & Francis Group

LONDON AND NEW YORK

First published 2016 by Routledge

2 Park Square, Milton Park, Abingdon, Oxfordshire OX14 4RN
711 Third Avenue, New York, NY 10017

Routledge is an imprint of the Taylor & Francis Group, an informa business

First issued in paperback 2017

British Library Cataloguing in Publication Data
A catalogue record for this book is available from the British Library

Library of Congress Cataloging in Publication Data
Eversole, Robyn, author.
Regional development in Australia: being regional / Robyn Eversole.
pages cm
Includes bibliographical references and index.
1. Regional planning—Australia. 2. Cultural landscapes—Australia. I. Title.
HT395.A9E94 2016
307.1'20994—dc23
2015029457

ISBN: 978-1-138-92020-0 (hbk)
ISBN: 978-0-8153-5987-6 (pbk)

Typeset in Times New Roman
by Book Now Ltd, London

For colleagues and students across regional Australia
With gratitude and respect

Contents

Introduction
Regional Australia

Regions

In my first job post-PhD as a regional manager in an international development programme, I worked across seven different Latin American countries. *Regions* in that context meant world regions: groupings of countries such as Latin America, Eastern Europe, or South East Asia. Later, when I started to engage with the field of regional studies, I discovered a very different definition of regions. These were *sub-national* regions: groups of localities, cities, and towns rather than countries. Like world regions, they were geographic units – places with something in common. But these *regions* were observable. They were local enough to reveal on-the-ground interactions among people and organisations. As an anthropologist, I was intrigued. I took a job as a regional development researcher in Australia. And I discovered that here, *regions* meant something different again.

In Australia, *regions* are not just a geographic category. They are also a cultural category. When I came to Australia, I discovered that living in a region meant certain things. On the one hand, regions in Australia are geographic places with particular characteristics – just like regions anywhere in the world. On the other hand, *regions* in Australia carry layers of meaning that have nothing to do with the particularities of a particular geographic place. Indeed, it is not uncommon for Australians to speak of 'living in the regions'. This does not mean they are living in multiple geographic places. Rather, they are living in a common cultural place: regional Australia.

I soon discovered that having chosen to base myself outside the capital cities where about two-thirds of the Australian population live, I was therefore *regional*. This quickly became a new thread in my identity: the *regional* researcher, based on the university's *regional* campus, living in a *regional* community. Being regional meant particular things in Australia. It came with a certain social and political positioning. It involved some explicit expectations – and often, thinly veiled assumptions. In the first years, I assumed these were simply character-istic of the particular region where I lived. But when I moved to other regions, very different ones, the trappings of 'regional' identity stuck. I was in a different region, yes. But I was still living in the regions.

So what are Australian regions? In a country of over 7 million square kilometres, regions are many and diverse. They have names like Riverina and Barossa, South West and North West, Illawarra and Pilbara. They are multiple and often overlapping. Some are functional economic regions – tied together by strong economic links as workers and firms interact. Often, however, regions are drawn on a map for administrative or marketing purposes, defined differently by different people and organisations. No one exhaustive list of Australian regions exists. Tourism regions (about 84 of them) are different from Natural Resource Management (NRM) regions (totalling 79).[1] Neither grouping necessarily corresponds with the regions defined by various regional authorities, development commissions, and regional development committees – of which there are many, at federal, state, and local levels.[2]

Any given Australian locality may thus belong to two, or three, or four different regions, each defined differently for different purposes.[3] Nor do these various regional boundaries necessarily coincide with residents' understanding of where they live – their own regional identity. Yet despite their fuzzy and contested boundaries, many of Australia's regions nevertheless have strong identity and history, and distinctive social, cultural, and environmental attributes. Regions in Australia are places 'large enough to have an impact in competitive globalised economies, yet small enough to capitalise on relationships of trust within the region and share identity as members of a regional community.'[4] They are like sub-national regions elsewhere in the world – with one exception: Australian regions are located outside the nation's capital cities. By definition, they are non-metropolitan.

In common parlance, Australia has no metropolitan regions. Regions in Australia are the 'areas outside the capital cities'.[5] By definition they are non-metropolitan places. People who live in Melbourne, Sydney, Brisbane, Adelaide, Perth, or Canberra are not *regional*.[6] People who live in rural areas of Australia are regional. Yet the terms *rural* and *regional* – often used together, as in 'rural and regional Australia' – are not synonymous. Australia has numerous significant regional cities: such as Newcastle, Albury–Wodonga, Geelong, Townsville, and Cairns, among others. It also has many large regional towns. Most Australian regions are a mix of cities, towns of various sizes, and countryside: cultivated farmland, uncultivated bush, and the remote outback. Regions range from populated coastal cities to remote outback deserts.[7] Capital cities are, however, intentionally excluded.[8]

It is a significant exclusion. Economically, Australia's fastest-growing and best-performing economies are metropolitan.[9] Two-thirds of the country's population – 66 per cent – choose to live in its eight capital cities.[10] The two biggest state capitals, Sydney and Melbourne, together contain about two-fifths of the nation's population.[11] In most Australian states – Victoria, New South Wales, South Australia, and Western Australia – more people live in the state capital than in the regions.[12] Australia's economic, social, and cultural activity is heavily concentrated in its capital cities; they are significant centres of population growth, and projections suggest that over the next decades the Australian population will become even more concentrated in its capitals.[13]

Being regional in Australia means being located outside these dynamic, growing centres. Australian regions are geographic places with distinctive social, economic, cultural, and environmental attributes, but there is one attribute they all share. The regions are all places on the nation's periphery, on the fringe of a metropolitan mainstream.

Regional issues

Australia's regions as a group have emerged from a particular historical and geographical context. This has generated some distinctly Australian regional issues – and some peculiarly Australian approaches to regional development. Internationally, regional development theory and practice have evolved in very different contexts. While the international literature speaks clearly to some aspects of the Australian regional development experience, on other aspects it is silent. An up-close look at Australian regional issues reveals some of the key differences.

First, regional issues in Australia have a particular geography. Australia's regions are located in a large, sparsely populated, and at the same time highly urbanised continent: very different to the United States, the United Kingdom, or Europe. Next, regional issues in Australia have a particular history: English colonialism, then a post-colonial administration that retained many of the features of top-down, centralised ways of working. Together, geography and history have set the stage for many of Australia's regional issues today: creating particular cultural attitudes about regions and capital cities.

Over the past 200 years, the nation's elites, investment, and decision-making apparatus have been concentrated in a handful of coastal cities.[14] Meanwhile, the vast rest of the country has provided the raw resources to create a successful colony and nation. From the early days of colonisation, Australia has been divided into administrative centres and their working hinterlands, separated by deep social, economic, and geographic divides.[15]

In the colonial regime, new forms of government and economic activity were layered over existing Aboriginal societies – rendering them invisible and appropriating their resources.[16] New settler communities were dispersed across the landscape to produce food and wool for urban centres and for export.[17] These communities were often geographically isolated and highly resourceful – by necessity – at the local level, while ultimately dependent on commodity markets and government decisions in far-off urban centres.

In this way, Australia's regions were created as servants of the capital cities. Each state capital became the economic and political gatekeeper for diverse but largely rural regions, mediating their access to goods and markets, while limiting the development of local infrastructure, institutions, and leadership.[18] This is a 'dependency' argument, that Australian regions were structurally created to be dependent on the capitals. Yet dependency is only part of the story.

Australian regions did not quietly accept a position of dependency. At the local level, in a far-flung continent, local communities had to rely on themselves.

They developed considerable independence, and strong identities apart from – and often in opposition to – the capital cities. Resentment at the power of distant capitals led to various political movements for 'new states' that would decentralise control to more regional scales.[19] Yet these new states movements were ultimately unsuccessful. Australia's six states stayed geographically large, and still administered from their coastal capitals.

Australian regions are simultaneously dependent, and independent-minded. Despite their diversity, they share a common identity as part of the Australia that lies outside the capital cities. It has been observed that Australia's non-metropolitan regions are largely under the control of city-based social, political, and economic forces, and yet 'in other important respects, non-metropolitan Australia is another nation'.[20] It does not seem to matter whether the region in question is a wealthy ex-squatter district or a once-booming manufacturing centre, regions are always very different places than capital cities.

The divide between the nation's regions and its capitals sits at the heart of regional issues in Australia. It has grown deeper than geography and history to become cultural, part of how Australians see the world. Today, it is possible to stand 60 kilometres outside the central business district of a capital city, or 600, in a rural crossroads or a bustling business district, and be regional. 'Regionalism' – the articulation of a regional identity – has two components in Australia. The first is identification with a particular geographic territory – one's own region. The second is the shared identity, the common condition of being beyond the capitals, in a shared place called *regional Australia*.

Regional issues in Australia are thus a mix of place-specific concerns – the constraints and opportunities that face particular regions – and the issues and concerns that are shared across all of Australia's non-metropolitan regions. If regional Australia is another nation, its common language is a sense of isolation, of distance from the centres of decision-making. Its shared issues revolve around questions of *equity* – between the regions and the capital cities – and *sustainability* – economic, social, and environmental.

These regional issues burst onto the Australian scene with particular vigour in the late 1990s and the turn of the new millennium. Threats to the sustainability of Australian regional communities launched regional issues to the forefront of public debate. A volatile cocktail of industry deregulation, global competition, service rationalisation, and environmental issues was bringing rapid change to many regions. A state of 'regional emergency' began to pervade the national consciousness.[21] It was observed at that time that: 'Many of Australia's regional people are confronting – and are confronted by – a period of fundamental change…. They are finding their communities depleted and their social relationships disrupted…. They are feeling increasingly insecure.'[22]

While these changes affected different regions differently, they gave rise to a common public discourse of Australian *regional issues*. These issues generally revolved around the withdrawal of services from regions, demographic threats to local populations, and downsizing or loss of significant regional industries. The debates focused on equity for regional Australians – who in many cases were clearly being disadvantaged by these changes – as well as the ultimate sustainability of regional communities.

Previous writing about Australian regional issues has focused disproportion-ately on rural areas, especially small towns dependent on agriculture.[23] This is because the stories of rural Australian communities losing their banks, schools, football clubs, services, and people have provided particularly stark expressions of what it means to live in the part of the Australia that lies beyond the capital cities. 'At risk' farming communities are not just a historical fact; they are potent cultural symbols of the issues that people grapple with regularly in Australia's non-metropolitan regions.

While not all Australian regions face such stark conditions, all share the same positioning vis-à-vis the nation's capital cities. Regional Australia is not nec-essarily rural or agricultural, but it is always peripheral to the nation's social, economic, and cultural centres. This leads to an ongoing quest for equity: for equal voice, equal investment, and an equitable level of services. It also leads to looming questions of sustainability – even for regions that are growing. In the end, sustainability is negotiated on the ground, but many of the key decisions are made elsewhere.

Regional development policy

In recent decades, the Australian government has made repeated efforts to achieve regional development in its non-metropolitan regions.[24] Politically volatile narra-tives of regional disadvantage and inequity emerge on a regular basis in Australian public discourse. The regions as a collective demand a 'fair share' of services and investment, while particular regions struggle through downturns that threaten their economic and social sustainability.[25] The imperative to act in favour of Australian regions ebbs and flows with the political climate, creating a fragmented landscape of regional policy initiatives.

Ideas from overseas about regional development find a ready audience here. Ideas like endogenous development – development driven from within regions – and regional-scale governance mechanisms have been widely adopted. Regions are regularly encouraged to leverage their peculiar attributes to create innovation from within. Yet while borrowing generously from overseas policy approaches, regional development in Australia is in many ways unique.

Regional development in Australia starts from the understanding that capital cities are always the dominant places. Thus, the underpinning frameworks guid-ing regional development assume that *regional development* is always about non-metropolitan regions. In turn, all non-metropolitan regions share an essential state of disadvantage – regardless of their other attributes, they are not capital cities.[26] This peculiarly Australian framing of regional development has made it possible to simultaneously follow international policy trends and execute them in quite distinctive ways.

First, Australian regional development policy, as in many other countries, seeks to address regional disadvantage through endogenous development: stimulating and facilitating development from within, rather than primarily through external investment or industry attraction.[27] As elsewhere, there is a recognition that less-advantaged regions can grow their capabilities and advantages by harnessing their distinctive regional attributes. In the Australian context, however, the starting point for endogenous development is always deficit-based. Regions all have specific attributes; the organisations, institutions, knowledge, and resource configurations that can potentially act as unique drivers of growth are there. Yet these attributes are subsumed under the common identity of *regions* grappling with shared *regional issues*. The focus is on shared problems, rather than specific opportunities. While in the European Union regional development policy 'seeks to replicate or nurture the positive environmental conditions that the best-performing regions offer', Australia does not.[28] Its best-performing regions are not, in fact, regional.

Second, Australian regional development policy places considerable emphasis on regional-scale governance and 'place-based' policy solutions. According to the OECD, 'a necessary condition for implementing regional development policy is strong regional governance'.[29] Yet despite the dizzying array of regional agencies, authorities, committees, and other regional development bodies that can be observed on the landscape, there is very little actual regional governance in Australia. In Australia, regions are sites of poorly coordinated, multi-layered intervention by three non-regional tiers of government (federal, state, and local). Despite the proliferation of regional programmes – and central programmes that affect regions – there is no real decision-making authority at regional level. Rather, there is a 'general unwillingness of central governments (either State or Commonwealth) to devolve real responsibility for regional development to regions themselves'.[30]

Regional development policy in Australia thus emphasises regional-scale action, but it sets effective limits on what regional actors can actually do. Furthermore, the policy positioning is reactive, dealing with problems and issues rather than opportunities. It is unsurprising that commentators generally give Australian regional policy poor marks. They observe that 'fragmentation is one of the defining characteristics of the Australian model of regional development' and that Australian regional development agencies are usually ephemeral, with high birth and death rates.[31] In the end in Australia, 'much of what passes for regional strategy consists of regions seeking largesse from central governments'.[32] With most resources controlled from the centre, regional organisations can do little else.

In Australia, international ideas about endogenous development and place-based solutions have permeated the regional development landscape, but they have been implemented in particular ways. Australian regional development policy devolves responsibility to regions on the theory that they know their own development potential best. Yet ultimately, resources and decision-making power are retained in the capital cities. This contradiction sits at the heart of Australian regional development efforts.

Re-imagining regional Australia

Australia's regions can be described as peripheral outposts in a peripheral country. Yet seen up close, region by region, each has its own distinctive attributes and potential. Australia's regions have breathtaking coastlines and mountains, rich soils and clear waters, ancient heritage and vibrant contemporary cultures.

When viewed through the lens of capital-city administrators, however, these distinctive attributes blur and disappear. The regions become distant and largely undifferentiated. Regional issues and problems fill the foreground. The regions themselves reinforce this: they regularly parade their deficits to bid effectively for centrally managed resources. Australia's regions become an undifferentiated landscape of disadvantage, rather than a highly differentiated landscape of possibilities.

Australian regions do face some common issues, born of distance, dispossession, and voicelessness in the nation's – and the world's – centres of power. Yet these need not define them. Every region is a different place, with different potential. Northern tropics, central desert, or temperate rainforest are different landscapes with different opportunities. Emerging regional city, established inland town, or tiny coastal hamlet are attractive in different ways. Each Australian region has distinctive attributes, and many are distinctive on the world stage: tropical agriculture in a first-world economy; world-leading universities in friendly coastal towns with vast beaches; artists, innovators, and entrepreneurs who could live anywhere but who live – by choice – in Australia's regions.

Every day, distance matters less. The globally distinctive attributes of Australia's regions have the potential to be springboards for competitive advantage and ultimately, sustainably high standards of living for regional Australians. Yet the way Australian policy makers see *the regions* renders the opportunities invisible. Regional development policy in Australia is caught in the gap between capital cities and the regions, and it continually reproduces this divide. Those who live and work in Australia's regions regularly observe that they have little say in the decisions that affect them, while those who make the decisions have limited understanding of conditions on the ground.[33] Regional opportunities are hard to see from far away.

In the national imaginary, regional Australia is continually framed as a deficit category. It is defined by what it is not: *not* metropolitan, *not* the hub of the nation's economic activity, *not* up to par with education and health, and in some cases facing severe sustainability challenges.[34] The cultural logic of regional development in Australia is that the nation's non-metropolitan regions need development because their economies, communities, and physical environments are potentially in grave jeopardy. A pervasive narrative of decline suffuses regional development conversations in Australia.

Yet these narratives of deficit and decline are starting to be challenged. Recent research draws attention to the diversity of Australian regions and their experiences; declining regions are only one story among many. In recent decades, many Australian regions have grown, and grown rapidly – and not just from the mining boom.[35] Diverse regional economies have emerged in Australia, including strong regional cities with global connections.[36] Moreover, recent research has highlighted that regional Australians tend to want to stay regional; if they move, they will generally choose another region, rather than a capital city.[37]

Australia's regions are real, diverse places. Only by spending time there is it possible to see what the issues and opportunities really are. On the ground in any particular region, it is possible to observe its particular attributes – and the linkages among the economy, the community, and the environment. Moving beyond the stereotypes of deficit and decline, there is much to be learned from an up-close view of regional Australia.

Four stories

This book takes an up-close look at regional development in the Australian context. It adopts an anthropological approach, using on-the-ground observations of people and organisations to explore how Australian regional development efforts work in practice – and why the results are often not as hoped.

The book starts from the insight that development policy and practice are always framed by particular ways of thinking and understanding the world. Regional development in Australia is underpinned by a particularly Australian understanding of regions, with all that entails. This leads people to 'do' regional development in certain ways, with certain practical consequences. While this book focuses specifically on the Australian context, the analysis presented here can shed light on similar issues in peripheral regions internationally.

Regions in Australia are both geographic facts – real places – and socially constructed ideas about what it means to be regional. Those who live and work in non-metropolitan Australia see themselves, and are seen by others, as regional Australians. They identify with their own region, but also with the wider universe of Australia's non-metropolitan regions. Being regional is one of the cultural ideas that frame how Australians see the world – and how they see themselves.

Anthropologists are interested in how these kinds of shared ideas guide people's actions. In terms of regional development, these ideas give rise to particular 'development logics' or approaches to regional development.[38] These logics influence how people – from policy makers to regional residents – see regional issues and choose to address them. Development logics are not immediately obvious; they are internalised but seldom articulated. They can best be understood via long-term immersions in particular places, where it is possible to observe on-the-ground actions, interactions, and the language that people use to explain what they do.

This book draws on 15 years of living in regional Australia and being involved in regional development work.[39] Each chapter begins with a story from these on-the-ground experiences. The stories have been chosen to illustrate themes that have recurred frequently during these years of involvement in Australian regional development contexts. Each story describes, in detail, experiences and practices in a particular region, where regional development initiatives are implemented and impacts felt.[40] These stories have been written to share insights provided by long-term immersion in the Australian regional development landscape: to enable readers to see, hear, and understand how Australians see *regions* and do *regional development*.

In Australia, when regional development is discussed, certain themes always surface. These are recurring patterns on an otherwise complex and diverse landscape. First, there is the question of *regional community sustainability* – economic, environmental, and social, often articulated at the geographic scale of towns. Then there is the question of *industry transition*, or what to do when a region's linchpin industry is declining. Next, conversations inevitably turn to *education for the regions*, and the need to upskill regional communities to survive and prosper in the knowledge economy. Finally, some conversations probe deeper, to the types of *institutions and governance arrangements* that might support better regional outcomes. These themes sit at the heart of Australian regional development work.

The chapters of this book have been organised around these four themes. Chapter 1 on *Regional Towns* explores the theme of regional community sustainability in Australia. It shows how the logic of isolated, town-scale community action has historically limited the impact of Australian regional development efforts. Next, Chapter 2 on *Regional Industries* unpacks the constant threat of industry decline in Australian regions. It illustrates how the logic of 'old' regional industries in decline systematically renders the new faces of resource-based regional industries invisible.

From there, Chapter 3 on *Regional Universities* describes the multiple roles played by regional university campuses in Australia and how they have been prevented from realising their full regional development potential. Finally, Chapter 4 on *Institutions and Communities* analyses why Australian regional development institutions and governance processes have been ill-equipped to drive place-based development. The concluding chapter summarises the development logics that guide Australian regional development policy and practice, and argues for the need to rethink what it means to be regional in Australia.

Australia's regions have rich assets and enormous opportunities, yet they are typically framed as disadvantaged and lacking. Delving beneath the popular images and debates about regional Australia, the following chapters reveal the on-the-ground experiences of regional communities, industries, and organisations, as they grapple with the contradictions and challenges of being regional. Over and over, regional disadvantage is actively recreated, as policy and practice fragment the knowledge and linkages that are needed to drive regional innovation.

Notes

1 There were 78 tourism regions as at 2011, and 79 Natural Resource Management (NRM) regions (ABS 2011); TRA 2011 includes additional regions, bringing the total tourism regions to 84. The most up-to-date breakdown of Australian tourism regions, with maps, is available at ABS 2014a.

2 For instance, at Commonwealth level there are 55 Regional Development Australia Committees which report to the federal Minister for Infrastructure and Regional Development. Previously there were other iterations of nationally defined regional authorities such as Area Consultative Committees (ACCs). At state level, Western

Australia has nine Regional Development Commissions. Tasmania has an organisation for each of its three regions: the Cradle Coast Authority in the North West, Southern Tasmanian Councils Authority, and Northern Tasmania Development. Queensland and the Northern Territory have a regional tier of local government known as Regional Councils (see ABS 2014b). Regional Development Victoria recognises five Victorian regions and has 17 offices across regional Victoria. The New South Wales state government formerly had its own Regional Development Boards but now works with the federal government on the appointment of RDA Committees, as does the South Australian government.

3   Budge *et al.*'s 1992 study of regional housing observed that 'many country communities find themselves split between a number of regional groupings of various departments' (p. 35). The study cites 'dissatisfaction with regional arrangements, frequent changes to regional boundaries and the fact that different departments use different regions' as important concerns expressed by regional Australians at that time (Budge *et al.* 1992, pp. 33–34).

4   Eversole and Martin 2005, p. 3.

5   This common parlance has also been reflected in much of the academic work on regional Australia. McManus and Pritchard 2000, p. ix use the term 'rural and regional Australia' to refer to 'areas outside the capital cities', noting that this 'is consistent with current usage by Australian governments and the media'. Similarly, in *A Future for Regional Australia*, Gray and Lawrence 2001, p. 2 use the term *regional* to refer 'to that part of Australia and its population which has a distinctive relationship … with metropolitan Australia', and Beer 2000, p. 183 notes that the regional development agencies 'are generally limited to the non-metropolitan parts of each State'.

6   For instance, the recent *Regional Wellbeing Survey* focused on 'all areas outside the major metropolitan centres of Sydney, Melbourne, Adelaide, Brisbane and Perth' (Schirmer and Berry 2014, p. 3). People who live in the smaller and more remote state and territory capitals (Hobart and Darwin) occupy an ambivalent position. Some claim that they, too, are regional, but the accepted usage of regional in public and policy discourse excludes all capital cities from the definition.

7   For a discussion of the diversity encompassed in the term 'regional Australia', see Hugo 2002.

8   One notable exception is the annual *State of the Regions* report, which uses an international definition of regions. These reports specifically include metropolitan regions (both core and dispersed) (NE/ALGA 2014).

9   See e.g. PWC 2014, p. 5.

10 ABS 2014c. Capital cities are defined based on the Greater Capital City Statistical Areas (GCCSA); each state and territory is split into a capital city (including suburbs) and rest of state region. As at 2013, 66 per cent of the Australian population was living in a capital city – that is, Sydney, Melbourne, Perth, Brisbane, Adelaide, Darwin, Hobart, or Canberra. This proportion has held reasonably constant over the last 40 years; in 1973 it was 65 per cent of the population. The actual numbers of people living in cities have, however, nearly doubled over this time.

11 ABS 2014d, np states that: 'In 2013, just over one fifth of Australia's population lived within Greater Sydney, while just under one fifth lived in Greater Melbourne.'

12 ABS 2014c. This is also the case for the Northern Territory; Darwin was the fastest-growing capital city over the period 1973–2013. Greater Perth now accounts for 78 per cent of Western Australia's population, up from 71 per cent in 1973. In Queensland and Tasmania, slightly less than half the population lives in the capital: 42 per cent of Tasmanians live in Hobart; 48 per cent of Queenslanders live in Brisbane.

13 ABS 2015 observes that the combined population of Australian capital cities between 30 June 2013 and 30 June 2014 represented 79 per cent of total national population growth. This capital-centred growth pattern is nothing new; Hugo 2002, pp. 17–18 observed that the country's four largest capital cities (Sydney, Melbourne,

Brisbane, and Perth) each grew by over a million people since the 1970s. ABS 2014c, Series B projections show the proportion of people living in a capital city increasing from 66 per cent in 2013 to 72 per cent in 2053.

14 Sher and Sher observed this back in 1994: 'Australia has the vast majority of its population, its corporate headquarters, its government offices, its universities, and its cultural institutions based within a handful of large metropolitan areas. So, it is only natural to assume that Australia's major cities are the places around which the nation as a whole revolves ... (creating a) mental map of powerful urban centres (the strong core) and relatively powerless hinterland communities (the weak periphery) (which) has guided – albeit often subconsciously – the portrayal of, and policies toward, the nation's rural people and places' (Sher and Sher 1994, p. 6).

15 For an excellent historical overview of the city–country divide in Australia, and its contemporary political manifestations, see Brett 2011.

16 They were rendered invisible via the legal fiction of *terra nullius*, the occupation of so-called 'empty land'; and exclusion from access to land, water, hunting rights, etc. Given the evidence of extensive pre-colonial Aboriginal settlement of Australia, many in Indigenous Australian circles now refer to the 'colonisation' of Australia as an 'invasion.'

17 Pritchard *et al.* 2012, p. 542 note that: 'agriculture developed not to furnish food for local populations (as in Europe), but to produce barely transformed commodities for export to distant urban populations, often a hemisphere away'. The focus of Australian agricultural policy from the 1930s encouraged land settlement and the establishment of family farms with a strong export focus (Gray and Lawrence 2001; Pritchard *et al.* 2012).

18 Gray and Lawrence 2001, p. 6, for instance, have observed that in Australia, 'The capital cities became conduits for the inflow of money and the outflow of goods. The regions ... were never to be self-directing.' Pritchard *et al.* 2012, p. 542 argue that this historical relationship created the conditions for structurally dependent regional towns, as 'relatively little of the surplus made its way back to the producing regions, thus truncating the establishment of diverse service economies in local towns'.

19 Given the large geographic areas covered by Australia's six states (and various territories), new state movements sought to form new states that more accurately reflected regional identities. See Brown 2005 for a discussion of new state movements and a history of regional-scale governance debates in Australia.

20 Bowman 1981, pp. xxvi–xxvii.

21 McManus and Pritchard 2000, p. 1 note that, 'the concerns of rural and regional Australians are now planted in the national consciousness'. Brett 2011 describes how these concerns manifested in the following election.

22 Gray and Lawrence 2001, p. 41.

23 For instance, Cocklin and Alston 2003; Gray and Lawrence 2001; Pritchard and McManus 2000; Rogers and Jones 2006; and others.

24 Regional development in Australia has been defined as 'The deliberate attempt by government (at any level) and/or regional actors to influence regional outcomes, either in in relation to the economy, the community or the environment, or all three, with varying objectives that generally relate to some notion of "regional well-being"' (quoted in Collits 2015, p. 20). Paul Collits provides an overview of Australian regional policy since World War Two. He notes that: 'Following an early focus on decentralisation, more recently regional policy has clearly shifted toward the support of regional competitive advantage and community driven development strategies. There is a shared commitment by governments to assisting (still mainly) rural places to diversify their economies. As well, in the last decade, there has also been a shift away from productivity focused policies towards "sustainability" and "liveability"' (Collits 2015, p. 29).

25 On regional equity and a 'fair share', see Brett 2011. On structural adjustment in reaction to downturns as Australia's de facto regional development policy, see Beer 2015.

26 Paul Collits has observed that 'there has been a broad focus on non-metropolitan regions in policy interventions, reflecting a long standing historical emphasis on the country–city divide and a sense that in Australia, the "regional problem" is the overconcentration of population and economic activity in the capital cities' (Collits 2015, p. 29).

27 See e.g. OECD 2009, pp. 50–51 for a description of international trends toward endogenous development approaches.

28 Quote from OECD 2009, p. 64. Collits 2015, p. 30, in his overview of Australian regional policy, explicitly contrasts Australian and European Union regional development policy, noting that 'the overall preference of Australian Governments has been for relatively limited interventions'. Most interventions of any substance have tended to be reactions to need rather than intentional efforts to build upon regional strengths (see also Beer 2015).

29 OECD 2009, p. 108.

30 Collits 2015, p. 31. Andrew Beer 1999, pp. 187–188 has also documented the complexity of the regional development landscape in Australia, observing that: 'There are numerous agencies and multiple programs operating unevenly across the nation' and that 'Local and regional development agencies are supported by all tiers of government in Australia and by individual communities'. While local government has some involvement in regional issues, its positioning in the Australian political system makes it largely a servant of state government.

31 Beer 1999, pp. 188–190.

32 Collits and Rowe 2015, p. 79.

33 See e.g. Faulkner *et al.* 2013, p. 21; Gross 2015, p. 299; and various examples in Eversole and Martin 2005 and Dibden *et al.* 2001.

34 The analysis provided by rural sociologists Gray and Lawrence 2001 is typical: they have observed that 'pressures are being exerted which "force" regions to exploit both their people and their natural resources' (p. 12) and that 'The challenge for regional Australia at the beginning of the twenty-first century is not just to fix its social and economic policies, but rather to build socially, economically and environmentally strong communities which have the necessary linkages with global capital, but which have a prospect beyond this season's price for traditional products like coal, beef or wheat' (p. 188).

35 For instance, Race *et al.* 2010, p. 4 summarise two broad-brush trends: 'The sustained decline in viability of commodity farming for small/medium-sized businesses has led to depopulation in large swathes of the rural landscape, while the increasing wealth of urbanites who can afford and value a rural lifestyle has led to re-population in attractive, "liveable" parts of the countryside.'

36 It is now possible, for instance, to work in Cairns and ski in Japan. While the nation's population was traditionally concentrated in the south and east of the continent, some of the thriving regional cities are now in the north (e.g. Rockhampton, Townsville, Cairns). Furthermore, the development of northern Australia has emerged as an important regional policy issue (Kinnear and Charters 2014, p. 1; NE/ALGA 2014, pp. 59–80).

37 The *2013 Regional Wellbeing Survey* found that of respondents living in regional Australia, 'More than 80% of those who were likely to move in the next 12 months planned to move to a country area or regional city, while less than 20% planned to shift to a large city' (Schirmer and Berry 2014, p. 7). This study 'suggested a majority of rural and regional Australians felt good about their community and its future … find their local community a good place to live in, are proud to live in it and feel it has a positive future' (Schirmer and Berry 2014, p. 5).

38 See e.g. Olivier de Sardan 2005, who also distinguishes between the 'notional' and 'strategic' logics of development actors (pp. 149–151).

39 For over 15 years I lived in Australian regional localities and towns, worked on regional university campuses, and occupied professional academic roles in university-based

regional development centres and institutes. I have lived and worked for extended periods of time in three Australian states and, previously, in the Northern Territory; and have spent time in every state. While my experience is certainly not inclusive of every part of regional Australia, I have been fortunate to experience and work in a cross-section of Australian regions and localities.

40 The stories are framed as ethnographic narratives, using a form of auto-ethnography in which the author describes a cultural setting in which he or she is a long-term participant.

1   Regional towns

A story about towns

When I arrived in Australia in the winter of 2000 to take a research role in a new university-based Centre for Regional Development, I was lent a university car and advised to take to the two-lane roads and visit some *regional communities*. These 'regional communities' were, I discovered, towns: small towns from one hundred to several thousand people, scattered across the landscape of the South West, Wheatbelt, and Great Southern regions of Western Australia. Each town had its own place on the physical landscape, separated by wide swathes of sparsely populated forests, farmland, and coast. Visiting these *regional communities* on the far edge of the Australian continent was, I was told, the logical starting point for my work. Here, I was told, was where I would learn about regional development issues first-hand.

The Centre that employed me was new, tiny, and located in a small city of about 30,000 people: a 'regional city'. This Centre was located on a 'regional campus' of a public university with headquarters in the state capital of Perth. Perth was a capital city, but mostly it was just *Perth*: the centre, the head office of nearly everything. Our Centre had been established on the University's regional campus as a vehicle for the university to explore regional development issues and opportunities. From the start, however, the most compelling *regional development issues* were understood to be located not in the regional city itself, but further afield: in the much smaller regional communities scattered across the Western Australian countryside.

These small towns each had a distinctive character and identity. Once learned, their names each conjured a particular image: of forests or mines, dairy farms or beaches, broad acre crops or wineries. Harvey was a dairy town (though it had wineries and citrus as well), while Busselton was known for its beach culture. Wagin was a wool-growing area, while Narrogin had broad acre cropping, primarily wheat. Manjimup was a forestry town (though forestry was restructuring and a new 'Regional Forest Agreement' has recently been signed).[1] Collie was a mining town, but one that was looking for new economic options. Regional communities were known for certain things: Bridgewater for its blues festival, Balingup for its medieval festival, Margaret River for its wine. Towns not known for anything in particular – or whose identity was rooted in transitioning industries – were regional communities at risk.

One of my first efforts at getting to know regional communities involved a dusty several-hour trek up a narrow highway to a small Wheatbelt town, where I had been invited to attend a community meeting. There, a group of farmers was exploring a new industry opportunity that would allow them to diversify beyond traditional broad acre agriculture, another industry in transition. The community meeting had been called to discuss the economic potential of raising fish and shellfish in farm dams and local weirs. The concept was referred to as *inland aquaculture*. For colleagues in my home Centre, *inland aquaculture in the Wheatbelt* was exactly the kind of regional development we were looking for. It was an example of a regional community instigating a process of regional development, drawing on their local resources to create something new.

The meeting had been organised by a local business development advisor and a representative from the local Shire. The aim was to explore the potential of inland aquaculture for the local community. In a farming context where salinity was a growing problem, having slightly salty water in farm dams and local weirs could actually be an asset. The meeting focused on how to tap into this asset to diversify the local economy. The meeting attendees were mostly farmers – both men and women. An invited speaker from the state fisheries department discussed the issues and opportunities involved in inland fish production. Farmers from other Wheatbelt towns shared their experiences of raising trout in farm dams and tanks; they had recently participated in fish-raising trials with the fisheries department. Observing the meeting, different agendas quickly became apparent.

The speaker from the fisheries department spoke on the business potential of inland aquaculture, and encouraged the meeting attendees to look beyond fish production to value-added products such as tinned smoked trout, shown to be popular with consumers. The farmers focused on the logistics of farming trout, querying the details of fish production and its feasibility: cost of fingerlings, likely profits, seasonality, and scale of production. The meeting organisers, meanwhile, placed the focus on the local weir and the potential for the town to stock it with trout and become a destination for recreational trout fishing. To accommodate visitors, the business development advisor suggested, the community could construct straw-bale holiday cottages – he would be happy to help build them. With such an icon, this small Wheatbelt town 'could become the straw-bale capital of the state'.

The meeting culminated in the formation of a community committee to explore the feasibility of inland aquaculture for the town. Most of the discussion in the latter part of the meeting focused on ensuring that this committee was properly composed: not too small, not too large, not obviously dominated by men, and not forgetting to include a representative from the local Shire. Of the eight nominated committee members, some were present; others were nominated as community representatives in their absence. The mandate of the Committee was to 'look into whether it was worthwhile' to proceed with the ideas discussed – not specifying which ideas. One representative later assured me that he would make sure the weir was stocked with trout for fishing, regardless of any other initiatives. The farmers, meanwhile, continued to discuss the details of fish production logistics. Their questions were practical; many had no easy answers. It was suggested, therefore, that such details should be left to the new Committee to resolve. Over and over, attendees were told that whatever the initiative, 'the community has to do it'.

Even in these very early visits, I was intrigued by this idea of regional communities as key economic actors. The communities themselves were clearly diverse, with multiple interests and agendas. Yet as a united entity – a committee, stocked with representatives – they were charged with diversifying their local economic base. Town-level action seemed, on first impression, to involve ad hoc committees of volunteers (and those volunteered in their absence), tasked with sorting out complex business decisions. At the same time, other conversations in the area suggested that some people were simply getting on with the process of economic diversification – starting up and sustaining new business ventures on their own farms, such as raising aquarium fish or yabbies.[2] There was evidence of individual entrepreneurship, but much of it seemed to fly under the radar. Regional development discussions focused, rather, on regional communities.

Soon thereafter, I had a chance to extend my first impressions about regional development in Australia. 1 was invited to a rural leadership conference that brought together young people from across Western Australia. The conference seemed a good opportunity to get an overview of regional development issues from those around my own age who were grappling with them first-hand. I attended various sessions, listed to motivational speakers, and even learned the conference theme song. The message was clear, repeated persistently over the two days: rural leaders could change the future of their communities. Exemplars of success abounded. One young man had established an iconic parade – dogs in rural utility vehicles – as a charity fundraiser in his local community. Another couple had started a niche flour business to diversify their community's economy. Another community, repeatedly mentioned, had established itself as an iconic tourism destination based on the possession of a large rock.

Definitions of success were enthusiastic and uncritical. Generating energy and community spirit in local towns was as valuable as generating infrastructure or jobs. Often, the aim of local initiatives seemed to be to come up with something that the town could be known for. Success stories included both individual business ventures and community-run initiatives; all were small and localised. There was a strong focus on farming communities specifically; most initiatives involved farm-based value-adding or agriculture-related community events. Many were local festivals; the most memorable was Western Australia's answer to Pamplona, the Running of the Sheep.[3] Success stories were presented as community successes, even though many were initiated by a single individual. Rural leaders were those who took the initiative to make things happen and collaborate with others. Above all, conference participants were encouraged to *maintain their enthusiasm* when they returned to their own communities.

Over the next months I visited many towns. Time after time these towns – described as 'regional communities' – were cast as key regional development actors.

The language of *community action* and *community initiatives* was omnipresent. There were numerous community committees, local organisations and groups. The general understanding was that regional development initiatives came from 'the community' – locally – in order to 'support the community'. At the same time, the key actors at the centre of these initiatives were often individuals. Community initiatives took a range of forms, from community-run enterprises to private businesses. Some were run by a single entrepreneur or family, some by a community volunteer or voluntary committee. They varied widely in both innovativeness and feasibility, an outpouring of clever and sometimes bizarre ideas from regional communities.

My visits to regional Western Australian towns normally started at a central 'community' institution: a telecentre (online access centre), progress association, or local shire office. In most, it was possible to observe a scramble to identify ideas that would help local towns to reinvent themselves and their fortunes. Sometimes the ideas focused on developing new industries or adding value to existing ones. There were projects exploring the potential of telework to provide local employment options, projects exploring how 'micro elemental mapping' could identify new cropping options for local areas, projects assessing the potential to start a local cheese industry, and even a project exploring the possibility for a local steam train. These ideas were assisted by the availability of some government funding for feasibility studies. Many local projects, however, were simply about generating novelty and distinctiveness. They focused on creating a festival, painting a toilet block, or establishing some other kind of local icon to put 'our town' on the map.

Without exception, it was local people who were expected to meet the challenge of generating ideas and driving change. While the language of 'assets based community development' or 'leveraging regional attributes to construct advantage' was not in common use, local people were clearly expected to leverage their assets and attributes to generate regional development solutions. Local volunteer committees were regularly charged with generating ideas, seeking funding to develop them (usually from the government or the quasi-governmental regional development body), and ultimately bringing their entrepreneurial ideas to fruition.

One town, for instance, possessed a wide-ranging menu of locally driven projects spearheaded by various committees and groups. The town was undergoing downsizing in its traditional mining industry; thus the aims of these community projects included creating employment, reversing population loss, and reinventing the image of the town. One group led the conversion of old mining infrastructure into a motor sports complex; another sought to turn an old post office into a gallery. The tourist train was at feasibility study stage, while there were plans to convert an old goods shed into a rail museum. Meanwhile, another group was conducting trials on the feasibility of viticulture, and another study was exploring the potential for aquaculture in old mine cuts.

There was no shortage of interesting regional development initiatives and ideas in this town; indeed there, as elsewhere at the turn of the millennium, the generation of ideas seemed to have reached a frenetic pace. Yet there was little communication among the different community groups – even among groups working on similar topics. Each idea or project had its own champions, with little or no coordination across projects. All town communities contained multiple communities, and different community groups championed different initiatives. In some towns, community projects even faced opposition from other parts of the local community. Meanwhile projects that linked communities across two or more different towns were practically unheard of. Regional communities addressed their issues separately, not together.

At the same time, the heavy reliance on voluntary committees was starting to tell in many towns. Often, the reality of *regional community action* was that a single person or a very small group was working in isolation to generate and sustain momentum for a community initiative. It was hard for local leaders to *maintain their enthusiasm*. Unsurprisingly, many promising projects never came to fruition. As a farmer in one South West Town observed, 'There's a lot of good ideas about, but they often don't get past stage one. The same people end up on the same committees all the time, and they get burnt out.' Local volunteers also often lacked specialised skills (such as marketing) that they needed to make good ideas succeed. Regional development initiatives were highly localised, small in scale, and usually lacked key resources. Many were never implemented. Few had any long-term impact.

On the ground in Western Australia at the turn of the millennium, *regional communities* were working hard to make regional development happen. Western Australian towns and others like them across Australia were under pressure to inno- vate. They were expected to generate their own solutions to a range of economic, social, and environmental issues. And they responded: not as towns per se, but as leaders, entrepreneurs, voluntary committees, and community-minded groups.

These people successfully identified a range of local assets and attributes, from heritage buildings to landscapes. They leveraged these assets, actively pursuing the funding and business opportunities available to them. They mobilised local energy to generate and develop new ideas – exactly the sort of community-based regional development leadership my colleagues and I had hoped to see. Yet their efforts did not reverse the fortunes of regional towns. Rather, these experiences illustrate how regional development in Australia is defined and implemented in particular ways – with particular consequences for Australia's regional communities.

Regional towns and their issues

> There was hardly a word written about regional development in the late 1990s Australia which did not exhort people to take their futures in hand, because nobody else will.[4]

By the year 2000 the situation facing Australia's small towns had taken centre stage in public and policy imagination. The plight of small, rural towns had become '*the* regional development issue of the 1990s'.[5] Many towns originally established as agricultural service towns were facing multiple threats. Declining employ- ment, shrinking populations, and the centralisation of services and facilities in larger population centres meant that many regional towns were facing a stark choice: change quickly, or die. This focus on declining towns had a profound effect on how policy makers and academics thought about regional Australia and its regional development issues.

Academics have typically explained the situation of regional Australia at the turn of the millennium as the fallout of a cocktail of global economic forces, neo-liberal government policy decisions, and social and demographic trends favouring urbanisation. The result was that resources and people withdrew from many small towns. Small towns became smaller, and some disappeared altogether: leaving empty shops, empty houses, shells of communities with the life sucked out.

It was dubbed the 'crisis of the bush'. Researchers reported deteriorating quality of life in rural areas, and suggested that towns were on a path to becoming 'fewer in number, older and poorer' as well as 'increasingly disadvantaged' if abandoned to market forces.[6] Meanwhile, politicians and commentators argued over what comprised 'a fair share' of resources and services for non-metropolitan communities in a highly urbanised nation.[7] Should regional towns be saved, or should natural attrition prevail? And what could regional communities do to help themselves?

By the turn of the millennium, Australian regional development was focused on peripheral small towns, their decline, and the action that regional communities could take in response. At the same time, another set of regional towns was quietly emerging on the landscape. These were the larger 'regional towns' or 'regional centres'. Through the 1990s, these towns had attracted services and facilities from their smaller neighbours, along with some of their exiting population, leading to the disparaging name of 'sponge centres'. These larger regional towns generally had several thousand residents, often tens of thousands – and a handful of regional cities in the hundreds of thousands. These towns were not 'small' or even 'rural', and they were not necessarily declining. Yet they were still very much regional.

The plight of declining rural towns is only part of the story of regional Australia. Towns in Australia are diverse: they vary in population size, demographic trajectories, key industries, and the economic and social roles they play. Not all regional towns in Australia have an agricultural base or a rural identity. Not all are declining: indeed, many are stable, growing, or growing rapidly. Nevertheless, all identify as *regional*, and all share common issues.

The issues documented in the 1990s with reference to declining rural towns have been ongoing concerns across regional Australia. Many have a long history. They are not confined to towns that are declining, rural, or small. To some extent they affect towns of all sizes. These issues can be summarised as:

1   access to services and service-related disadvantage (the 'regional equity' question);
2   flight of youth and ageing regional populations (the 'regional decline' question); and
3   sustainability pressures on traditional industries (the 'regional transition' question).

As the 1990s' 'crisis of the bush' has evolved into the new millennium's Regional Australia question, these issues continue to loom large. Service equity, demographic decline, and industry transition are core regional development issues in the Australian context. And these issues are all typically grappled with at the level of regional towns.

1. Services and 'regional equity'

> Small-town Australians ... do not compare their public amenities with those of a Vietnamese village or Zulu kraal, but to those of an Australian city.[8]

The question of equitable access to services has been a persisting issue in regional Australia for decades. For towns of all sizes, quality services located in quality infrastructure make a town viable, vibrant, and attractive to residents and investors. Services are central to a town's identity and its future. Furthermore, there is a broad policy position that all Australians should have access to basic services regardless of where they live: funding to local governments is premised on this idea of service 'equalisation'. Services are important, and they are something Australian regional towns have had to fight for.

For smaller towns with declining populations, the main issue in recent decades has been the *loss* of services – closure of the local bank, primary school, or hospital, for instance – and the flow-on effects on employment, population, and overall town viability. For larger towns the issue is often about retaining and attracting the services that are found in larger population centres, and ensuring that local services and associated infrastructure are of a comparable quality. The question thus becomes: Does the town have a university? An airport? A full range of health services? How good are the schools?

Australian towns nearly always lack services that are taken for granted in the metropolitan capitals. This is because lower population densities work against economies of scale. In regional Australia, therefore, it is not uncommon for communities to take collective action around acquiring, retaining, or upgrading the quality of their services. Back in the 1970s, the anthropologist H.G. Oxley documented how people in Australian towns used community fund-raising efforts, government lobbying, and working bees to obtain such things as a local swimming pool, X-ray equipment and air conditioning for their hospital, and audio-visual equipment for their school.[9]

Equity and sustainability of services for 'the regions' are persisting leitmotifs in Australian regional policy. Perhaps at no time was this so visibly illustrated as in the 1980s and 1990s, when a range of services and facilities were rationalised and consolidated across regional Australia. At that time, both public and private sector organisations actively reduced their large numbers of local offices and service-delivery shopfronts into a few, larger regional offices. This process was widely referred to as *regionalisation*.[10]

'Regionalising' services in Australia did not mean devolving central functions to the regions. Rather, regionalisation meant centralising services from a local to a regional level. The aim was to reduce the number of branch offices, enhance efficiency, and lower costs. Numerous government departments and government-owned services, as well as private providers such as banks, regionalised in the 1990s. In Victoria, for instance, the number of local governments shrank by over half, leaving many towns without a local government office. At the same time state government departments were regionalising into larger towns and closing their local offices. It was possible to observe 'constant and increasing downsizing, rationalising and restructuring for regions', along with 'the anger that services cuts and the centralisation of economic functions have caused in regional communities'.[11] In some places regionalisation was visibly manifested on the landscape in the form of empty shops and abandoned public infrastructure.[12]

Arguably, this process of regionalisation has been a key driver of the shape of regional Australia today. First, regionalisation established many of the multiple and overlapping regional boundaries that are still apparent on the administrative landscape today. Regionalisation typically involved creating new regions from multiple towns and then adopting a regional approach to policy and planning.[13] In some cases regionalisation included the amalgamation of local government areas into fewer, larger council areas. New regional administrative boundaries were drawn by various organisations for different purposes in a generally uncoordinated way. As a result, regional boundaries in Australia often do not coincide: either with each other (a particular locality may belong to several different regions) or with any functional economic or community-based definition of region.[14] The existence of multiple, often externally imposed, administrative regions continues to complicate Australian regional development policy and practice.

In addition, regionalisation of services created a situation in which some towns were winners and others losers. For smaller towns, regionalisation was generally synonymous with service withdrawal. The loss of a service could be significant; it meant more than simply not having that service. Losing the bank, the school, or the government department branch office also created a range of flow-on effects. These included the loss of professionals and their skills from towns (including leadership and financial skills), loss of jobs and training sites for rural young people, and increased unemployment.[15] Flow-on impacts also included decreased attractiveness of towns to shoppers, investors and new residents.[16] Research in small towns in the Latrobe valley in Victoria concluded that 'hospitals have many layers of meaning for their communities'; people who never used the hospital services were still affected by hospital closures.[17] One commentator summarised the impacts of service regionalisation in the 1990s as 'a domino effect of collapsing services which has brought many small communities to the brink of extinction'.[18]

While regionalisation threatened the identity and autonomy of many smaller towns, other towns reaped benefits. For larger towns that became centres for newly regionalised services, the effects of regionalisation were generally positive. These towns of several thousand or more people took on a more complex service role and a wider economic base.[19] These so-called 'sponge centres' did indeed 'soak up' some of the population from surrounding smaller towns, but their growing range of services meant that they attracted population in from a range of places – including from the metropolitan capitals.[20] Thus some towns gained significant benefits from regionalisation, though this was often perceived to be at the expense of neighbouring towns. Regionalisation exacerbated the rivalries among towns and further fragmented the regional landscape, creating the impression that larger towns and their smaller neighbours were competitors who did not share common interests.

Ultimately, while the regionalisation of services may have achieved greater efficiency, it has also left scars. The legacy of regionalisation is a complex landscape of externally imposed administrative regions, in which service equity is an ongoing bone of contention. Into the twenty-first century, there is immediate and fierce community resistance to any suggestion that services might be removed from local areas or consolidated across towns. Regional-scale planning is common, but still largely viewed with suspicion at the local level. Efforts to bring towns of any size together to discuss services often translate as: *What are we going to lose?* Furthermore, externally imposed regionalisation processes reinforced the idea that metropolitan-based decision makers could not be trusted to look after the interests of regional communities.[21] Thus regionalisation fomented distrust both among regional towns, and between regional towns and capital cities.

In the twenty-first century, access to services remains a key issue mediating the relationships among regional towns and capital cities. Even in prosperous and growing regions, local services such as schools and hospitals are still often perceived to be 'dependent on policies and policy makers from far away'.[22] Meanwhile, debates on what comprises a fair and sustainable level of services in regional Australia remain essentially unresolved. These debates are characterised by two entrenched positions. The 'regionalist' position proposes that services should be subsidised to ensure equity among citizens living in different places. The 'rationalist' position proposes that services should be provided only where it is efficient and economically sustainable to do so.

These debates on regional service equity have been played out again and again, with no resolution. The lesson of the 1980s and 1990s was that strongly rationalist approaches to regional services were socially unsustainable and led to fierce political backlash. This paved the way for the ascendance of a regionalist position in the 2000s, with greater political attention to service provision in regional Australia.[23] In 2011, Judith Brett observed:

> But will Australia's regions ever be sustainable? Sustainability still carries within it the ideal that the country should stand on its own, without subsidies, or at least not too much in the way of them. The nation needs to confront the possibility that rural and regional Australia might always need a fair degree of subsidisation, that it will always be more expensive to deliver services to many parts of Australia than to the city, that we do all live in a big country with a difficult geography, and that we do all need to share the cost.[24]

Nevertheless, the question of service equity is more complex than simply whether services can be provided to far-flung towns in an economically sustainable way. Services are deeply intertwined with the identity of towns. In strategic planning conversations across Australia, services are always a key theme: *What if we lose our airport? How can we attract more doctors? Can we get a university?*

Thus, while regional-scale service solutions make sense in thin markets, they meet strong cultural resistance. People remember externally driven regionalisation – where services were suddenly withdrawn and located sometimes hundreds of kilometres away. They equate loss of local services with a loss of autonomy and identity. Gaining services, on the other hand, equates to gains in recognition, status, and autonomy. In this context, it is unsurprising that towns compete rather than collaborate. Services matter, and in regional Australia services are dreamed for and fought for at town scale.

2. Flight of youth and 'regional decline'

> The regions have ageing populations. Their best and brightest young people often leave for the city, and many never return.[25]

A second persisting issue in regional Australia has been the question of demographic imbalance between the old and the young. The loss of young people – often described as the 'flight of youth' to metropolitan centres – is a longstanding and persisting concern in regional Australia. It is mirrored by a parallel trend of population ageing: on average, regional communities are getting older. These demographic observations in turn lead to concerns about the overall social and economic sustainability of regional communities. Can older populations, lacking the energy of the young, maintain and grow productivity? Can regional towns sustain the services that ageing populations will require? How can regional communities keep their young people?

Policy concerns about the 'flight of youth' and 'population ageing' in regional communities have been remarkably persistent over the past decades. In some towns they are also intertwined with concerns about population decline. Population decline and loss of services can quickly create a vicious circle – loss of services leads to a loss of population, and a smaller population can no longer sustain services.[26] The vicious cycle is likely to be exacerbated if the population 'left behind' in regional towns falls into certain undesirable policy categories: such as old or welfare-dependent.

In towns where populations are not declining, there are still concerns about the flight of youth and population ageing – the decline of the young and working-age population. Writing in 2002 on New South Wales, Margaret Alston observed that:

> Even in the Bega Valley and Leeton despite population growth there is a loss of young people over time and therefore the aging of the rural population is evident…. If rural communities are to be sustainable, ways of retaining and supporting young people to return are essential. The loss of young people

signals the loss of future leaders, small business owners, entrepreneurs and community drivers.[27]

Demographic imbalances – too few young people, too many old people – are typically portrayed as putting the sustainability of regional communities at risk. 'Decline' in this context might not mean a numerical population decline, but rather decline in the social and economic sustainability of the community as a whole. This is because young people are seen to be the social and economic drivers for the community's future. Furthermore, the flight of young people from the regions to the cities is often construed as a kind of 'brain drain' in which their knowledge, skills, and energy are lost to the regions.

A 2007 study of youth migration to cities in Australia commenced with the observation that:

> Around Australia today, there is concern in rural and regional communities about the rate at which their young people are leaving their communities. The majority of young people who move away from their original non-metropolitan location move into a metropolitan area.[28]

This longitudinal research project found that there is 'a general movement of young people from non-metropolitan areas to the major cities of Australia', primarily but not exclusively for educational purposes.[29] More young women were moving to the cities than young men.[30] Research in the South West region of Western Australia in 2000 also demonstrated that access to education was a major factor influencing the decision of young people to leave regional towns.[31]

While the loss of young people equates to a loss of energy and future leadership, the presence of older people is, conversely, taken as a measure of economic dependency. Areas outside Australian's capital cities usually have demographically older populations when compared with the capital cities, and this trend of regional population ageing is expected to continue.[32] Projections that 'by 2056 there will be less than two people of working age for every person aged 65 years and over' in areas outside capital cities raise alarm bells with policy makers, as it suggests that the ratio of 'productive' to 'unproductive' people is becoming less sustainable over time in many regional towns.[33]

Up unto the present day, the loss of young people and the ageing population have continued to be a central concern across regional Australia. The National Party's 2013 policy document paints this in broad-brush terms as 'the regions have ageing populations' and 'the best and brightest young people often leave'.[34] In 2012, the out-migration of youth aged 15 to 30 years was a key regional development issue raised by over two-thirds of the nation's Regional Development Australia Committees. They observed that young people 'leave the region to pursue education, training and employment opportunities and because of a lack of recreational facilities.'[35]

The flight of youth and the spectre of population ageing are regularly portrayed as key challenges to the sustainability of regional towns of all sizes. Nevertheless, these concerns tend to oversimplify the situation, and overlook key assets. First, the focus on 'youth' (usually defined as aged 16–24) overlooks the role of working-age people in slightly older age cohorts – late twenties, thirties and forties. Yet in-migrants to many regional areas are often under 45, including families with young children.[36]

While people in their teens and early twenties may leave home for educational or other early-life-stage opportunities, working-age people often move back to regional areas, attracted by job opportunities, family connections, or lifestyle considerations for themselves and their children. Thus, the more nuanced question is not how to 'keep' young people in regional communities, but how to entice them home with the skills, knowledge, and networks acquired elsewhere. As a 2009 study of university students in Victoria observed, decisions about where to live are in part dependent on life stage:

> Melbourne's events and entertainment offerings are reasons not to go home…. [Nevertheless] there was an overwhelming consensus among these respondents that once they reach their thirties they will settle down in regional Victoria to raise children of their own. They are not committed to living in their original hometowns; rather they are willing to relocate to a new regional area.[37]

The issue then becomes, can regional towns attract and retain the slightly less young? One initiative from North West Tasmania was the establishment of a Young Professionals Network in 2007. This initiative recognised that while a number of young professionals in their twenties and thirties were moving into the region, they often felt socially isolated – and social isolation was discouraging them from remaining in the region.

There is also a tendency to take a deficit-based view of population ageing. Ageing populations need not constitute a threat to either social or economic sustainability. The 'older people' that are an increasingly large share of regional populations are typically defined as aged 65+, assumed to be retired, and portrayed as constituting a drain on scarce resources and services. Yet many people post age 65 continue to participate actively in the labour force, volunteering, business ownership, and other forms of productive activity.

Furthermore, the human capital represented by older people with extensive life experiences is often an untapped asset in regional communities. As recently observed in Tasmania, Australia's fastest-ageing state, there is a need to take an asset-based view of ageing:

> There is a lot of expertise amongst the retirees living here. So many retirees are willing and able to pass on their skills but there is no outlet for that. We have built a men's shed and craft cottage but it strikes me that these guys want to do more and many are very skilled.[38]

Recent work in South Australia has emphasised that baby boomers 'can bring wealth, expertise, demand for services and new ideas into regional areas and they create, rather than need, jobs'.[39] It is often surprising to scratch the surface in a regional town and discover the high-flying professional backgrounds and skills of some quiet local retirees. Yet venues for people to use and share these skills are often lacking. Furthermore, older people's demand for services, amenities, and leisure activities creates numerous business opportunities. Retirement living, leisure, and aged services have been identified as among Australia's future economic growth waves[40] – waves that many regional Australian towns may be well positioned to catch.

Concerns about the flight of youth and population ageing are persistent leitmotifs of regional development in Australia. Yet the threatened 'decline' of regional towns is ultimately neither a question of youth or age. Rather, the question becomes whether or not these communities are able to recognise, retain, and leverage the human assets they already have.

3. Sustainable industries and 'regional transition'

> For the majority of Australian towns, the reason for their establishment is no longer the reason for their present existence.[41]

A third persisting regional development issue for towns is the economic and environmental sustainability of their industries. Many Australian towns have faced significant threats to their traditional industry base. These threats, and the need to develop new industries and new ways of working, have had a deep impact for many communities. Sustainable industries influence a town's ability to retain and attract services, population, investment, and skilled human capital in the local area. Transitions that affect local industries thus loom large in conversations about town sustainability and town futures.

Decline in traditional regional industries, discussed in detail in Chapter 2, has been a persisting feature of regional Australia in recent decades. The bulk of attention has focused on agricultural industries: wool, wheat, dairy, and others.[42] This is because agriculture is a significant component of many (though certainly not all) regional economies, and because changes in agriculture have been significant. Many government protections have been removed.[43] The number of farmers has decreased dramatically, even as the volume of food produced has grown.[44] Australian agriculture is export-oriented and plays in global markets. It thus faces pressures to continually produce more efficiently. The demands of the global marketplace are further complicated by the environmental fragility of much of the land under production, including susceptibility to drought and land degradation.

Agriculture is not the only industry that has faced sustainability challenges and transition, however. Other key regional industries such as mining, forestry, and manufacturing have too. In many ways mining is in a permanent state of transition, characterised by dramatic swings of boom or bust in response to global demand and exchange rate fluctuations. Employment opportunities grow or shrink accordingly. Forestry employment has plummeted in recent years, and the land available for logging has decreased.[45] Manufacturing has also faced transitions, as numerous firms have moved their operations offshore and others have down-sized or closed altogether. And energy and telecommunications companies have restructured, creating employment impacts in regional towns.

In regional Australia, a single large firm may provide a highly significant employment source; threats of a downsize or whispers of a closure are quickly splashed across the front page of local newspapers, and economic multipliers calculated accordingly. Moreover, regional manufacturing is often located in sectors such as food processing, textiles, pulp and paper, or agricultural or mining equipment. These sectors are closely tied to other regional industries like agriculture, mining, and forestry. The interdependencies among regional industries can create either virtuous or vicious cycles.

Economic transitions in regional Australia are not just challenges for individual firms and industries: they are challenges for town communities. Across Australia, most towns have a population of fewer than 50,000 people.[46] At this scale, change in a single industry – even, the closure or downsizing of a single firm – can have deep impacts. Companies shedding jobs make front-page news because their impacts are felt, not only by the redundant employees, but by those who sell them groceries, cut their hair, and school their children. Negative economic multipliers are the stuff of regional transition: fewer jobs mean fewer working people and fewer services: vicious circles spiralling downwards. The link between sustainable industries, sustainable services, and sustainable communities is keenly felt in regional Australian communities.

Often, large distances between towns of any size mean that there is not easy access to other employment options. People may simply leave: in Burnie, Tasmania, the significant downsizing of the town's paper mill in the 1990s can be tracked in a measurable population drop: between 1996 and 2001, Burnie's population fell by over a thousand people, from 19,283 to 18,145. As the economy diversified, the population gradually recovered and by 2011 was back up to about 19,300.[47] Similarly, the effects of the privatisation of the State Electricity Commission in Gippsland, Victoria in the late 1990s could be tracked in population losses; loss of local jobs had visible impacts in Gippsland towns, in the form of empty shops and young people leaving.[48]

Environmental sustainability issues further complicate the transitions facing regional industries. Irrigated agriculture – and the agricultural service towns built around these industries – are one example. Under the Murray–Darling Basin Plan in 2012, the Australian government bought back water rights from irrigators and established a system of piped water (in lieu of open channels) to increase the flow of water in a river system under severe pressure. The Basin Plan process became a serious and divisive issue in regional Australia. While it was generally recognised that something had to be done about the damaged state of the Murray River, the effects of limiting the water available for irrigated agriculture in one of Australia's food bowls had impacts across regional communities – affecting farms, farm-support businesses, processors, and a range of other businesses and services.[49] A recent media report notes that while river health is slowly improving, 'Western New South Wales towns are struggling to adapt to having less water'.[50]

Similarly, in Tasmania, efforts to reduce logging in native forests have led to the closure of a number of timber mills and significant economic pressures on regional towns where forestry has traditionally been a key employer. A 2011 statement by the Tasmanian Local Government Association notes:

> There is a strong and genuine concern within Tasmanian councils that no-one is recognizing the impacts of what occurs when people leave the forestry floor. Communities are being devastated and the impacts are already being felt directly and indirectly with 1000 jobs gone from the industry since October last year. ... There is significant concern about the ongoing viability of essential services in some of the areas impacted by the forestry downturn. ... The social fabric of these communities is under severe threat. [51]

Retail spending, schools, and medical and dental services were among the services flagged as potentially under threat due to transitions in this regional industry.

In Western Australian towns at the turn of the millennium, several important industry transitions were taking place. The dairy industry had just been deregulated, with the government no longer guaranteeing a farm-gate price for milk. The forestry industry had been in negotiation with environmental interests and federal and state governments, culminating in a Regional Forest Agreement that limited the available land for logging. Meanwhile, broad acre cropping was facing not only a competitive economic environment, but significant environmental pressures from increasing soil salinity. These challenges were regularly grappled with at town level.

People were acutely aware that a failure to stem the decline of traditional industries would feed the negative spiral of service loss, flight of youth, and smaller, ageing populations. Thus, they sought to reinvent their economic options. Quests for new industries – from aquaculture to tourism – were understood as the place to start. New industries would provide jobs for young people, attract new residents, and ultimately make local services more viable. These issues were all intertwined.

Local leaders, entrepreneurs, and voluntary committees could see these connections. Their ability to create options with limited resources was frequently impressive. At the same time, other kinds of transitions were happening around them that were making a much bigger impact on the landscape of regional Australia.

Small-town diversity: sea, tree, and ICT

Seen one town ... seen one town. [52]

As regional communities were coming up with ideas to reinvent their economies, larger cultural forces were quietly changing the shape of regional Australian towns. Small coastal towns were being 'found' by wealthy professionals and retirees from the cities. The ability to work, shop, and socialise online was challenging the central role of local communities in mediating economic and social relationships. [53]

Changing work patterns, lifestyle aspirations, and technological advances meant that people were moving more, travelling more, and creating different kinds of connections in and across places. In the second decade of the new millennium, the story of regional towns is a story of diversity.

Nearly two decades after the survival of Australia's small towns became a topic of popular speculation, the evidence for regional small-town sustainability is mixed. Through the 1990s, some of Australia's towns lost population; others gained population.[54] Towns along the coast have tended to grow, as have some of the larger regional centres and towns within commuting distance of urban centres.[55] Small agricultural service centres have not disappeared, as many farm households and businesses continue to support their local towns.[56] Yet the spectre of regional decline has not gone away; the Australian Bureau of Statistics (ABS) tells us that: 'Many of the largest population declines in 2012–13 were in regional areas.'[57]

In the early 2000s, Australian demographer Graeme Hugo observed that: 'Australia's nonmetropolitan population is becoming more heterogeneous.'[58] This has continued to hold true. A number of towns have benefitted from regionalisation or other economic opportunities such as mining or tourism. They have created a more diverse set of local industries, and in turn, a more diverse landscape of Australian towns.[59] Many, like Albury–Wodonga and Wollongong, are 'significant urban areas' in their own right.[60] Furthermore, despite a longstanding tendency to conflate *regional* with *rural* – and *rural* with *agricultural,* there has always been a range of town types on the Australian regional landscape.[61]

Different towns have had different trajectories. In addition to their industry base, the diverse trajectories of Australia's regional towns are in large part guided by two key characteristics: whether they are attractive places to live (their amenity), and their physical and virtual connectivity to other places. *Amenity* is especially, though not exclusively, characterised by natural amenity: for instance the appeal of small towns in coastal environments with nice beaches. *Connectivity* refers to towns with ease of access to other places, both physically (e.g. access to highways, airports and larger urban centres) and virtually (e.g. broadband connectivity and mobile phone coverage). Regional Australia varies enormously in both amenity and connectivity, and these two characteristics can explain a great deal about the diverse trajectories of towns.

A number of Australian studies have explored the role of natural amenity – 'such as sea views, proximity to towns and a pleasant climate' – in driving in-migration, population growth, economic diversification, and rising land prices.[62] Many of Australia's regional towns that have a physically attractive setting have increased their populations and diversified their economies accordingly. Attractive environments appeal to in-migrants, who include both retirees and young families. In regional Australia, 'one of the most evident trends is the high rate of in-migration to coastal areas. This is one of the migration streams that is playing a major role in the redistribution of regional populations.'[63]

In Australia, amenity migration to attractive coastal environments is referred to as 'sea change' – after a popular Australian television show. The twin concept 'tree change' recognises that some people choose, not the sea, but inland environments such as the Dandenong Ranges in Victoria or the Blue Mountains in New South Wales. Amenity migration is one of the drivers of recent population growth in the historically sparsely populated Australian north, as one study observes:

> The landscapes of Far North Queensland, in particular in the Wet Tropics bioregion, are increasingly attractive places for people seeking a sea- or tree-change. … it is not labour market considerations that drive migration in these areas. Instead it is a combination of lifestyle factors, such as recreational opportunities, attractive landscapes and views, a pleasant climate and a good place to bring up children.[64]

Natural amenity has been cited as a new and significant source of advantage for regional Australian towns.[65] Nevertheless, the importance of amenity migration should not be overplayed, as migration decisions may relate to a range of other factors besides lifestyle: such as where family members live and where work is available.[66] Furthermore, other forms of amenity, such as the availability of local services (schools, hospitals), can also influence the attractiveness of towns.

Connectivity is a second key factor influencing the trajectories of Australian regional towns. In regional Australia, large distances prevail. In general, towns that are close to other places seem to do better than towns that are remote and isolated.[67] Those close to capital cities and larger inland towns tend to grow.[68] In remote areas, by comparison, even when jobs are available, people often prefer to commute in rather than relocate to these areas.[69] Given cultural trends toward greater mobility, access to transport amenities such as airports can also be an important consideration.[70] Indeed, having residents who regularly travel has been associated with greater levels of innovation in regional towns.[71]

Mobile phone coverage and communications infrastructure are important aspects of connectivity. Internet usage in Australia is growing and will likely continue to do so, particularly in the context of the growth of flexible working arrangements.[72] Yet many areas of regional Australia – even areas quite close to urban centres – are still subject to painfully slow Internet speeds and mobile phone black spots.[73] The National Broadband Network is ambitious but high-speed broadband still does not reach many areas. Overall, the twenty-first century's globally connected world has manifested unevenly in regional Australia; some areas are highly connected, others disconnected.

In addition to physical and virtual connectivity, small towns often have a reputation for social and community connectivity. The image of small towns as offering opportunities for community involvement can provide an incentive for some people to move in.[74] This image is somewhat borne out in the statistics; a recent study in Western Australia found that regional respondents rated their sense of community, and their involvement in volunteering and community activities, higher than respondents in the metropolitan area.[75] Furthermore, 2011 census data documented that regional Australians volunteer at much higher rates than capital-city residents.[76]

Overall, when seeking to understand the diverse trajectories of Australia's towns, it is notable that towns with high amenity and high connectivity have tended to grow, while remote, poorly connected, inland areas have tended to decline. Today, thriving Australian regional towns may vary in size from hundreds to tens of thousands of residents, but nearly all have some combination of amenity and connectivity characteristics. Together, these create liveable towns. Nevertheless, these characteristics are not deterministic; there is scope for community action to influence the trajectories of towns.[77] In Western Australia at the turn of the millennium, regional communities were attempting to do just that.

Reinventing regional towns: self-help development

> Many rural communities have reversed long-term patterns of decline using local knowledge, skills and ingenuity.[78]

Regional Australian towns are increasingly diverse. Some have grown to become regional centres, diversifying their local economies. Others have stayed small, but have developed a new population or industry base. Many towns have reinvented themselves in response to the challenges of economic transition or the opportunities linked to amenity and connectivity. In regional Australia, there is a sense that towns can take charge of change: that they can generate new economic trajectories from within.

While this focus on endogenous community-driven change can be partially attributed to cultural traditions of self-help development – such as the self-provisioning of local services – it has also reflected a very strong policy position by Australian governments over the past two decades. A number of academic commentators in the late 1990s observed the growing influence of 'bottom-up' or 'self-help' regional development policies in Australia. It was noted that 'bottom up' policies 'have become fashionable both in Sydney and Canberra, the new mantra being local leadership and community ownership of the economic development process. Governments now facilitate regional development, they do not direct it.'[79] Equally, 'the approach of Commonwealth and State governments over recent years has been to simply provide guidance to communities attempting to help themselves'.[80]

One of the early examples was the Commonwealth-funded Country Centres Project in the mid-1980s, 'which sought to develop effective models for the participation of community groups in self-help local development'.[81] These kinds of approaches gathered momentum through the 1990s. By October 1999, the Regional Australia Summit held in Canberra was 'laden with the philosophies of community self-help and the social resilience of rural Australia'[82] and 'replete with the stirring rhetoric of "community empowerment", "capacity building" and "partnership" between all levels of government, business and community'.[83] A major theme of the summit was leadership: leadership from within regional communities that could help these communities respond to change and transition.[84]

In regional towns facing the intertwined issues of service loss, demographic decline and economic restructuring, the policy response was: *reinvent yourself.* Towns were expected to create their own successes. Self-help development policies did not distinguish between towns that had – perhaps accidentally – caught the wave of larger 'sea change' amenity trends or the benefits of connectivity to larger urban centres, and those that had fewer resources or amenities that they could leverage. Such considerations were out of scope: the focus was on what regional communities could do for themselves.

'Success' in turn was defined quite broadly. A number of popularly cited examples of self-help development were captured in the 2001 report *Who Dares, Wins*, which profiled 14 case studies of small-town renewal. These towns, most with populations under 2,000 people, had ostensibly 'won' by mobilising community energy behind a range of local and enterprise development initiatives such as new streetscapes, tourism enterprises, and local events.[85] The sharing of these success stories served to motivate other communities, showing them that they, too, could constructively do something about the issues they faced.

Town reinvention efforts often attempt to create something distinctive that a town can be known for: an activity, event, or piece of infrastructure that could put a town on the map. Beechworth has its famous bakery. Margaret River has wine. Tiny Coleraine is known for its chocolate factory; New Norfolk and Strathalbyn are unofficial antique capitals (of Tasmania and South Australia, respectively). The small town of Clunes, Victoria established the *Back to Booktown* festival as a rural renewal project; the initiative was led by a local committee, later formalised as 'Creative Clunes', that borrowed an idea from the UK to apply locally:

> *Back to Booktown* … has brought a new lease of life to Clunes, with its heritage buildings providing impressive venues for the 50 or so book-sellers, growing numbers of high profile writers, and thousands of visitors who flock to the town.'[86]

The story at the start of this chapter showed how, in regional communities in Western Australia at the turn of the millennium, there was a strong push for self-help development. In town after town, local people were grappling with the imperative to do something, innovate, identify and leverage their assets, mobilise support, and put their town on the map. Many rose to the challenge, churning out an impressive range of ideas and options. At the same time, on-the-ground observations in these regional towns raised a number of issues about what was being asked of these towns and their leaders, and what could feasibly be delivered.

First, the on-the-ground impacts of self-help development initiatives were generally small. This is because self-help development devolved responsibility to communities without corresponding resources. In fact, several commentators noted trenchantly that these responsibilities were falling on many communities just as resources were being actively withdrawn.[87] 'Resources' were not just money, but the leadership and skills needed to get initiatives underway. As services withdrew and industries downsized, many skilled people moved away, leaving communities with limited human resources to drive change. As an interviewee in one Western Australian town put it, admitting to the lack of marketing skills in a local initiative, 'I don't think there's anybody here that actually has those skills'.

While some government funding was available, it was typically on a small scale and often on a 'pilot project' basis. Typical initiatives included main street beautification efforts, small local tourism ventures, or local sports and recreation facilities.[88] These efforts were highly localised and seldom in line with the scale of the challenges facing towns. As Lynda Cheshire observed for the town of Austin, Queensland, 'local efforts to develop alternative industries in Austin have done little to reverse the population decline facing the town'; despite this, the town and its local action committee were frequently cited in the press as a success story of rural renewal.[89] Such uncritical assessments of success were common; policy makers regularly cited initiatives such as a sound-and-light show or a local festival as signs that declining towns were reversing their fortunes.

Next, self-help development mobilises local assets, energy, and leadership, but generally overlooks the role of external support and extra-local networks for communities and their leaders. As traditional institutional infrastructure such as government offices and banks withdrew from many towns, so did the extra-local linkages that towns had relied on for access to information, assistance, and influence. Local action groups, development committees, and other groups ran on the energy of under-resourced volunteers.[90] Many promising efforts floundered on the lack of time, skills, and market intelligence.

When communities sought out external support, many discovered that they had 'no members with political or economic clout in the greater systems'.[91] They could not get the ear of decision makers. One study of community leaders observed: '... local regional leaders find that their interest in what needs to be done if their regions are to survive, let alone prosper, often clashes with the beliefs and practices of the external decision-makers on whom they depend.'[92]

The tensions between self-help development and limited external support was documented in a case study of Ouyen, Victoria, in 2007, a town with no local government representation facing the spectre of an unwanted toxic waste dump:

> The limitations to what small communities can do for themselves is also evident. . . . Local people see this as a 'can-do' town with 'a vibrancy . . . that you don't see in other Mallee towns', but ... locals feel that 'we don't have the voting power' to influence policy. Given the policy environments within which they must work, there is only so much a 'can-do' community can do.[93]

Communities cited as 'successful' have often enjoyed institutional or financial support from government or other influential organisations.[94] Yet on the ground in Western Australia, external support for regional community efforts was seldom apparent beyond an occasional small tranche of funding, available on a competitive basis to those in a position to apply. Multi-year funding commitments for locally driven development efforts of the type seen overseas are unknown in Australia.[95]

Finally, while self-help development policy has strongly emphasised *regional community* action, on-the-ground observations showed that town communities seldom act – and almost never act together. Town communities are comprised of numerous sub-groups and individuals with different interests and agendas.[96] As the story at the start of this chapter illustrated, individual entrepreneurs and small groups were all championing their own ideas and projects. Different groups typically worked in isolation from (or even in opposition to) each other, even in the same regional community.

The existence of numerous sub-communities and interest groups creates a challenge when the task is to reinvent a town. For instance: 'Different communities within small towns may have different ideas about what their town's image should be. Is Balingup to be known for its small farms and scarecrows, its Medieval Fayre, its Tree Park – or all of the above?'[97] Many regional communities have responded to this conundrum by hosting planning days, 'search conferences', or other forms of community visioning exercises designed to get different sectors of the community to agree what the future of their town should be. Yet while such activities generally produce long lists of possible initiatives, few if any come to fruition.

When things get done in communities, it is often because there is a driver willing to make things happen.[98] Many of regional Australia's stories of small-town innovation were originally catalysed or instigated by a single entrepreneur. The iconic Penguin market in Tasmania, the famous Beechworth bakery in Victoria, and the gourmet chocolate factory in Coleraine, Victoria – all were established by entrepreneurs, not community committees. Often, these were outsiders who arrived in local towns and spotted an opportunity. King Island cheese is another product that has put an isolated regional Tasmanian community on the national map. Yet this success story was the result of efforts by a single entrepreneur to leverage endogenous place attributes into a successful, marketable product.[99] Wynyard, Tasmania, has a successful annual tulip festival that has been documented as an example of community-led social enterprise.[100] Yet the iconic tulips at the centre of the festival are the result of the efforts of a private entrepreneur who established the industry on Tasmania's North West Coast. Governments focus on community action, but it is often individuals who make things happen.

Towns of all sizes dot the landscape of regional Australia today, and most are in no immediate danger of disappearing. Arguably, however, the ability of regional towns to reinvent themselves owes less to the – admittedly impressive – self-help efforts of local communities, and more to the demographic, economic, and cultural shifts that have placed many towns in a position to succeed. The location of some towns near sea, trees, and centres of population and connectivity has meant they have been well placed to attract a diverse population base, including resident entrepreneurs, energetic volunteers, and new (often service-based) industries. Many such well-positioned towns have leveraged assets and opportunities; they have 'successfully reinvented' themselves.[101] Even less-favoured towns have created a sense of amenity through local streetscapes, parks, and facilities, or enhanced their connectivity through festivals, events, or services such as community banks. But the potential of self-help development is ultimately limited by the resources at hand.

Regional towns as peripheral economies

> It is often too easy to focus on the grassroots while ignoring the role of rain, sun, and frost: i.e. the extra-community relationships that mediate a community's access to resources.[102]

This chapter began with a story about regional communities – small towns – across three regions of Western Australia. In the early 2000s all of these towns were facing a number of significant economic transitions. In response, community groups were scrambling to identify ideas – botanical gardens, town murals, medieval festivals, cultural centres, tourist trains – that could provide new opportunities. In the face of the intertwined issues of regional industry restructuring, demographic decline, and service loss, community groups and individuals were actively seeking out ways to ensure their economic and social sustainability from the ground up.

These communities' on-the-ground efforts tried to identify and configure local and regional assets to create new economic options. The experiences of self-help development in regional Australian towns are examples of endogenous development – development driven from within. All were attempts to leverage local attributes to intentionally 'construct' advantage.[103] All mobilised local leaders, entrepreneurs, and voluntary civic groups in order to generate innovation from the ground up. These approaches echo ideas from mainstream regional development theory. Yet the experiences of Australia's small regional towns have often yielded very different results from those that mainstream regional development theories would suggest.

As per endogenous development theory, individuals and groups in these towns did leverage their resources – physical, cultural, social, and human – from within. As per the idea of 'constructing advantage', they did intentionally identify and actively pursue opportunities to leverage these attributes to create new sources of advantage vis-à-vis other places. These processes, observed on the ground in Western Australia, were mirrored in other regional communities around Australia.[104] People took on board the message that they could change their future economic and social trajectories. They sought to create new economic options by mobilising their distinctive attributes. Yet in the end, their results were typically small: drops in the ocean on a regional landscape that in many ways was being transformed around them.

According to the economic competitiveness index developed by the Regional Australia Institute, the bulk of rural Australia still sits within categories of limited competitiveness.[105] In 2015, many towns of all sizes still struggle with the regional equity question, the regional decline question, and the question of industry transition. Most are actively seeking to gain or retain services that are taken for granted in the metropolitan centres. Most are concerned about population ageing and their ability to retain young people and highly skilled professionals. And most have economies that are closely linked to the ups and downs of primary industries. Some towns are advantaged by their natural amenity and/or connectivity, others disadvantaged by remoteness. Nearly all face one or more of these persistent regional development issues.

Why have Australian endogenous development efforts ultimately been so limited in their impact? Clearly, one factor has been the relatively sparse resource base of many towns – particularly the 'small, rural' communities-under-pressure that were most often the focus of self-help initiatives. As Jacqui Dibden has observed, 'the assumption that rural communities are capable of engaging in self-help, bottom-up development is often at odds with the real disadvantages experienced by many rural areas'.[106] Small rural communities are often resource poor: in terms of human capital, financial resources, amenity, connectivity, and political influence. Even when they are doing all the right things – working together to identify sources of advantage, identifying and leveraging resources and unique attributes – they may simply not have enough ingredients to create a distinctive source of advantage.

This is certainly the case for many small and historically disadvantaged places. Yet being regional does not necessarily mean being small. Many regional towns have a broad population base of thousands or tens of thousands of people, across a range of ages and life stages. Many are well positioned vis-à-vis the population drivers of amenity and connectivity. Nevertheless, the endogenous regional development activities described in this chapter missed much of this diversity and failed to realise how it could be leveraged. Rather, regional development efforts were based in deeply held assumptions about what it means to be *regional* in Australia. The Western Australian experience is illustrative.

First, in the heyday of self-help development, almost no regional development initiatives were focused on the larger regional centres – those with populations over 10,000 people. The discourse of regional development assumed that the relevant *regional communities* were all, by definition, small towns. Seen from the desk of capital-city decision makers, regional Australia was a largely undifferentiated landscape of small, rural towns in crisis. It was a landscape of problems, not opportunities: a peripheral economic space.

Regional development initiatives were not rolling out in the state capital of Perth, nor did they tend to appear in regional centres like Bunbury and Albany – themselves the centres of larger functional economic regions. Rather, Australian regional development – in Western Australia as elsewhere – was intentionally framed as the province of smaller and peripheral places: towns of a few hundred or at most a few thousand people that found themselves on the receiving end of the 'familiar and well-rehearsed narrative of global capitalism and its disregard for regional and local communities'.[107]

Next, regional development activities were motivated first and foremost by the survival and sustainability of individual regional communities. As *regional community* in practice meant a locality or town, regional development was not truly regional at all. On-the-ground initiatives were all highly localised. Despite various attempts to promote initiatives across towns, at regional scale, these existed only at the level of plans and strategies – not sustained action.

Furthermore, regional development action always started from the pervasive narrative of towns-under-threat. Thus, regional development was primarily defensive, aiming to ensure towns maintained their population, services, and economic base. Neighbouring towns were framed as irrelevant at best, competitors at worst. In the end, the imperative was to ensure the sustainability of one's own town. This was more than common parochialism; it was entrenched peripherality: learned over time through the repeated need to defend local communities against externally initiated threats.

Finally, the peripherality of small communities' scattered development efforts was reinforced by framing regional development as a voluntaristic community activity. Self-help regional development efforts were poorly resourced and poorly linked into larger systems. They were typified by the community committee or community progress group – voluntary groups that embodied the ideal of communities acting together to take charge of change. Yet placing isolated community committees and their limited resources at the centre of regional development efforts pushed these initiatives even further into the periphery.

Community committees often have no legal status or political voice. They comprise volunteers with day jobs and multiple other roles, for whom committee activities are not core business. Regional development thus became an ad hoc activity conducted by volunteers with little time or influence. Links between such groups and larger government, industry, or university organisations and networks were usually non-existent. Funding, when it arrived, was minimal. Further, the expectation that communities drive development initiatives often served to quietly disguise the role of individual entrepreneurs in bringing successful initiatives to fruition.

Overall, endogenous 'self-help' regional development in Australia has followed many of the prescriptions in the mainstream regional development literature, but only to a point. In Australia, economic actors in local places have sought to identify and leverage their distinctive, place-based attributes to construct new sources of advantage. They have often mobilised local resources and brought together people across sectors to assess their situation and identify opportunities for the future. Observations on the ground in Western Australia demonstrated no shortage of energy and local agency to create change from within. Yet in most cases, little came of these efforts. Regional communities were defined as, and remained, peripheral economic actors.

Policy makers saw regional development as ultimately a problem of the periphery, to be solved by small-scale pilot projects in small communities. Regional communities in turn saw themselves as peripheral, and so shaped their strategies as self-defence tactics in isolation from each other – and from the larger economic and political systems that had consistently failed to support them.

The end result was that regional development initiatives were, indeed, endogenous, but they were limited to the efforts of small community groups working in isolation from each other and from larger networks. Most lacked the resources they needed to bring their good ideas to fruition. A project on the sustainability of Australian rural communities conducted by the Academy of Social Sciences in Australia concluded that *'towns and communities do not exist and operate independently of other places'*.[108] While undeniably true, the need to point it out says volumes about being regional in Australia.

Notes

1 The *Regional Forest Agreement for the South-West Forest Region of Western Australia* is one of ten Regional Forest Agreements around the country. They are 20-year agreements between the state and Commonwealth governments on the sustainable use and management of the forests. See: http://www.dpaw.wa.gov.au/management/forests/managing-our-forests/74-wa-regional-forest-agreement-progress-report (viewed 1 June 2015).

2 Yabbies are a type of small freshwater crayfish, the species farmed in Western Australia is *Cherax albidus*. See Western Australia Department of Fisheries: http://www.fish.wa.gov.au/Fishing-and-Aquaculture/Aquaculture/Aquaculture-Management/Pages/Farming-Yabbies.aspx (viewed 1 June 2015).

3 An internet search reveals that the idea has apparently taken off; South Australia and New South Wales have similar festivals.

4 Gray and Lawrence 2001, p. 118.

5 Collits and Gastin 1997, p. 20.

6 Quotes from Forth and Howell 2002, p. 4; see also Alston 1996; Gray and Lawrence 2001.

7 See Brett 2011.

8 Oxley 1981, p. 9.

9 Oxley 1981, pp. 9–11. These are not just observations from 40 years ago. Only last month, a community group where I live bought a defibrillator with the proceeds of a local fund-raising event and matching funding they had requested from local government.

10 See e.g. Budge *et al.* 1992; Collits and Gastin 1997; Henshall Hansen Associates 1988, p. 32.

11 Collits and Gastin 1997, pp. 9–10.

12 For example, hospitals, as observed by Fletcher 2001, p. 22, reflecting on Gippsland in Victoria.

13 Trevor Budge and colleagues, writing in 1992, note that: 'Most states have increased their regionalisation of services and region based planning' and that 'The findings of most studies and reviews undertaken of the delivery of programs and services has lead [sic] to recommendations that services be further regionalised and that needs identification and planning be undertaken at the regional level' (Budge *et al.* 1992, pp. 33–34).

14 Budge *et al.* 1992, pp. 33–34 note that: 'One of the most frequently raised issues in the consultation program was dissatisfaction with regional arrangements, frequent changes to regional boundaries and the fact that different departments use different regions.' For an analysis of Functional Economic regions (FER) in Australian labour markets, see Mitchell and Stimson 2010.

15 See e.g. Alston 2002, p. 9; Argent and Rolley 2000, pp. 157–158; Beer *et al.* 2003, p. 203; Collits and Gastin 1997, p. 9; Gray and Lawrence 2001, p.3; and Wainer 2001, p. 48.

16 See e.g. Collits and Gastin 1997, pp. 11, 12; Fletcher 2001; and Wainer 2001. Further, Beer *et al.* 2003, pp. 202–203 note that the closure of bank branches resulted in reduced retail trade, decreased local investment and confidence, and limited access to finance.

17 Fletcher 2001, p. 22; see also Wainer 2001, p. 46. Schools arguably have similar roles, as has been evident in the recent outcry over the closure of rural schools in Tasmania.

18 Cribb 1994, p.13, quoted in Collits and Gastin 1997, p. 13.

19 Pritchard *et al.* 2012, pp. 544–545 describe this 'flight of functions from smaller to larger centres', especially 'a few larger and more spatially accessible regional centres with populations greater than about 8000 people'. They also note that in the mid-1990s, the term 'sponge centre' was coined to describe 'the process whereby larger regional cities grew at the same time as smaller adjacent towns were experiencing population decline.'

20 See Beer *et al.* 1994 quoted in Argent and Rolley 2000, pp. 141–142.

21 Wainer 2001, p. 46 summarises the general tenor of this distrust of metropolitan decision makers, observing that with regionalisation: 'Definitions were developed external to the rural communities about what those communities needed, and answers provided for questions that rural communities had not asked.'

22 Eversole and Martin 2006, pp. 694–695, writing on Hamilton in Victoria's Western District.

23 See e.g. Brett 2011, p. 6*ff*; Dibden 2001, p. 5.

24 Brett 2011, p. 56.

25 The Nationals 2013, p. 70.

26 'Rural decline in Australia, as in many other Western countries, is often precipitated or exacerbated by the loss of services and infrastructure' (Dibden 2001, p. 5).

27 Alston 2002, pp. 5–6.

28 Hillman and Rothman 2007, p. 1.

29 Hillman and Rothman 2007, p. 21. About 36 per cent of the young people in this survey moved from non-metropolitan areas to major cities, though a small proportion of these later returned.

30 Hillman and Rothman 2007; see also Alston 2002.

31 Eversole 2001.

32 ABS 2009a.

33 ABS 2009a, np. These data are for the non-capital-city areas of New South Wales, Victoria, South Australia and Tasmania. By comparison, by 2056, Australian capital cities are projected to have three people of working age for every one aged 65 years and over.

34 The Nationals 2013, p. 70. The National Party of Australia has traditionally been the political party representing rural areas of Australia. Australia's two major political parties are the Australian Labor Party and the Liberal Party.

35 Faulkner *et al.* 2013, p.14. The issue of the out-migration of young people was raised in 37 of the nation's 55 Regional Development Australia committees. Furthermore, 'Population decline and sustainability in rural and remote areas' was specifically raised by 19 of the committees (p. 14).

36 An analysis of the 2006 census data for North West Tasmania documented, for instance, that 62 per cent of in-migrants to this region were under the age of 45 (IRD 2007, p. 39). Burnley and Murphy 2004, p. 36 note that in sea-change areas of New South Wales, around 70 per cent of those moving in are of working age. State Government of Victoria's nd, p. 31 analysis of the 2001–06 census data found that: 'The age structure of interstate migrants to large regional centres (e.g. Geelong, Bendigo and Ballarat) and growth areas (e.g. Wyndham, Melton, Hume, Whittlesea, etc.) is more typical of families, as indicated by the higher numbers of persons in the age cohorts 25–39 years, and of children (whose migration decisions are governed by their parents).'

37 Sweeney Research 2009, pp. 35–36.

38 Eyles *et al.* 2014a, p. 78.

39 Hugo *et al.* 2013, p. 5.

40 Deloitte Access Economics 2014.

41 Plowman *et al.* 2003, p. 8.
42 There is a tendency for perceptions of rural and regional Australia to favour agriculture and farms; for example, Lockie 2000, p. 23 notes that 'beyond the five-yearly census of the Australian population, the collection of statistics about rural and regional Australia is overwhelmingly dominated by the collection of agricultural production and financial statistics'.
43 For a review of agricultural policy in Australia see Smith and Pritchard 2015.
44 ABS 2012a.
45 Forestry shed about 15,000 jobs nationwide between 2008 and 2013, but regained about 9,000 jobs between 2013 and 2014 (ABARES 2014a, p.1). The annual area of multiple-use public native forest harvested for wood decreased by 32 per cent between 2006 and 2011 (MPIGA 2013, pp. 8–11).
46 According to ABS 2014e data, only six significant urban areas outside Sydney in New South Wales had populations over 50,000 people: Wagga Wagga (54,679), Coffs Harbour (67,519), Albury–Wodonga (86,274), Wollongong (286,581), Central Coast (comprising 29 different towns, with a total population of 320,266), and the regional city of Newcastle – Maitland (425,895). Victoria had only four: Geelong (181,853), Bendigo and Ballarat (each around 90,000 people), and Melton (54,483). Western Australia had one large regional town (Bunbury, population 72,464) and South Australia had no town over 30,000. Queensland had the largest number of towns over 50,000, nine: Gold Coast–Tweed Heads, Sunshine Coast, and Toowoomba are located in the South East Queensland growth corridor, Hervey Bay and Bundaberg are on the northern edge of it, while Rockhampton, Mackay, Townsville and Cairns are spaced at intervals along the coast toward the north.
47 IRD 2007; ABS 2013a.
48 See Birrell 2001, Fletcher 2001.
49 EBC *et al.* 2011, p. 2. Another recent study found that 'Most residents of irrigation communities, particularly in southern New South Wales, felt the Basin Plan would have negative effects on their community' (Schirmer and Berry 2014, p. 10).
50 Woodburn 2015.
51 LGAT 2011, pp. 3–4.
52 Quoted in Martin 2007, p. 62.
53 See e.g. Collits and Rowe 2015.
54 Tonts 2000, p. 55 observed that between 1991 and 1996 nearly 40 per cent of Australia's rural settlements between 200 and 20,000 residents experienced a decrease in population, while 60 per cent gained population. Butt 2011, p. 61 has noted that between 1986 and 2006 in Victoria, 21 towns with between 2,000 and 15,000 inhabitants experienced a decline in population, while 36 towns of that size grew.
55 Australian Bureau of Statistics data (ABS 2007) highlight that the largest growth outside Australian capital cities between 1996 and 2006 occurred along the coast. At the same time, a number of inland regional centres were also growing. ABS 2014e observed that in the 12 months to 2013, larger inland towns like Wodonga and Mildura in Victoria and Bathurst and Orange in New South Wales were growing, as well as smaller towns like Northam in Western Australia.
56 They 'continue to make extensive use of their local towns for everyday "maintenance purchases" and for a range of other supplies' (Pritchard *et al.* 2012, p. 554).
57 ABS 2014e.
58 Hugo 2002, p. 11.
59 Argent and Rolley 2000, p. 143 observe that Australia originally lacked 'the intermediate-sized centres needed to blur the distinction between "Sydney and the bush"'. Pritchard *et al.* 2012 reflect on the historical development of Australian settlement patterns and observe that: 'Increasingly, there is a stark distinction between the economic structures and fortunes of regional towns that have "moved beyond" dependence

on agriculture (typically, coastal, near-city and amenity rich spaces), and those that have not' (p. 543).

60 'Significant urban areas' are 'concentrations of urban development with a population of 10,000 people or greater, which include a dense urban core and some surrounding hinterland' (Commonwealth of Australia 2014a, pp. 5–6).

61 Sher and Sher 1994, pp. 10–11 make the point strongly that most government officials conflate 'rural' with 'farms' despite the fact that 'all rural places are not farms, nor are all rural Australians farmers'. They note, rather, that 'The diversity among Australia's rural communities and rural economies is nothing short of staggering' (p. 12). A 1988 town study identified dozens of types of towns in Victoria alone, and six distinct types of resource bases: dryland agriculture, irrigated agriculture, tourism, services (government and private sector), manufacturing, and commuter towns (Henshall Hansen Associates 1988, pp. 35–38).

62 Barr 2001, p. 5, quoted in Budge 2006, p. 43. See also, Argent *et al.* 2007, 2010; Barr 2009, pp. 49–57; Bohnet and Moore 2010; Race *et al.* 2010; Ragusa 2010; Smailes *et al.* 2012; and Burnley and Murphy 2004. Burnley and Murphy 2004 note that the 'sea-change' population turnaround in Australia started as early as the 1960s.

63 Argent *et al.* 2010, p. 29. They note that 'virtually all of the coastal Statistical Local Areas (SLAs) in New South Wales, Victoria and South Australia recorded in-migration rates of at least 20%' during the period of their study.

64 Bohnet and Moore 2010, pp. 46, 53. They cite other Australian studies that have generated similar results on the role of amenity migration.

65 For example, McGranahan 1999, quoted in Smailes *et al.* 2012, p. 37.

66 For instance, Collits and Rowe 2015, p. 85 quote a 2009 Regional Development Victoria study that found that '48% of Melburnians planning to relocate to a regional setting were doing so for (mainly) family reasons, 44% for employment and only 27% for lifestyle'. They also observe that 'in Queensland, the boom towns in recent times are those where people are moving for work, rather than for lifestyle. Key centres in this context are Mackay and Gladstone' (p. 85).

67 See Bohnet and Moore 2010, p. 53; they discuss the importance of 'closeness to other places' in interviewees' migration decisions. Murphy 2006, p. 35 uses the term 'metro proximals' to describe the connectivity advantages of being close to a metropolitan area.

68 It is notable that Victoria's total population growth from 2001 to 2011 was 816,500, yet only 52,500 or 6 per cent of this growth occurred in Victorian regions located outside 2 hours' drive from Melbourne (SGS 2014a, p. 2). Budge 2006, p. 39 has observed, for Victoria: 'The reality is now a divide between those areas that are part of an extended Melbourne area or sphere of influence, embracing nearly all areas within 150 kilometres of Melbourne, and largely the remainder of the state.' Martin *et al.* 2011, p. 5 observe that: 'Of the 50 fastest growing towns in Australia between 2001 and 2006, 20 were coastal and 19 (some overlap) were within 50 km of a metropolitan city – with some others close to smaller regional cities.' Commonwealth of Australia 2014a, p. 184 demonstrated that inner regional areas had a net population gain of 85,106 from internal migration, while both major cities and outer regional and remote areas as a whole lost population from internal migration.

69 The phenomenon of 'fly-in–fly-out' (or 'drive-in–drive-out') is discussed in Chapter 2.

70 For instance, Bohnet and Moore's 2010 study of lifestyle migration in far north Queensland highlighted that towns attracting in-migrants were close to Cairns International Airport, 'which was mentioned frequently in the interviews'. They observed that: 'This makes the context in which the sea- and tree-change phenomena occur even more complicated', noting that analysis of coastal growth based on 'distance to a capital city' may also apply 'to distance to regional service centres and transport networks/hubs' (Bohnet and Moore 2010, p. 53).

71 Plowman *et al.* 2003 found that innovative towns in Queensland were characterised

by such factors as younger, more transient and more highly educated populations, residents who travelled overseas, access to adequate products and services, higher proportions of owner-occupied accommodation, and upward trends in population and employment levels.

72 According to one index, internet activity in Australia doubled in the four years to 2011 (Deloitte Access Economics 2011).

73 See e.g. RAI 2015, p. 3; lack of high-speed broadband connectivity in many regions has been identified as an issue influencing their development potential.

74 For instance, Butt 2011, p. 72 explored reasons commuters moved to Castlemaine (on the outskirts of the larger regional town of Bendigo) and found that they included 'notions of community connectedness'.

75 Government of Western Australia 2013, pp. 18–31. This study also found that compared with an earlier study in 1997, 'a greater percentage of people wanted to stay in regional Western Australia' (p. 6). Though it is impossible to demonstrate causality, the level of ICT connectivity in regional Western Australia grew exponentially during this period.

76 People in inner regional, outer regional and remote areas volunteer at much higher rates (between 21 per cent and 24 per cent of the population) than those in major cities (16 per cent of the population) (Commonwealth of Australia 2014a, p. 64). Interestingly, however, between 2006 and 2011 the rate of volunteering grew slightly in major cities and fell slightly in regional and remote areas.

77 Smailes *et al.* 2012 found that existing variables such as amenity, proximity, and town size were able to statistically explain 57 per cent of the variance in population in South Eastern Australian towns over a ten-year period. They note that while these variables were important, there was 'scope for some communities to buck the trend, or to exploit the advantages' (p. 39).

78 Tonts 2000, p. 69.

79 Collits and Gastin 1997, p. 17.

80 Tonts 2000, p. 66.

81 Garlick 1999, p. 182.

82 McManus and Pritchard 2000, p. 219.

83 Dibden *et al.* 2001, p. 7.

84 Rogers and Barker 2001, p. 3.

85 Kenyon and Black 2001.

86 Kennedy 2011, p. 208. In a visit to Victoria in 2015 I observed the *Booktown* festival still going strong.

87 See e.g. Alston 2002, p. 9, who observes: 'It is difficult to rationalise the preferred message of the neoliberals, that community self-help is the key to rural survival, when government commitment to rural community infrastructure is not strongly evident and policies of cross subsidisation between city and country areas are being withdrawn.' Collits and Gastin 1997, p. 20 note that: 'It make little sense for governments to, on the one hand, encourage self-help through regional development policies and community economic development programs, while at the same time allowing small towns to waste away through the cumulative impact of a denuding of essential service infrastructure.'

88 Tonts 2000, p. 67 gives examples of 'rural revitalisation projects'. He notes that: 'Although the projects undertaken are usually small in scale and limited in scope, their impact in some country towns has been positive and has prompted further entrepreneurial development in some cases.'

89 Cheshire 2006, p. 14.

90 See e.g. Eversole 2007; Gray and Sinclair 2005; O'Toole and Burdess 2004.

91 Oxley 1981, p. 21.

92 Gray and Sinclair 2005, p. 50.

93 Eversole 2007, pp. 121, 136.
94 Dibden and Cheshire 2005, p. 225; see also Eversole 2003.
95 For instance, the Quebec Rural Policy, which takes a self-help approach and provides generous funding to towns over a five-year period (see MAMR 2006).
96 Dibden and Cocklin 2005, p. 11 note that there is a 'tendency to view rural communities as homogenous and unified by common interests', assumptions that do not hold true on the ground, where 'many are in fact characterised by socio-demographic heterogeneity and disparities in power and influence' (p. 11).
97 Eversole 2003, p. 81.
98 Other studies have identified the importance of individual civic leadership in providing a catalyst for local change, e.g. Sorensen and Epps 1996 quoted in Sorensen 2015.
99 The history of the King Island dairy industry is documented in Coates 2014.
100 Eversole *et al.* 2014.
101 Forth 2000, p. 3.
102 Eversole 2003, p. 78.
103 See e.g. European Commission 2006 for background on constructing advantage as a regional development approach.
104 Such as the Queensland communities documented by Cheshire 2006; the Victorian communities documented by Kennedy 2011 and O'Toole and Burdess 2004; and the various small-town renewal 'success stories' profiled by Kenyon and Black 2001.
105 Cited in Sorensen 2015, p. 45.
106 Dibden 2001, p. 9.
107 Cameron and Gibson 2001, p. 133.
108 Cocklin and Alston 2003, p. 6; see also Dibden and Cocklin 2005, pp. 9–10.

2   Regional industries

A story about industries

When I arrived in Tasmania in 2007, I had already spent seven years observing regional industries in Australia. They ranged from traditional broad acre farming and pastoralism to mining, forestry, retail, trades, and niche tourism enterprises. Most were 'in transition' from old ways of working to new. In Western Australia, broad acre farms, dairy operations, and towns built around forestry and mining were all looking to diversify their economies into new areas like tourism, orcharding, or viticulture. In Victoria, where sheep farms had once dominated the economy, the economy no longer rode on the sheep's back; key new industries in the Western District included plantation forestry, canola production, tourism, services, and a new mineral sands mine and processing facility.

A first look at North West Tasmania showed that industry transitions were well underway here too: in manufacturing, forestry, mining, and especially in agriculture. This was a green, temperate farming and dairying landscape. Agriculture was dominated by commodity vegetables – potatoes, carrots, and onions. These were, however, interspersed with newer arrivals such as poppies – taking advantage of a policy environment permitting poppy production – and pyrethrum. It created a beautiful patchwork landscape of green hills and ploughed red-soil fields, distinctive and productive. Yet it felt, from day one, under threat. There were carrots, and potatoes, and brassicas, but were there markets, and incomes, and futures for the family farms that dominated Tasmanian agriculture? Could Tasmanian agriculture survive and compete successfully on the world stage?

The Tasmanian hills were dotted with cows grazing lush temperate grasses, and milk tankers plied the roads regular as clockwork; but the price of milk had just dropped again. Dairy farmers were in the newspapers looking worried, lamenting the sustainability of their farms and the uncertainties they faced as price-takers. Meanwhile, about the time I arrived in town, a group of local farmers were taking their tractors to Canberra for a protest. Large companies had been sourcing their vegetables more cheaply offshore; the *Fair Dinkum Food* campaign wanted policy makers to actively support Australian-grown vegetables. In North West Tasmania, vegetable processors followed the mantra of *value adding* I had learned well in Western Australia. They were turning a portion of the local crop into frozen vegetables and chips. Nevertheless, one of these processors was about to move its operations offshore to cheaper climes, shedding enough jobs to make front-page news – and instigating yet another regional task-force.

Everything in the local farming economy seemed to be outside local control. I attended seminars at the then Tasmanian Institute of Agricultural Research to hear that the only solution to current pressures was for farms to get bigger and more efficient. The language of 'get big or get out' had achieved the status of unquestioned wisdom in many agricultural policy circles. These ideas were reflected on the ground in the state government's guidelines on the Protection of Agricultural Lands (PAL). PAL was a state government planning tool designed to stem the tide of rural residential developments by placing restrictions of the subdivision of quality agricultural land. Under PAL, a viable agricultural block for development purposes was defined as 40 hectares or more; the assumption was that anything smaller was not viable for agriculture. Nevertheless, these state-level planning rules met sharp resistance on the ground.

Over and over in local communities across Tasmania, it was observed that these planning rules were standing in the way of new rural enterprises. Tasmania's comparatively abundant water, rich soils, and a 'clean green' environment were sources of competitive advantage and they were attracting agricultural entrepreneurs – locally, from interstate, even from overseas. These entrepreneurs were coming to local Councils with proposals for agricultural business developments, but many of these proposals were being knocked back because they were not compliant with PAL. Agriculture on comparatively small parcels of land was dismissed as hobby farming, not serious business. Yet many of the proposed crops, from berries to walnuts to heritage pigs, could be cultivated intensively: 40 hectare blocks were not required.

A closer look over the next months showed that the agricultural landscape of North West Tasmania was much more complex than the surface image of commodity vegetables, big processors, and dairy. On the ground, entrepreneurs were leveraging red soil and a cool, wet climate in a range of innovative ways. Many producers had already diversified into a range of new, so-called 'niche' crops. There were raspberries, cherries, capsicums, wasabi, saffron, walnuts, ginseng, cut flowers, tulips, and salmon. There were rabbits, herbs, dairy goats, gourmet chickens, heritage pork, and specialty beef – a wide range of non-traditional products.

Then, there were the value-adding operations, often linking in strong local supply chains of producers: flavoured cheeses, local beer and cider, freeze-dried vegetables, gourmet chocolate, jams and sauces, even baby food. Most businesses were spearheaded by an entrepreneurial individual. Some had diversified their operations from larger agricultural properties; some adapted existing rural premises to new ventures. None were overly large in land area or staff, but many were successfully competing in markets in Tasmania, interstate, and overseas.

This landscape of 'niche' enterprises seemed to directly contradict the agricultural mantra of 'get big or get out'. Most did not require large tracts of land or large processing factories. Many even relied on hand-work – such as the painstaking harvesting of saffron. These products found markets, often lucrative ones: whether supplying direct to chefs, independent supermarkets, interstate buyers, via websites, or direct to the public at farmers markets or retail shops. Tourism promoters started to call attention to those with retail outlets, and to promote the state as a gourmet holiday destination. Yet on the landscape of Tasmanian agriculture, these businesses were largely invisible. Strategies did not mention them. Planning schemes did not take them into account. When the government talked about agriculture, only the traditional commodities were visible. Capsicum, wasabi, gourmet chickens, and walnuts were not conceptually part of the *agricultural industry*.

Nor was this kind of invisibility limited to agriculture. The story of invisible businesses repeated itself again and again in the region's other 'old' industries: manufacturing and forestry. Both were – and still are – undergoing significant transition, with question marks over their futures. The visible face of forestry-related manufacturing in the region is pulp and paper mills. The town of Burnie was long known for its large paper mill, which downsized significantly in the 1990s and ultimately closed in 2010. Nearby Wesley Vale also lost its paper mill that year. These 'old' manufacturing operations were understood to be out-of-date, uncompetitive in a global market. Increasingly, they have been portrayed as environmentally problematic as well: a proposal for a new wood pulp mill at Bell Bay in the north of the state has given rise to considerable conflict around the projected environmental impact – both of the facility, and of continuing to turn Tasmania's forests into pulp. Yet largely invisible in these forestry debates are the firms that produce high-value timber products, such as specialty wood veneers and handmade furniture, from Tasmanian timbers.

In North West Tasmania the closure of the region's paper mills, weaving mills, and vegetable processors has been constantly in the news, dominating the public and political imagination. Over and over again, the headlines proclaimed *jobs axed* and *more bad news for Tasmanian workers*. Large manufacturing firms – many owned by overseas-based multinationals – seemed to be perpetually struggling to compete. Some regularly sought government funding to prop up their ailing operations. Threat of possible and actual downsizing in one single large machinery manufacturing firm warranted regular front-page news in the North West over several years. The firm finally closed, a decision made overseas, after an emotional rollercoaster of *threats*, *hopes*, and *axed jobs*.

The visible manufacturing sector in North West Tasmania was, therefore, in a precarious situation. The main firms were always on the precipice of being downsized, relocated offshore, or closed. Yet alongside this landscape of struggling larger manufacturers, there was a less-visible manufacturing sector of small, locally owned manufacturing firms. These firms were producing innovative farming equipment and precision irrigation systems, road sweepers and trucks, watercraft, remote area housing, even components for space shuttles. Many were set up to manufacture specialty items to order for a range of applications: equipment components, art installations, skate parks. These firms were generally SMEs (small and medium enterprises), many with fewer than five employees. They had identified specific, high-value 'niches' where they could compete successfully. Nevertheless, they did not appear in the visible public discourse – in newspapers or in policy statements about manufacturing in the North West.

For every industry I observed on the ground, there seemed to be two: one visible, one invisible. There were the visible industries that policy makers saw – generally, the large, traditionally structured firms – and the ones that flew under the policy radar, too small to notice, and yet often the most interesting and innovative. Every policy document I read painted the region as mired in *old industries* (agriculture, manufacturing, mining, forestry), with low-skilled workforces, lacking innovation.

It was true the overall levels of formal qualifications in industries like manufacturing and agriculture were low, particularly at university level. Yet a visit to any shop floor or working farm showed workers with well-honed skills, many learned on the job, not formally credentialed. Equally, many entrepreneurs who were moving into the region to start businesses were highly educated. And I heard numerous stories of local back-shed inventors who had built pieces of equipment to solve a practical problem. Some went on to market their inventions interstate and overseas.

The industry transitions in this region weren't just about 'old' industries struggling, closing, or moving offshore. Rather, the view at ground level revealed a number of transitions. Locally owned, small-scale firms with agile business models were showing they could compete on the world stage. Embedded in the local region, these firms were unlikely to suddenly move offshore. Other transitions were simply cyclical, as markets waxed and waned. For these industries, as the Tasmanian road sign says: *Expect the unexpected*. Milk prices were low; now they are buoyant. Forestry was riding the wave of expected pulp mill investment; now forestry employment has declined dramatically. Mining is lucrative but highly cyclical; months of lament over mine closures have turned cheerful again this month with the promise of a new mine. Meanwhile, one of the most significant recent investments in the region has been in offshore fish-farming: a multi-million dollar industry that was, until recently, invisible to the public eye.

In the past eight years, applied researchers in the Institute for Regional Development have drawn attention to the existence of niche agriculture, nimble niche manufacturing, and other industry trends in North West Tasmania.[1] Nevertheless, there is still a large chasm between how distant decision makers see Tasmania's regional industries – typically large, old, under-skilled, and under threat – and this diversity on the ground. Micro and small businesses, for instance, make up about 95 per cent of the region's businesses, but they still fly largely under the policy radar.[2] Newspaper headlines are still reserved for big firms, though the local farming newspaper has started to tell the stories of successful niche enterprises.

On the ground, talking with local people, there are stories of lost jobs, but many more tales of interesting regional businesses doing clever things. Firms, often small, are leveraging unique skills and attributes to create new, high-value market niches: the beef farmer that supplies (guaranteed disease free) bovine heart valves to the United States, the eel grower that exports to Asian markets, the IT business with its world-first internet security program, the family firm exporting medicinal plants to Europe – the list goes on. Some firms struggle and fail, but the overall story is of dynamism, not decline.

Regional industry issues

> Industry fortunes affect regional fortunes, and hence the prosperity of communities of all sizes.[3]

Transition, restructuring, change: these are the leitmotifs of industries in regional Australia. It seems to matter little whether the conversation is about wool, wheat, dairy, forestry, or manufacturing – these 'traditional' industries are all changing, and have been for some time. Regional communities in turn are caught in the nexus of change. Industry sustainability is perhaps the central regional development issue for Australian communities: Can the region's key industry (or industries) survive the twin pressures of global competition and local environmental constraint?

Australia's longstanding regional industries – farming, forestry, mining, and related manufacturing – are heavily dependent on natural resources, and they tend to trade primarily in global commodity markets.[4] These industries have been in transition for decades, as new technologies, transport links, domestic and trade policies, and natural resource pressures have continually shifted the playing field, creating both challenges and opportunities for regional producers.

The 1980s and 1990s represented a particularly acute period of change, as government policies removed price protections on agricultural commodities like wheat and wool, restructured state-run enterprises, and began to grapple with a new set of environmental sustainability concerns. Yet up until the present, with every farm buyout, milk price drop, forestry agreement, or manufacturing plant closure, industry restructuring is rediscovered. In the end it can be said that Australia's regional industries operate in a perpetual state of change.[5]

Regional industries in Australia, despite their diversity, share a set of common characteristics that create challenges when grappling with change. First, there is a high level of economic and social interdependence between regional communities and their industries. In agricultural areas, many businesses are closely tied to the agricultural economy as suppliers, contractors, and so forth. Downturns in the farming sector are felt far beyond agriculture. Equally, towns with a single large manufacturing firm or mining enterprise often have many smaller firms who rely on the large firm's business – as well as those who provide retail, education, food, and other services.

Regions with heavy reliance on a single industry – and worse, a single large company – suffer economic multipliers with a vengeance when there is a downturn. For instance, an economic forum in a large Tasmanian town remarked with reference to one firm, that 'a change in the company affects the whole community'.[6]

In 2012, the most commonly identified economic threat in Australian regions was the lack of economic diversity.[7]

The interdependence between regional communities and industries goes in the opposite direction too: industries in lightly populated regions depend upon a limited pool of human capital. It can be difficult to access the range of skills and labour needed to diversify. When transitioning industries enter a downturn and shed jobs, commuting catchments struggle to absorb the retrenched workers. The few jobs available are usually a poor match with workers' skills; despite the best intentions of training providers fluent in the language of *reskilling the workforce*, few retrenched miners are keen to serve cappuccinos.

Often, workers move out of the region. When an upturn comes, they and their skills are gone.[8] The common language of 'regional skill shortages' is often a gloss for this mismatch between skilled workers and available opportunities over time. As a result, many mining companies now rely on 'fly-in–fly-out' (FIFO) workforces. FIFO allows companies to source their workers and suppliers from anywhere; it essentially removes the interdependence between regional communities and industries.

A second characteristic of Australian regional industries is their generally high level of interdependence with their natural environments. Most regional Australian industries are resource dependent: either primary production, or industries closely linked to primary production such as food and fibre manufacturing or minerals processing. The natural environment is thus both a key resource – indeed, in many cases a source of competitive advantage – and a key limiting factor.

Poor management of the resource base can seriously damage productivity over the long term, illustrated in problems like soil salinity in agriculture. In addition, environmental issues like drought create an additional layer of uncertainty quite apart from global market conditions. Furthermore, in recent decades Australian policy has focused on achieving sustainable industries that do not exhaust their resource base or damage surrounding environments. This has been a particular challenge in areas where strong regional industries have been built around high levels of resource consumption: such as irrigated agriculture in the Murray–Darling Basin, or the logging of old-growth forests in Western Australia and Tasmania.

The interdependence between regional industries and their environments often gives rise to social conflicts on the ground in regional communities. Water and trees are both scarce and valuable resources in the Australian context. Policy moves to protect river and forest ecosystems have come into direct conflict with important regional industries. Public debate typically creates an either/or opposition between industry interests – often glossed as 'jobs' – and environmental, or 'green' interests.

Thus, it is not uncommon to see bumper stickers promoting one camp or the other: *support the pulp mill* versus *save our forests*. While mining companies have proven adept at managing conflict through active community engagement and mine site remediation, other industries regularly fall foul of the environment–industry divide: even supposedly 'green' industries like wind farming.[9] Meanwhile, government environmental regulations tend to be complex, costly, highly prescriptive, and imposed from the capital cities with limited local input. None of this endears them to regional communities or industries.[10]

A third characteristic of regional industries, alongside their interdependence with regional communities and environments, is their high level of isolation. Australia as a whole can be said to suffer from a certain degree of isolation on the world stage, and this situation is greatly compounded for those working outside the nation's metropolitan centres. Regional firms are often disconnected from both capital cities and global networks. The sheer physical distances between places in Australia, and between Australia and the rest of the world, mean that transport options can be costly and/or inadequate for business needs.[11] Virtual distance is also an issue; many parts of regional Australia still only have poor broadband and mobile phone coverage, severely limiting connectivity.[12]

Political and social distance matter too: regional firms sit outside the nation's hubs of knowledge, investment, and decision-making. It is not uncommon for business owners in regional areas to observe that they make little or no use of government programmes and services and don't really know what services are out there.[13] Equally, many – particularly smaller firms – struggle to access market intelligence that would permit them to identify and exploit emerging market opportunities.[14] Perhaps because of this the rate of new business entries is lower across regional Australia than in the major cities.[15]

Regional industries are thus deeply embedded in their regional communities and environments, yet disconnected from resources beyond their region. This creates a particular set of issues. On the one hand, they must strike a delicate balance to ensure economic, social, and environmental sustainability on the ground. On the other, they must navigate in globalised markets where many key resources are out of reach.

The situation is complicated by the fact that most regional industries comprise very small firms with limited human resources. Most are not even SMEs by international standards.[16] Regional locations thus provide the ingredients for success, yet put firms at a disadvantage in accessing the information, resources, and support they need to succeed.

Old industry myths

> Australia still has an old economy. To this day, much of its wealth comes from raising plants and animals and digging stuff out of the ground.[17]

The most common industries in regional Australia are often called 'old' industries: resource-dependent activities such as agriculture, forestry, mining, and manufacturing. Agriculture of various kinds – grains, grazing, horticulture, viticulture, or tropical agriculture – has been particularly important over Australia's history, though not in every region. In different regions, different industries predominate. In some regions agriculture is the biggest employer; in others it is manufacturing, mining, retail, or construction.[18] So-called 'new' industries like tourism and services are also important in many regional economies. An emerging major employer in Australian regions in recent years is health and social assistance services.[19]

Contemporary regions are often exhorted to look past their traditional economic base in old industries and seek out new industries. Downturns and job losses feed a narrative of old industries inevitably in decline. Furthermore, old industries are portrayed as *resource based*, while new industries are *knowledge based*.

Traditional regional industries extract the natural resource base (soil, water, minerals, trees) and sell the product into global commodity markets, where the recipe for success is to produce more, more cheaply. This can create a vicious cycle of resource exploitation, efficiency-driven job cuts, and dwindling earnings margins – damaging firms, environments, and communities. Over time, sustainability concerns weave a compelling narrative of old industry decline: the idea that old, resource-based industries are not just in transition, but on their way out.

This portrait is, however, only a partial story. While Australia's resource-dependent regional industries are in transition, they are not necessarily in decline. Agriculture, manufacturing, forestry, and mining have not disappeared, nor have they ceased to operate in global commodity markets. Nevertheless, they are changing.

Firms are becoming more diverse and more clever. They are developing and adopting new technologies and value-adding processes to achieve quality and efficiency gains. In many cases they are stepping outside the commodity mould and identifying new economic 'niches' where they can compete on quality rather than on price. Looking beyond the dominant narrative of regional industry decline, it is possible to discern the new face of old industries.

1. Agriculture – the myth of small farm demise

> Get big or get out.[20]

Agriculture is Australia's classic old industry. Since European colonisation it has constituted the economic base of much of regional Australia. Yet agriculture is less important than it once was. While regional Australia once *rode on the sheep's back*, relying heavily on the lucrative wool industry, it has since dismounted and gone on to other things. Other industries have grown: such as manufacturing, mining, and services. Data on diminishing agricultural employment and declining farm numbers suggest that regions need to look to new economic options beyond agriculture. Nevertheless, a closer look at agriculture on the ground reveals that this old industry contains considerable diversity – and numerous new industries.

It is clear that agriculture's *relative* economic contribution to the Australian economy has dwindled quickly in recent decades. In the first half of the twentieth century, agriculture accounted for up to 80 per cent of Australia's exports; in 2010–2011, only 11 per cent.[21] Between 2006 and 2011 alone, agriculture was the fastest declining industry in many regions, shedding over 30,000 jobs across regional Australia.[22] Every time a count is taken, there are fewer farmers – in the 30 years to 2011, Australia lost over 100,000.[23] These data raise the spectre of a declining, and potentially disappearing, farm sector in regional Australia.

Yet Australian agriculture is not an industry in decline. The value of agricultural production is significant – $48 billion in 2013, and growing.[24] Australian farm exports were worth about $8.2 billion in 1980–81; 30 years later in 2011 they were worth $32.5 billion – four times as much.[25] Other exports have grown faster, so the relative importance of agriculture has fallen, but agriculture is still a significant export industry. Furthermore, Australian agriculture produces 93 per cent of all food consumed in Australia.[26]

Agriculture is not in decline, but it has undergone a period of very rapid change. The state of rapid transition that characterises many regional Australian industries is particularly notable in agriculture. Writing from her on-the-ground work with farming women in New South Wales in 1991, Margaret Alston observed that some of the older women she interviewed could remember farming with draughthorses.[27] Not only has farming become much more technology-driven very quickly, but the institutional and policy landscape has shifted dramatically.

Australian farmers have moved from a highly protectionist regime to one highly exposed to the open market.[28] As tariff protections have been removed, industries deregulated, and marketing boards disbanded, farmers in traditional sectors such as wool, wheat, and dairy have landed on a very different playing field: from guaranteed farm-gate prices for their grain, wool, or milk to dealing with the uncertainty of global price fluctuations and post-farm-gate customer expectations. Many, unsurprisingly, have left the industry.[29]

Other changes have also affected agriculture. Costs of inputs have grown more quickly than the prices farmers receive, meaning that terms of trade have declined and farmers earn less.[30] In many cases, lower real earnings have meant a series of trade-off decisions for farmers and their families: to continue farming full time, or take off-farm work to supplement their incomes; to grow the farm, often by buying out neighbours, or to maintain an acceptable level of consumption for the family.[31]

Meanwhile, two major supermarket chains now exercise a duopoly in the domestic food market, limiting market options. As a result, farmers can be forced to sell below the cost of production.[32] Land prices have also risen in much of regional Australia.[33] Farmers now compete with a range of other land uses such as plantation forestry and rural residential development.[34]

These kinds of pressures raise questions about the sustainability of small farms and farming communities over the long term. Various authors have written eloquently about the strain that participation in global, competitive agriculture puts on farmers and farming communities: the impact of personal financial stress, the declining populations in rural communities as farmers leave, and the environmental consequences of production-intensive farming regimes.[35] In some cases, it has been observed that farming families are 'working harder and longer for less return', and that their 'economic well-being, health and family lives are under constant pressure'.[36]

These portraits describe the situation facing a sub-set of the agricultural industry: farmers who produce for global commodity markets, particularly on smaller farms or environmentally marginal land. For this part of the industry, the common mantra of 'get big or get out' can ring very true. Growth-oriented farms buy out their neighbours, leveraging economies of scale to remain competitive.[37] Farmers exit the sector and farms consolidate, leading to fewer but larger farms.[38] Small farms struggle to compete. There is a sense that the small-farm sector is doomed to disappear.

Nevertheless, there are other trajectories for farms. Rather than sell up or consolidate, some farms change what they produce, or diversify into a broader range of products. They explore new products, new markets, and/or new business models. The story at the start of this chapter described a diverse landscape of agricultural producers in one Australian region: the high-rainfall, temperate-climate landscape of North West Tasmania. There, environmental attributes have given rise to considerable experimentation around new products, new markets, and new businesses models. Tasmania started Australia's wasabi industry, its quinoa industry, its truffle industry, and its poppy industry. In the face of a rapidly changing landscape, the agricultural industry has diversified.

Diversification and niche industries are particularly easy to observe at ground level in Tasmania, with its varied topography and climate. Nevertheless, there are many other examples: Western Australia has been a leader in on-farm aquaculture, an industry which produced about $8 million worth of freshwater crayfish in 2011, many in farm dams.[39] Queensland has spearheaded the production of numerous tropical fruits and nuts such as macadamia nuts, and significant new industries have emerged.

Across regional Australia, agriculture has diversified into a wide range of new, non-traditional products. These stories of agricultural diversification are often missing from popular and policy narratives of agriculture in Australia. Agriculture is an old industry, but it has many new products. Little by little, they are beginning to attract attention.

In 2014 the Rural Industries Research and Development Corporation (RIRDC) released a report on emerging agricultural industries in Australia – new industries, often valued in the millions of dollars, and often with significant growth potential in international markets.[40] The results confirm the significance and diversity of emerging agricultural industries in Australia. Some of these are already producing significant value: such as the truffle industry, worth over $5 million per year; the culinary herb industry, worth $46 million; and the olive industry, with annual production valued at $218 million.[41]

Nevertheless, this diversity can be hard to see. New agricultural industries often sit under the umbrella of larger traditional categories. Horticulture is a case in point. Horticulture in regional Australia embraces a range of agricultural practices: from commodity production of potatoes for processing, to a range of high-value and technologically sophisticated practices such as controlled climate horticulture. The horticulture industry produced about $3.8 billion of food in 2013, comprising everything from carrots and onions to capsicums and melons. Notably, however, about a third of these products – $1.3 billion worth – was made up of numerous niche and emerging varieties too small to classify.[42] Asian vegetables, for instance, are one important suite of products not reflected in mainstream statistical counts.[43] These are not typical horticultural commodities, but high-value niche products.

Furthermore, the language of agricultural niches can be misleading; 'niche' products are high-value and targeted, capable of competing on attributes other than price. Yet 'niche' does not necessarily mean small. Fruit and nuts, for instance, are typical niche agricultural products in Australia, but Australia's fruit and nut sector as a whole is worth more than horticulture – close to $5 billion per year, and growing at about 20 per cent.[44] Nor are 'commodity' and 'niche' necessarily opposites; both approaches can co-exist within the same firm.

Dairy, for instance, is a significant commodity industry, but dairy firms have developed numerous value-adding ventures in regional communities in recent years, such as gourmet cheese production. Farmers have also explored and gone on to exploit a range of high-value yet high-volume non-traditional products such as canola and poppies, often planting these in fields alongside more 'traditional' agricultural activities. Bright yellow canola fields on the wool-growing landscapes in regions like Victoria's Western District yield good returns – $2.3 billion Australia-wide in 2013.[45] The Tasmanian poppy industry, established in the 1960s, has achieved high levels of productivity and innovation: including a recently released variety of poppy which manufactures codeine in-field.[46]

Thus, the supposedly 'old' agricultural industry in regional Australia has a number of 'new' faces. These new faces are increasingly apparent in a range of clever and highly competitive regional businesses from hothouse capsicum to clever dairy farms, and from oilseed production to cut flowers.[47] Even small cocoa, coffee, and tea industries have emerged.[48] Honey is now an established industry and also demonstrates innovation: for instance, a world-first online tool using current satellite imagery to help beekeepers predict where and when eucalypt trees will flower.[49] The new face of agriculture in Australia also includes growing food in water; aquaculture is a significant industry, worth about $1 billion annually, that now comprises over 40 per cent of Australia's fisheries production.[50]

Cumulatively, the significance of Australia's new and non-traditional agricultural industries are easily on par with the value of traditional commodities such as wool, wheat, and beef. Yet as single products, traditional agricultural categories dominate, and with them the dominant narrative that Australian agriculture is primarily broad acre or pastoral, commodity based, and caught in a downward spiral. The diversity and innovation in Australian agriculture is too often overlooked.

Furthermore, the new faces of the agriculture industry often have different business models, resource requirements, and skill needs. Business models that suit broad acre farming – where it is often necessary to 'get big or get out' – do not necessarily hold true in other kinds of agriculture. The nature of many niche and emerging crops means that they do not require large spaces to be viable. Policy makers tend to calculate the minimum land size required for a serious agricultural business based on the requirements of broad acre agriculture. Yet many of Australia's new and emerging crops are cultivated much more intensively, and can be commercially viable on smaller parcels of land.[51]

Equally, policy makers tend to assume that farms must be full-time and high-turnover to be serious businesses.[52] Yet today's agriculture is characterised by diversification of income streams; even traditional farmers with large properties now diversify their crops and/or take off-farm employment to supplement their incomes. Meanwhile, new farmers are entering agriculture, seeking to identify and exploit new market niches.[53] These new farmers are often older – with dollars and business experience behind them. Though often dismissed as 'hobby farmers', they are well positioned for business success; they do not require the same level of income as a young family, and so can ride out the low-turnover start-up phase to build new businesses from the ground up.[54]

The skills that are needed in these new agricultural industries are not necessarily the ones that spring to mind with the words 'agricultural industry skills'. They often extend past the farm gate and along the value chain: skills in research, food science, engineering, transport and logistics, manufacturing, and marketing, to name a few. One workshop in North West Tasmania, for instance, named the top priorities for future agro-food research and development to be post-farm-gate considerations such as value adding, logistics and distribution, branding and marketing, and the science to support the state's 'clean green' marketing image.[55]

Perhaps more than any other regional industry, agriculture is deeply embedded in regional communities and environments. It is clear that traditional commodity-based farm business models have created sustainability challenges for family farms and farming communities. In response, the agricultural industry has diversified. On the one hand, there are large farms that successfully 'got big' and are producing commodities viably on a large scale. On the other, many farms have moved to diversify what they produce and have transitioned into higher value production, often at physically smaller scales.[56]

In the end, it is clear that agricultural industries in regional Australia have been innovative and flexible in response to rapid transition. Yet many of the positive stories of agriculture go unnoticed. The new faces of agriculture do not correspond with the expected face of an old industry in decline. While the existence of a viable, high-value small-farm sector is slowly being documented, its implications for sustainable regional economies are only starting to be explored.[57]

2. Manufacturing – the myth of industry decline

> The ordinary citizen could be forgiven for believing that it is inevitable that the nation will no longer build anything.[58]

Manufacturing is another 'old industry' which, like agriculture, has been in the throes of transition over a number of decades. It is an industry where job losses have often been dramatic; in the decade 2003–13 manufacturing in Australia lost over 100,000 jobs.[59] These job losses were spread across both metropolitan and regional Australia, but were felt hardest in the less-diverse economies of Australia's regions.

Certain manufacturing sub-sectors have experienced particularly dramatic job losses, and many of these are closely linked to regional economies: such as paper and wood product manufacturing and textiles.[60] At the same time, other sub-sectors of manufacturing with close ties to regional economies, such as food and beverage manufacturing, are strong and growing.[61]

Manufacturing is a significant economic player in many parts of regional Australia. Currently, about a third of all Australia manufacturing workers are employed in regional and remote areas.[62] Manufacturing employment tends to be concentrated in particular regions: for instance, Shepparton, Victoria, and North West Tasmania, regions where manufacturing is the top employer.[63] In some regions, however, manufacturing employment has been important but is declining: such as the Illawarra (New South Wales), Ballarat, Geelong and Hume (Victoria), and Fitzroy (Queensland).[64] Even in North West Tasmania, where the manufacturing industry is still the largest employer and economic contributor to the region, several major firms have closed in recent years.[65]

At one time most regional communities had small manufacturing enterprises providing local value adding. The landscape of regional Australia was full of butter factories, abattoirs, textile mills, and so forth, built upon local primary industries, and serving primarily a local market. Some of these enterprises have survived, but most have not. Over time, the location of value-adding processes has shifted away from local areas. While many regional Australian towns still support local bakeries and butcher shops as part of their retail landscape, many manufactured staples now travel: at least within the same state, and often between states and internationally.[66]

While the closure of smaller and less-competitive local manufacturers has been an ongoing process over time, recent declines in Australian manufacturing have been fast and dramatic. Manufacturing plummeted from Australia's largest industry in terms of economic value in 2003, to fourth largest in 2013 – and it was the only industry that actually shrank over that time period.[67] During this decade manufacturing suffered from a combination of decreasing cost-competitiveness – in line with the quick-rising Australian dollar – which, alongside the fast expansion of manufacturing capacity in emerging economies, made it increasingly difficult for firms to compete, and tempting for many to move operations offshore to cut costs.[68] Large, foreign-owned manufacturers are notoriously fleet-footed. A recent report on Australian manufacturing observed: 'One out of every ten manufacturing jobs disappeared over the last four years ... Many firms, and the supply chains they support, are only just holding on.'[69] The language of 'just holding on' suffuses the conversation about manufacturing in regional Australia and a 2014 report on the manufacturing industry notes that 'transition' in the manufacturing industry is likely to continue for some time.[70]

The government's regional development policy response to manufacturing decline and job losses has been primarily in the form of structural adjustment programmes of various types.[71] Many of these programmes aim to assist displaced workers to transition to new roles.[72] Nevertheless, a longitudinal study of manufacturing workers conducted over the decade 2001–11 confirmed that a significant proportion of redundant manufacturing workers – over 17 per cent – simply left the labour force.[73] Equally, it has been noted that many workers who were left unemployed by closures of the textile, clothing, and footwear industries during the 1980s 'went onto social security and stayed there', unable to find alternate work.[74] Older workers and those with limited literacy and numeracy skills are often least likely to transition successfully into new jobs.[75]

Job losses in manufacturing thus represent serious human capital and productivity drains in affected regions. At the same time, job losses are not the whole story. Some parts of the manufacturing industry are doing surprisingly well. A number of manufacturing sub-sectors have experienced growth over the past decade: such as food and beverage manufacturing, where industry value added has increased, and employment grew by an impressive 32 per cent.[76] Other growing manufacturing sub-sectors include metal products, minerals, and petroleum and coal products.[77] These thriving sub-sectors are linked to the agricultural and mining industries in regional Australia. While Australia is a small player in global manufacturing, it has a competitive edge in low-to-medium technology manufacturing linked to its abundant natural resources.[78]

In manufacturing, stories of decline capture the headlines, and governments too often invest dollars in propping up ailing large firms or enticing them to stay. Yet these stories sit alongside a reality in which some parts of the manufacturing industry are managing quite well. The image of manufacturing as an old-economy industry in decline disguises these pockets of success and even significant innovation. Those involved on the ground with the manufacturing industry are increasingly articulating the need to address the 'perceptions issue' in Australian manufacturing – to counter the pervasive myth of manufacturing industry decline.[79]

North West Tasmania provides a case in point; the region's manufacturing heritage is typified by large firms such as the pulp mill and a paint plant known for regularly changing the colour of the Bass Strait. It has been observed that: 'In the popular imagination, "manufacturing" still involves traditional activities, infrastructure and products – large factories, smoke stacks, production lines, heavy machinery, and sizable unionised workforces.'[80]

In practice, however, contemporary manufacturing in North West Tasmania is highly diverse and agile, comprising primarily micro and small firms serving niche and custom markets. Despite the closure and downsizing of several large manufacturing firms, manufacturing in the region is alive and well, producing about $3 billion per year of product, far and away outstripping other industries including mining and agriculture.[81] Furthermore, manufacturing firms in North West Tasmania have 'a strong regional focus', including a preference for buying goods and services from within the region, thereby generating further economic multipliers for the region.[82]

As noted in a recent report on manufacturing in the region: 'The North West is in the midst of a shift from "smoke stack" manufacturing to a new "green manufacturing" future.... working with customers from concept to design, production and product support.'[83]

Manufacturing industry experts observe that 'niche' and 'knowledge intensive' manufacturing that can provide specialised, client-focused products at short notice are the new face of manufacturing – representing the future of the industry in Australia.[84] Moreover, these kinds of businesses are already present and competitive on the ground in Australian regions.[85] In comparison with the dominant narrative of manufacturing industry closures, recent research has highlighted 'a contrasting cohort of growing, highly productive clusters of manufacturing scattered throughout the country.'[86]

Regional Australia is well positioned to develop a next generation of globally competitive manufacturing firms. The most competitive and growing sub-sectors of manufacturing rely on raw materials from Australia's regions. Further, niche and high-value manufacturers are often able to overcome the competitive disadvantages of cost and distance in the way that traditional large-scale plants have been unable to do.[87] The combination of abundant natural resources and clever business models gives regional manufacturers traction on the world stage. Closures of large firms capture the headlines, but in the background, smaller and more agile firms are creating the new face of an old industry.

3. Extractive industries – the myth of prosperity

> Many regions both rural and urban would have been better off had the boom not taken place.[88]

The Australian economy still relies heavily on extractive industries: mining in particular. Mining is the biggest single contributor to the Australian economy – industry value added was $114 billion in 2013.[89] Coal and iron ore alone comprise about 45 per cent of all exports from Australia.[90] Other extractive industries such as forestry and fishing are also important to many regional economies: forestry contributed about $7 billion to the economy in 2013 and employed over 70,000 people Australia-wide, while wild-catch fisheries added an addition $1.4 billion of value.[91]

Extractive industries are often portrayed as quintessentially 'old economy' activities. They simply extract and sell what is already there. They are thus vulnerable to both the swings of commodity markets and the finite life of the resources themselves. In Australia, this combination of global market fluctuations and sustainability challenges has created a landscape of extractive industries in constant transition.

The forestry industry, for instance, has faced serious transitions; these have created a roller-coaster ride for forestry-dependent regions such as Northern Tasmania and South Western Australia. Forestry shed about 12,000 jobs nationwide between 2006 and 2011, about 14 per cent of its total workforce; but in Tasmania, forest-related employment nearly halved.[92] Part of this decline was due to competitive pressures on the industry from abroad, and part to growing public opposition at home to the logging of 'old growth' native forests. Over time the land available for logging in Australia has decreased, as has the amount of wood logged.[93] Transitioning to a smaller resource base has impacted the industry at the same time as it confronted pressures from rising input costs and competition from overseas.[94]

Mining, as well, is an industry prone to regular cycles of 'boom' and 'bust'.[95] In recent years the Australian mining boom has had a dramatic impact in some regions. In regional Australia, the opening or expansion of mines in response to high commodity prices can generate a great deal of excitement, investment, and in-migration.[96] At the same time, the trauma occasioned by mine downsizing and closures in regional communities is akin to that caused by the downsizing or closure of a major manufacturer.

Regions such as the Pilbara/Kimberly and Gascoyne/Goldfields regions of Western Australia and the Mackay region of Queensland have become boom regions on the back of mineral exports; mining is the largest and fastest growing source of employment in remote and Northern Australia.[97] Nevertheless, 'boom' regions have not benefitted as much as might be expected. Meanwhile, other regions have suffered when their agriculture and manufacturing industries have had to grapple with a higher Australian dollar.[98]

Mining is a complex, global industry with significant regional impacts. It relies intimately on the resources found in regional environments. Yet the industry is increasingly disconnected from regional communities. Most mining companies are foreign-owned multinationals. The bulk of mining's economic benefits flow to urban areas and overseas. Profits flow elsewhere, and most inputs – about 60 per cent of total investment – are imported from overseas, not sourced from regional or even metropolitan Australian economies.[99]

The main economic benefits for mining communities are in the form of relatively high-paid employment in mining and construction, a characteristic that has meant mining developments are often relatively popular with regional communities in spite of concerns over environmental impacts.[100] Nevertheless, in recent years the growing popularity of 'fly-in–fly-out' workforces has increasingly separated employment impacts from regional communities. Now, many of the employment benefits of mining developments are accruing to metropolitan centres such as Perth and Brisbane.[101]

Fly-in–fly-out mining refers to the growing tendency for mining workforces to live somewhere other than the mine site, and to fly in (or in some cases, drive in) to undertake intensive shifts over several days or weeks, interspersed with rest periods at home.[102] Thus, nearly 22 per cent of Australia's mining industry workforce now lives in the West Australian capital Perth; Perth is Australia's biggest mining town.[103] Equally, the Queensland mining sector provides more jobs in Brisbane (40 per cent of mining employment) than in any other region.[104] Fly-in–fly-out workforces give both workers and companies flexibility, and can lessen the economic transitions related to mine closures in regional communities. Nevertheless, FIFO can also be a source of frustration when much of the economic value-add of mining employment to the local area leaves town at the end of its shift.[105]

While mining is increasingly disconnected from regional communities, other extractive industries such as forestry and fishing remain deeply grounded in their regional contexts. It is interesting to observe that these regional industries are gradually transitioning away from pure extractive models. They are focusing on harvesting wild resources sustainably and, increasingly, cultivating new resources. Both aquaculture and plantation forestry are significant and growing segments of these industries, suggesting a more sustainably focused production regime.[106] Furthermore, an emerging trend toward growing seafood on artificial reefs proposes an interesting mid-point between aquaculture and wild catch: a cultivated resource in a wild-catch environment.

In regional Australia, patently unsustainable resource extraction, such as the opening-up of coastal waters to a 'super trawler' capable of huge wild catches, generates significant public outcry.[107] Yet even apparently sustainable production models can meet resistance on the ground in regional communities. Plantation forestry is one example. Though it is a sustainable form of wood production, tree farms give rise to a number of other sustainability concerns on the ground: about the loss of productive agricultural land as farms sell out to trees, the loss of population and employment that farms previously provided, and the environmental impacts of tree monoculture.[108]

On the ground in regional communities, sustainable resource use is not just about the industry itself, but the larger economic, social, and environmental landscapes on which it is located. Simply being 'sustainable' or 'green' is not enough if these on-the-ground relationships and impacts are not understood. Wind generation, for instance, has enormous potential in regional Australia, but it has attracted significant public resistance due to concerns such as the effect of wind turbines on public health or bird life. It is difficult to resolve these issues because there is often poor communication between wind farm developers – who are often from metropolitan areas – and regional communities.[109]

Among regional Australia's abundant natural resources are renewable resources like sun and wind that can be harvested sustainably. Renewable energy has been identified as a key 'economically disruptive' technology with the potential to create significant economic impacts.[110] Yet in practice, renewable energy projects in Australia are typically imposed from afar with little or no effort to explore how they interact on the ground with the regions that host them. Local partnerships and local ownership models in the renewables space are only beginning to be explored in the Australian context, and only at small scale. It remains to be seen whether future business models are able to link resources, capital, and expertise in a way that enables regional communities to benefit from the potential of renewable energy developments.

The promise of new industries?

> Today the Australian economy is no longer driven by what we make – the extraction and production of physical goods – but rather by what we know and do.[111]

Regional Australia's economy is dominated by resource-dependent industries. These are often portrayed as 'old' industries, rapidly losing ground in a global economy. Yet a closer look demonstrates that many 'new' industries are already present within the old: high-value agricultural niches, clever manufacturing, lucrative farming of fish and seafood, and so forth. These new faces of old industries are clearly visible on the ground in regions like North West Tasmania. Yet they are often overlooked in the economic narratives of regional Australia, where industry *transition* is synonymous with *decline*.

To replace declining old industries, economic recipes for regional communities often focus on the cultivation of new kinds of industries. Tertiary-sector services, especially tourism, and new 'knowledge-intensive industries' are generally prescribed to ensure the future of regional economies. Knowledge-intensive services, for instance, are significant and growing in the Australian economy, both in capital cities and non-metropolitan regions.[112] Tourism contributes about $39.9 billion per year to the economy and employs about half a million people across Australia.[113] These industries are present and indeed significant in many regions.

Nevertheless, there are significant barriers to the growth of knowledge-intensive industries in much of regional Australia. On the one hand, it is now possible to describe many Australian regions as service economies. Yet most of the services that dominate in the regions are not particularly knowledge intensive. Professional, scientific, and technical services are not the top employer or top growth industry in any single non-metropolitan region in Australia.[114] Rather, health care and social assistance is the top employer, and top growth industry, in many regions across Australia.[115]

Regional Australia's service economies are highly people intensive, rather than knowledge intensive. The services provided in regional communities – health services, personal services, local consultancies, and so forth – employ a large number of people, often in personally satisfying and socially useful occupations. They provide local, face-to-face service that increases the quality of life and the efficiency of firms in regional areas. Those offering these services are often strongly embedded in their local communities and deeply knowledgeable about local environments. They tend, however, to service only their local catchment, and struggle to compete further afield.

Knowledge-intensive service industries do exist in regional Australia but they are much weaker than in the nation's metropolitan centres.[116] This is unsurprising: the agglomeration economies of cities create a much more supportive environment for knowledge-based industries. Meanwhile, many regions still grapple with the basics, such as large gaps in mobile and broadband coverage.[117]

Furthermore, there are reputational considerations that are part and parcel of being regional. While many regional communities have good local consultancy firms, it is a common complaint that big contracts are nearly always awarded to capital-city firms – even for work that would benefit from the on-the-ground knowledge of local consultants.[118] Capital-city firms not only have the advantage of scale (they are in markets that can support large firms and diverse staff), but it is difficult for regionally based firms to compete against the prestige of a capital-city firm.

Tourism, on the other hand, is a people-intensive industry, one that is often portrayed as a comparatively easy way to turn local and regional assets into economic benefits. Tourism is an important employer in many regions – particularly coastal regions like Queensland's Gold Coast and inland wine-growing areas. Furthermore, market research has shown that the natural environment is a major drawcard for overseas visitors to Australia.[119] This would seem to represent an important advantage for many regions.

Nevertheless, it is difficult for any but a few regions to leverage tourism into a major economic driver. First, tourism in practice comprises a collection of diverse industries – retail trade, accommodation, cafes and restaurants, etc. Most tend to have low skills and pay levels. Attracting a high calibre of staff is thus a constant challenge for tourism firms, particularly in regions where tourism is highly seasonal.[120] Next, tourism in the regions also suffers from problems of isolation and poor connectivity. Poor linkages between regional areas and metropolitan cities mean that regional areas attract few international tourists, the bulk of whom remain in the capital cities.[121]

Across many regions, service industries have grown to supplant traditional industries like agriculture.[122] Yet Australia's 'new' service economies are in many ways old service economies. Services are still produced locally, primarily for a local market. They survive largely on the loyalty and support of their local clientele, with few links to capital-city markets. Opportunities for smart, niche, and ICT-enabled services – for instance, in the health area – are only starting to be explored. In regional Australia, services are people intensive rather than knowledge intensive.

In the future, however, they could easily be both. It is notable that despite their isolation, service industries in regional Australia are not poor performers. Regional tourism, for instance, generates more revenue on a per-business basis than metropolitan tourism.[123] Regionally based service providers are often deeply knowledgeable about local contexts and the needs of their clients. At the same time, they are poorly connected with other places – particularly the capital cities, where many resources are concentrated. These disconnects limit the ability of regional service economies to thrive.

Regional industries as grounded economies

> Across regional Australia people talk of the dominance of the global economy over local and regional communities.[124]

Australia's regional industries operate in a global environment. Even though they are located in physically peripheral places, they are not isolated from global competition. In some regions, competition has led to a decline in traditional industries. These declines are real and have impacted regional people and communities. There can be a sense that forces far beyond local control are determining the future of communities and their livelihoods. Yet decline in 'old industries' is only one small part of a larger story of industries in regional Australia.

Across regional Australia, old industries are in transition – and they are developing new faces. Local firms are creating new niches where they can compete. They are leveraging local resources and know-how and mobilising new technologies to do this. As one commentator observed, there is 'plenty of new economy' in Australia's 'old economy industries'.[125]

Industries regularly press at the boundaries of their traditional categories. In growth areas such as niche food manufacturing, wine making, and minerals processing, the lines between primary production and manufacturing are increasingly blurry. The products sent to global markets are diverse and distinctive. From remote irrigation systems to salmon farming, regional industries are proving that it is possible to survive and thrive in global markets from a base in regional Australia.

Yet regional industries still face a battle of perceptions. They frequently get stereotyped, painted as needing to wake up and skill up for the new knowledge economy. The public image of agriculture and manufacturing is of old industries on the decline. Few young people aspire to careers in these industries. The media is full of stories of factory closures and disappearing family farms, yet has very few good news stories of successful firms doing clever things in the regions.

Many of the interesting industry innovations happening on the ground in regional Australia simply fly under the public and policy radar, noticed only by their neighbours. The firms in many cases are small, not big; and they come from places that are small, not big. While commentators wax effusive on the threatened closure of large factories or the value of global mega-industries like mining, they ignore the new faces of old industries – as well as the old problems faced by new industries.

Economic commentators observe that the Australian economy is driven from its dense urban clusters, dominated by Sydney and Melbourne.[126] In dollar terms, this is true. Nevertheless, the consensus seems to be that Australia's competitive strengths are linked to its physical environment and natural resources – based in Australia's regions.[127] Ultimately, Australia's advantages on the global stage are regional. They will depend on regional firms' ability to leverage abundant natural resources into high-value, sustainable industries. A recent European study came to a similar conclusion: in the end, the fastest growing industries were not biotechnology or ICT, but rather, 'old industries' that 'use innovation to reinvent themselves in a competitive international economy'.[128]

In Australia, these old industries are often deeply embedded in regional communities and environments. In many ways this is their great strength. They can mobilise local resources, and they often benefit from strong reciprocity with the region: enabling them to create, and leverage, multiple forms of value.[129] At the same time, embeddedness may seem like a weakness when regional communities actively resist the entry of new industries or the closure of old ones. Yet it is precisely this embeddedness – this groundedness in the region – that supports social and environmental sustainability goals.

Regional economies are deeply grounded. In many ways they illustrate the potential of triple bottom line decision-making: decisions that consider economic, social, and environmental outcomes. In the regions interconnections among community, industry, and environment are easy to see on the ground, where all are in close proximity and highly interdependent. There are still conflicts – especially around environmental issues and trade-offs – but the issues are always on the table. From a distance, decisions can be made in isolation, on the basis of numbers alone. On the ground, it is impossible to ignore the wider impacts of industry decisions.

Regional industries are grounded, and perhaps because of their on-the-ground connections, they are surprisingly innovative. Local firms regularly leverage local resources to identify new products, processes, and markets. Yet their innovation rarely takes the form of formal patents or high-tech engagement.[130] Many of Australia's regions seem unable to turn their considerable potential into high levels of competitive success on the international stage.[131] The problem is not so much that firms are small; internationally, it has been observed that small firms are often more aware of niches or emerging markets than larger firms.[132] The core problem is that while firms are deeply grounded in their local places, they are still often disconnected from other places.

While firms in regional Australia participate in global economies, they do not work from a position of strength. They are often physically far – and socially disconnected – from metropolitan-based decision makers and urban knowledge hubs.[133] Poor ICT infrastructure in many areas further affects the ability of industries to connect, communicate, and access information.[134]

Often firms in regions are unsure where to go to get the information they need.[135] Tony Sorensen has recently observed that regions 'offer fewer of the vital networking opportunities which help in both the adoption of new technologies and the integration (or blending or fusion) of ideas leading to the formation of new technologies.'[136] In regional Australia, those who can provide targeted advice and decision support in specialist areas are fewer, farther between, and more often than not, based in the capital cities.[137]

In important ways, Australian regional industries are still disconnected from the resources and support they need to succeed on the global stage. A recent commentator has highlighted that improving competitiveness will require strengthening ties between Australia's metropolitan knowledge hubs and their 'hinterlands'.[138] Yet such connections are hard to forge in Australia. Regions do not see themselves as hinterlands of the capitals, but as vibrant places in their own right. They understand that the value generated by regional industries is more than their economic value added, and they can see the flow-on impacts of industries in regional communities.[139]

In the capital cities, where most policy decisions are made, these on-the-ground connections are often missed. It has recently been observed, yet again, that people living in non-metropolitan areas often 'feel disenfranchised and left out of critical decision-making processes which impact on the viability of their livelihoods'.[140] Deep disconnects persist between Australia's capital cities and its regions, with ongoing consequences for regional industries.

Notes

1 See e.g. Allison *et al.* 2013; Bonney *et al.* 2015; Castles 2014; Coates 2014; Eversole *et al.* 2015; and Woolley and Eversole 2013.
2 ABS 2012, cited in Woolley and Eversole 2013, p. 11. As an example, the Tasmanian Innovation Census excludes firms with under five employees.
3 NE/ALGA 2014, p. 200.
4 NE/ALGA 2011 notes that the Australian economy is heavily dependent on non-mining, trade-exposed industries, which suffered from the high Australian dollar driven by the recent mining boom.
5 The Australian Government Department of Infrastructure and Regional Development uses a structural change index to measure the change of the mix of employment between industries in a given time period. This index shows that across all states and the Northern Territory, regional Australia consistently demonstrates higher rates of structural change than capital cities (Commonwealth of Australia 2014a, pp. 296–300).
6 Future forum session notes, 2009, p. 1 (unpublished document).
7 Faulkner *et al.* 2013, p. 10: 'The most commonly raised economic threat – identified by 39 regions – was the reliance on one or few main industries and the need to diversify the region's economy. Many regions reported that their key industries were seasonally dependent and vulnerable to influences, such as climate and commodity cycles. Other economic threats included fragmented industries, the availability of land for industrial and commercial activity, the cost of freight transport, a lack of value adding to raw commodities and a lack of business expertise.'
8 Thus, while Australian regions do not have significantly higher unemployment than metropolitan areas, they do experience quite a bit of population churn as people move in and out (see e.g. Collits and Rowe 2015, p. 88). Commonwealth of Australia (2014a, pp. 81–85) documented that the employment rate across both metropolitan and non-metropolitan areas averaged around 94 per cent in 2011, and that employment was slightly higher in regional areas of Victoria, South Australia, and Western Australia than in the capital cities. Nevertheless, labour force participation is higher in capital cities (62.6 per cent) than in most regional areas (58–59.5 per cent on average), with the exception of remote areas (Commonwealth of Australia 2014a, p. 117). Equally, the ratio of people receiving income support is higher in non-metropolitan areas (with the exception of remote areas) than in capital cities (Commonwealth of Australia 2014a, pp. 229–233).
9 On community opposition to wind farms in Australia, see e.g. Gross 2007; Hindmarsh 2010.
10 While a certain degree of catchment planning has been delegated to regional representatives through Natural Resource management committees and major environmental policy changes such as the Murray–Darling Basin Plan undergo community consultation processes, there is limited room to influence outcomes within pre-set regulations and policy agendas. See for instance, Craig and Vanclay 2005 on decision-making in New South Wales Water Management Committees.
11 Nearly all (54) of the nation's RDA committees 'recognised issues associated with transport infrastructure. These issues can be divided into three categories: public transport, road and rail.' (Faulkner *et al.* 2013, p. 22). It has been observed that, 'Australia's scale and remoteness work against competition, innovation and export growth' (Commonwealth of Australia 2014b, p. 38).
12 'Poor mobile phone or broadband coverage was an issue raised by RDA committees in 45 regions' (Faulkner *et al.* 2013, p. 24). See also RAI 2015, p. 3 on poor internet coverage.
13 These observations were documented in Western Australia field notes in 2000 and in a business survey in Tasmania in 2012 (Braddon Business Centre 2012, pp. 10–11).
14 See e.g. Eversole *et al.* 2015.

15 For 2011–12 the new business entry rate (rate of new business entries relative to existing businesses) was nearly 15 per cent in capital cities, compared with 10–11 per cent in non-remote regional areas, and 11–12 per cent in remote areas (Commonwealth of Australia 2014a, p. 86*ff*).

16 Microenterprises with less than five employees make up 88 per cent of all business in Australia, and only 2.5 per cent of all firms employ 20 or more people; this figure is only slightly higher in major cities (2.6 per cent) than in regional areas (2.2 per cent) (Commonwealth of Australia 2014a, p. 306). It has recently been observed that Australia has a 'unique industrial structure … large multinationals in resources and food, large domestic services oligopolies and a long tail of SMEs' – the bulk of which in fact are owner-operated microenterprises (Commonwealth of Australia 2014b, p. 38).

17 *The Economist*, 2000, online article.

18 Commonwealth of Australia, 2014a.

19 Commonwealth of Australia, 2014a.

20 A common mantra in agriculture, referring to the need for farms to increase their scale in order to be efficient and economically sustainable; it was quoted in Barr 2009, p. 9.

21 ABS 2012a. This decline is paralleled in other high-income countries around the world. Barr 2014, p. 9 cites the international data on the relationship between per capita national income and the economic role of agriculture, concluding that 'improved standards of living within a nation are almost always associated with a decline in agriculture's relative share of GDP and of the nation's workforce, despite increases in the volume of agricultural production'.

22 The number of people employed in agriculture fell by 13,134 in inner regional areas, 14,974 in outer regional areas, and 3156 in remote areas between 2006 and 2011. It was the fastest declining employer (Commonwealth of Australia 2014a, pp. 287, 292–294).

23 ABS 2012a, np documents that 'there were 19,700 fewer farmers in Australia in 2011 than in 2006, a fall of 11% over five years. Over the 30 years to 2011, the number of farmers declined by 106,200.'

24 It grew at about 3 per cent over the financial year 2012–2013 (ABS 2014f).

25 ABS 2012a.

26 ABS 2012a. Sixty percent of Australia's agricultural output is exported.

27 Alston 1995, p. 39 observed that: 'The changes within the lifetime of some women interviewed have been dramatic, and have seen farms metamorphose into technological business ventures linked to a world market.'

28 Smith and Pritchard 2015, pp. 58–59 note that the situation changed from one in which 'the Australian agricultural sector was one of the most protected in the developed world' to a situation where it is currently 'one of the most deregulated in the world'. Australian farmers enjoy very little in the way of government subsidy compared with other OECD countries. Government support for Australian farms represents just 4 per cent of farming income, compared with 61 per cent in Norway, 52 percent in Korea, 23 per cent in the European Union, 17 per cent in Canada, and 9 per cent in the United States (OECD 2010, quoted in NFF 2012, p. 17).

29 In some cases, the restructuring of industries included government incentives enabling struggling farms to exit.

30 DAFF 2010, p. 5 notes that: 'Declining terms of trade have been a consistent feature of the Australian farming landscape as prices for produce have grown more slowly than the cost of inputs. This has been the case on both the domestic market and internationally…. terms of trade have declined more than 50 per cent between 1980–81 and 2007–08.'

31 See Wilkinson *et al.* 2011, whose study in Victoria explored how farming families were grappling with these kinds of decisions.

32 Growcom, the nation's peak horticulture industry body, assesses that: 'The most significant (change in recent decades) has been the increasing dominance of the major

supermarkets chains (MSC) that now control in excess of 80% of the food retail market and are able to dictate terms to their suppliers in a way that no retailer was able to in 1980.... In a recent survey of our members, it was revealed that 45% of growers are forced to take the price set by the buyer, while 87% have been forced to sell below the cost of production at some time in the past three years' (Growcom 2012).

33 DAFF 2010, p. 2 observed that: 'The average total capital value (in 2007–08 dollar terms) of broadacre farms has more than doubled over the 20 year time period to be $3.5 million in 2007–08.'

34 These issues are discussed in Castles 2014.

35 For instance: Alston 1995; Barr 2009; Gray and Lawrence 2001; Pritchard and McManus 2000; and others.

36 Quotes from Alston 1995, p. 43 and Gray and Lawrence 2001, p. 9.

37 This process is described in Barr, 2009. The National Farmers Federation has recently observed that: 'It is likely that because of the costs of remaining competitive, the trend towards smaller farm businesses consolidating will continue' (NFF 2013, p. 26).

38 DAFF 2010, p.2 observed that over the 30 years between 1987–88 and 2007–08 Australia lost nearly 20,000 broad acre farms. According to Barr 2014, p. 45, the number of farms with a value of production over $50,000/year fell by 51 per cent between 1981 and 2011. See also Barr 2009 for a discussion of farm consolidation and its impacts on farming communities.

39 Foster 2014, pp. 50–51.

40 Foster 2014.

41 Australian grown truffles had a total value of $5.15 million in 2012 (Foster 2014, p. 150), and culinary herbs were worth $46 million in 2011 (p. 80). Olives, including those grown for oil, were worth $169.3 million in 2011 (p. 108), but ABS 2014f, np places the 2013 value at $218 million.

42 Data from ABS 2014f.

43 Foster 2014, p. 60 observes that: 'The gross value of production of Asian vegetables in Australia in 2011–12 is estimated to be around $85 million. The industry is mostly oriented toward the domestic market.' Nevertheless, 'the diffuse nature of the Asian vegetable industry makes it difficult to source comprehensive data' (p. 62).

44 Data from ABS 2014f: Value of production of fruit and nuts excluding grapes grew at 20 per cent between 2012 and 2013, while grapes grew at 12 per cent. Grapes were worth $1.2 billion in 2013 ($858 million for wine and $303 million for other uses) and other fruit and nuts were worth $3.7 billion – bringing the total value of fruit and nuts produced to nearly $5 billion (ABS 2014f).

45 Data from ABS 2014f.

46 State of Tasmania 2012, p. 97.

47 There were 980 establishments growing cut flowers in Australia in 2010–11 on 4,750 hectares, around 300 hectares of which were undercover; over half of the area planted was in the state of Victoria. The total value of the cut flower industry in Australia in 2010–11 was $291 million (Foster 2014, p. 153), which rose to $309 million in 2013 (ABS 2014f).

48 See Foster 2014, pp. 75–79 on Australian cocoa and coffee production, and pp. 122–125 for tea production. A green tea processing plant, focusing on export to Japan, was opened in the Victorian regional town of Wangaratta in 2004 (Foster 2014, p. 124).

49 RIRDC 2014, p. 32.

50 ABARES 2014b, p. 7. They observe that aquaculture contributes 43 per cent of gross value of all Australian fisheries production. In 2000, this figure was only 16 per cent, it grew to about 26 per cent by 2008 (DAFF 2010, p.2), and it has grown significantly since.

51 This point has been observed in Tasmania; it was echoed in the findings of a study in Queensland where the 60 ha required minimum lot size for agricultural land failed to

take into account 'that farms producing high value crops such as vanilla, tropical flowers or small crops require a lot less land for a viable enterprise than would traditional broad acre crops such as maize or sugar cane' (Bohnet and Moore 2010, p. 62).

52 For instance, Skills Tasmania 2008, p. 9 notes that about as many farmers enter vegetable growing as leave, but that 'closer examination shows that entries at the smaller turnover categories (i.e. smaller farms) are growing whereas exits are occurring in the medium and large farm category. This means that medium sized farms are being broken up into smaller lots for purchase by part-time and "hobby farmers". *This is a strategic concern for the state and is a common trend across the nation*' (emphasis in the original).

53 One study in Queensland identified a sector of tree changers that were farming tropical fruit, flowers and/or trees on their properties, and value-adding crops to produce juice, tropical fruit wine or ice cream (Bohnet and Moore 2010, p. 55).

54 Wilkinson *et al.* 2011, pp. 28–29 have calculated that 'there is a benchmark of approximately $400,000 gross farm income above which a farm business will on average be capable of generating a sustainable income for an average family with no off-farm income'.

55 Workshop notes, 2009, unpublished document. ABARES, 2014c, p. 26, made a similar point, noting that: 'The NASIS [National Agricultural Statistical Information System] is being asked to meet information needs that extend beyond the farm gate.'

56 One study in Victoria found that about a third of farmers studied were aiming to grow the productivity of their farm but not its scale (Wilkinson *et al.* 2011, p. 30).

57 In Tasmania, a few studies (Bonney *et al.* 2015; Castles 2014, pp. 168–170; Coates 2014; Eversole *et al.* 2015; and Gralton and Vanclay 2006) have documented the existence of 'niche' and high-quality food producers, often selling into national and international markets.

58 SGS 2014b, p. 1.

59 Commonwealth of Australia 2014b, p. 77.

60 Commonwealth of Australia 2014b, p. 143, notes that: 'Large job losses have been experienced in 10 of the manufacturing sub-sectors over the past decade to 2013. These were Pulp, Paper and Converted Paper Product Manufacturing (–45.4 per cent), Textile, Leather, Clothing and Footwear Manufacturing (–41.4 per cent), Fabricated Metal Product Manufacturing (–40.0 per cent), Wood Product Manufacturing (–33.3 per cent), Polymer Product and Rubber Product Manufacturing (–29.9 per cent), Transport Equipment Manufacturing (–28.8 per cent), Furniture and Other Manufacturing (–26.0 per cent), Printing (including the Reproduction of Recorded Media) (–22.6 per cent), Non-Metallic Mineral Product Manufacturing (–22.0 per cent), and Basic Chemical and Chemical Product Manufacturing (–5.6 per cent).'

61 Ibid, pp. 29–36. Food and Beverage Products made the largest contribution to total manufacturing gross value added in 2013 – 23.5 per cent, followed by Machinery and Equipment (20.6 per cent). See also Commonwealth of Australia 2012, p. 16 on growth in certain manufacturing sub-sectors, including food and beverages.

62 Commonwealth of Australia 2014b, p. 30: '33.5 per cent of manufacturing workers were employed in regional and remote areas: slightly below the all industry average of 34.1 per cent.' Most of the remainder of Australia's manufacturing is located in the suburbs of metropolitan regions, such as South East Melbourne, Western Sydney and Northern Adelaide: 'Over recent decades, much of manufacturing has shifted out of the high-cost areas of our major cities to the suburbs and regions as it, along with distribution functions, has been displaced by higher value business services' (Commonwealth of Australia 2012, p. 17).

63 Based on 2011 census data. Manufacturing employed 13.7 per cent of all workers in Shepparton and 12.3 per cent of all workers in North West Tasmania. It was also a top employer in parts of Greater Melbourne, Sydney, Brisbane, and Adelaide (Commonwealth of Australia 2014a, pp. 280–285).

64 In 2006 manufacturing was the top employer in these regions; it was superseded by Health Care and Social Assistance as the new major employer – or, in the case of Fitzroy, by construction (Commonwealth of Australia 2014a, pp. 280–285). Commonwealth of Australia 2014a, pp. 292–295 notes that in several of these regions, manufacturing was the fastest declining industry of employment between 2006 and 2011.

65 Woolley and Eversole 2013, p. 12 note that: 'The regional *Economic Development Plan* highlights that manufacturing is the number one economic sector in North West Tasmania 2010–11 in terms of value added … and thus it is a major contributor to Gross Regional Product … Manufacturing is responsible for more than half of all exports from the North West region.'

66 With food products, there is a growing consumer preference for Australian brands due to food safety concerns; most recently typified by food scares such as Australian consumers contracting hepatitis from imported frozen berries.

67 Jericho 2013, np.

68 'The emergence of Australia as a 'high cost economy' has coincided with the massive expansion of global manufacturing capacity in emerging economies' (Commonwealth of Australia 2012, p. 20). Popular lower-cost destinations have also included New Zealand: culturally similar but cheaper.

69 Commonwealth of Australia 2012, p. 21.

70 Commonwealth of Australia 2014b, p. 24. The recent announcement of major automotive industry closures in 2016 and 2017 are high on the list of challenges to the sector. Commonwealth of Australia 2014b, p. 84 predicts that: 'Regional employment will be hardest hit in the Victorian regions of Greater Dandenong, Ballarat, Hume, Greater Geelong and South East Melbourne, and Playford in northern Adelaide.'

71 Beer 2015 provides a detailed discussion of structural adjustment programmes in Australian regional policy, many of which have been developed for the manufacturing sector.

72 See e.g. Commonwealth of Australia 2014b, p. 15.

73 Commonwealth of Australia 2014b, pp. 146–147.

74 NE/ALGA 2014, p. 54.

75 Commonwealth of Australia 2014b, p. 24 observes that: 'Manufacturing in Australia is in transition. This transition will be difficult for some workers, particularly those in declining sectors or jobs that become obsolete. A relatively high proportion of the workforce do not have formal, industry-recognised qualifications or sufficient language, literacy and numeracy skills to meet the demands of the modern workplace, which will impact on their ability to find new jobs.'

76 The category is defined as 'food, beverage and tobacco product manufacturing' Employment growth data from the decade 2003–13 are sourced from Commonwealth of Australia 2014b, p. 77. Industry gross value-added data are sourced from Commonwealth of Australia 2012, p. 16: over the period 2001–11, the average annual growth rate of value added by food, beverage and tobacco products was 0.4 per cent.

77 Commonwealth of Australia 2014b, p. 16. The average annual growth rate of value added by non-metallic mineral products was 3.6 per cent, of metal products 2.9 per cent, and of machinery and equipment 1.9 per cent.

78 Commonwealth of Australia 2014b, pp. 29–30. Australia represents only 1 per cent of global manufacturing value added.

79 The Manufacturing Leaders Group (in Commonwealth of Australia 2012, p. 5) observed: 'We are particularly concerned that leadership and judgement is brought to bear on the "perceptions issue" about Australian manufacturing. With the loss of over 100,000 jobs since 2008 and more structural adjustment ahead the Manufacturing Leaders Group is particularly committed to exploring how the good news story about Australian manufacturing success can be presented.'

80 SGS 2014b, p. 1.

81 Enterprise Connect 2013, p. 8.
82 Enterprise Connect 2013, p. 2.
83 Woolley and Eversole 2013, p. 13.
84 Commonwealth of Australia 2014b, p. 23 observes that: 'The future of Australia's Manufacturing industry will increasingly lie in transitioning to a manufacturing base that incorporates advanced and niche manufacturing, with firms participating in global supply chains and offering lifetime services for their products.' This report also highlights the competitive potential Australia enjoys in high-value food and beverage manufacturing, particularly linked to emerging Asian markets (see e.g. p. 14).
85 AusIndustry 2013, p. 19 notes that: 'Businesses specialising in providing specific products at short notice appear to have maintained solid growth and remain insulated because of their inherent advantages over import competition. Overall, the GFC appears to have hastened shifts towards areas of competitive advantage.' AusIndustry also assesses manufacturing in Australia as a comparatively innovative industry: 'Around 39 per cent of manufacturers introduced some form of innovation in 2010–11, compared to 33 per cent of businesses overall' (p. 21).
86 PWC 2014, p. 9.
87 See e.g. SGS 2014b, p. 1, on niche urban manufacturing in the United States.
88 NE/ALGA 2014, p. 49.
89 ABS 2014g. Industry value added had declined from the previous year.
90 OECD 2014, p. 15.
91 Data on forestry from ABARES, 2014a, p. 1, for financial year 2012–13. The economic contribution of forestry had been stable at about $8 billion for several years previously. These data include forest-related manufacturing. Data on wild-catch fisheries from ABARES 2014b, p. 7.
92 MPIGA 2013, p. 11; these data include wood products manufacturing. The decline was 'from 85 thousand people in 2006 to 73 thousand people in 2011' and 'In Tasmania, forest-related employment fell by almost half between 2006 and 2011.'
93 MPIGA 2013, p. 8 note that: 'The area of native forest not legally restricted from wood harvesting decreased steadily over the period 2000–01 to 2010–11 as a result of the transfer of significant areas of multiple-use public forests to nature conservation reserves.' Between the years 2006–07 and 2010–11, 'the annual area of multiple-use public native forest harvested for wood decreased by 32%'.
94 See AusIndustry 2013, p. 27.
95 Measham *et al.* 2013, p. 185 note five 'major' mining booms over Australia's history – defined as 'significant increases in mining investment and/or mining output, which trigger macroeconomic consequences in the form of increased GDP, balance of trade and most recently, higher currency exchange rates'.
96 Argent *et al.* 2010, p. 32 note that: 'Strong global demand and high prices for commodities over the past decade has fuelled a rapid expansion of the minerals and petroleum industries in a number of SLAs across rural Australia.' They note that there are not many true 'boom' towns; but some towns in the Pilbara region of Western Australia and the Bowen Basin in central-eastern Queensland experienced a strong influx of population between 2006 and 2011.
97 See e.g. Commonwealth of Australia 2014a, p. 287. NE/ALGA 2014, pp. 165–167 note the extent of mining industry employment in each region: up to 40 per cent in the Pilbara/Kimberly region of Western Australia.
98 So-called 'Dutch disease' – see e.g. NE/ALGA 2011.
99 NE/ALGA 2014, p. 4 argue that the 'net benefit of mineral exports to the Australian public at large had been seriously overestimated, partly because the sector is highly capital-intensive and generates very few jobs in relation to the value of production and partly because much of its cash flow goes straight back to its overseas owners'. They note that: 'The surge in mining investment was quite largely overseas-financed and also had high import content. In 2007–08 approximately 48 per cent of mining

industry investment in Australia was spent on imported equipment and know-how; by 2013–14 this proportion had risen to 60 per cent' (NE/ALGA 2014, p. 48).

100 KPMG 2013, p. 15 notes that 13 per cent of the population in mining regions were high income earners (defined as earning $2,000 or more per week), compared with 5 per cent across the rest of regional Australia. In terms of environmental impacts and local communities, much mining in Australia occurs in very remote areas, but there are some areas, such as the Hunter Valley, where mining occurs close to population centres and competition between mining and other land uses can be observed (see Measham *et al.* 2013, p. 191).

101 As a result of the growth of fly-in-fly-out (FIFO), the greatest concentration of people who work in the mining industry now live in Perth and Brisbane (Australian Bureau of Statistics 2013, quoted in Perry and Rowe 2015, p. 140).

102 The growth of FIFO workforces has been documented particularly for Australian remote mining communities; see e.g. HRSCRA 2013; Perry and Rowe 2015; and others.

103 ABS 2013b.

104 SGS 2014a, p. 1.

105 Even more so when infrastructure and services must be provided for workers whose normal place of residence is elsewhere. This was a frequent observation when conducting regional planning conversations on the West Coast of Tasmania: not only does the area not attract 'drive in' workers' families or dollars, but the workers themselves are generally not reflected in local population statistics, because when they respond to the Census, their usual place of residence is elsewhere.

106 MPIGA 2013, p. 7 documents the growth in industrial forest plantations Australia-wide from 1.8 to 2 million hectares between 2006–06 and 2010–11. DAFF 2010, p. 2 observes that the volume of aquaculture production almost doubled between 1999 and 2008; over the same period wild catch declined. ABARES 2014b, p. 7 notes that despite slight declines in aquaculture in the 12 months to 2013, aquaculture now contributes 43 per cent of the value of Australian fisheries production, and farmed salmonids are the most valuable fisheries product.

107 See for instance, http://www.abc.net.au/news/2015-04-19/anti-super-trawler-protests-move-to-river-derwent/6403894 (viewed 1 June 2015).

108 The author observed these concerns on the ground in both Western Victoria and Tasmania; they have been formally documented by a number of authors; see e.g. Miller and Buys 2014 for a recent study. Eversole and Martin 2006 provide a description of the rapid growth in the plantation forestry industry in the Western District of Victoria, including the government tax incentives that led to large-scale investment in plantation forestry. They observe (p. 696) that: 'The publicly listed companies involved in the plantation industry are typically large, with their head office in an Australian capital city. These companies are not closely tied to the rural communities where their tree plantations are located, and they judge the success of their investment decisions primarily on economic criteria.'

109 See e.g. Gross 2007 for an exploration of social acceptance of wind farms, and Hindmarsh 2010 who discusses the limits of community engagement processes in wind farm developments.

110 McKinsey Global Institute 2013, p. 4 and elsewhere.

111 Kelly and Donegan 2014, p. 6.

112 For instance the 'professional, technical and scientific services' industry category grew 51 per cent in real gross value added between 2003 and 2013. See Jericho 2013, np.

113 TRA 2014, pp. 8–9.

114 Commonwealth of Australia 2014a, pp. 278–291.

115 Ibid.

116 In 2011 knowledge-intensive industries represented between 21 per cent and 27 per cent of all employment in regional areas in each state, compared with between 30 per cent and 36 per cent of all employment in the capital cities (Commonwealth of Australia

2014, pp. 311–315). Both Sydney and Melbourne were at 36 per cent. Nevertheless, there were some individual regions, such as Newcastle/Lake Macquarie (New South Wales), Ballarat (Victoria), and Toowoomba (Queensland) that had levels of employment in knowledge-intensive industries at or above that of the smaller capital cities. The definition of 'knowledge-intensive industries' used here includes high and medium-high technology manufacturing and knowledge-intensive services.

117 See NE/ALGA 2014, p. 105 for a coverage map. RAI 2015, p. 7 notes that: 'Access to ICT is not equitable across Australia. Large gaps exist in both coverage and quality of service throughout different regional and some metropolitan locations.'

118 In Tasmania, this generally has the extra dimension of 'mainland firms': even firms in Hobart struggle to compete with those in Melbourne and Sydney.

119 'Australia's biggest strength is its world class nature, well regarded from all markets and core to our global tourism offering ... The greatest drivers of international visitor demand to Australia are coastal (including beaches), aquatic and wildlife experiences' (TA 2012, p. 1).

120 See e.g. Eyles *et al.* 2014a, who discuss this issue in the context of the West Coast of Tasmania.

121 Hamper 2012, p. 50 observes that 'international tourists to Australia tend to concentrate their visit to capital city destinations, usually at the expense of the regions. Of course this means that the economic benefit is likewise concentrated in the big cities.'

122 As measured by employment, over the five years 2006–11. Commonwealth of Australia 2014a.

123 'Despite a larger proportion of tourism businesses being located in capital cities, tourism revenue was not generated proportionally in the capital cities.... Overall, 38 per cent of tourism businesses were located in regional areas, but they generated 44 per cent of total tourism revenue in 2012–13. This highlights the importance of developing strategic policy and investment initiatives to support business growth in regional areas' (TRA 2015, p. 2).

124 Cameron and Gibson 2001, p. 135.

125 Harcourt 2007, p. 1.

126 'Dense urban clusters continue to underpin the bulk of our economic activity. The CBDs [central business centres] of Sydney and Melbourne dominate the other areas in terms of economic contribution' (PWC 2014, p. 5).

127 'Our suite of national strengths across resources, food, health, engineering and the environment, when harnessed effectively, provides a platform for growth that is both uniquely Australian and globally significant.' (Commonwealth of Australia 2014b, p. 30).

128 Dodgson and Steen 2010, p. 111.

129 See e.g. Bonney *et al.* 2015 for examples from agriculture and food processing in North West Tasmania, Pritchard *et al.* 2012 for farmers' efforts to support other local businesses, and Commonwealth of Australia 2012, p. 43 for the example of large manufacturers helping SMEs access global markets. Bonney *et al.*'s Value Assessment and Development (VAD) Framework provides a way for policy makers to describe and leverage these interconnections in a particular region (Bonney *et al.* 2015).

130 Sorensen 2015, p. 49 cites a study which 'found considerable low-level business innovation activity among SMEs in the agricultural communities studied, but very little in the way of high-tech engagement indicating creativity, imagination and substantial risk-taking'. NE/ALGA 2014 note that: 'Judging by patent applications, Australia's most intensive knowledge-based regions are its metropolitan centres, though several of its independent cities are shaping up.'

131 The Regional Australia Institute's competitiveness index, for instance, ranks most of regional Australia comparatively poorly. See http://www.regionalaustralia.org.au/insight/ (viewed 1 June 2015) and Sorensen 2015, p. 45.

132 OECD 2007a, p. 84.
133 Kelly and Donegan 2014, p. 1 observe that: 'There is a reason intense economic activity is concentrating in CBDs and inner suburbs. Many businesses in these areas provide highly knowledge-intensive and specialised services such as funds management, insurance, design, engineering and international education. These businesses depend on highly skilled workers, and locating in the heart of large cities gives them access to the largest possible pools of them. Proximity to suppliers, customers and partners also helps businesses to work efficiently, to generate opportunities and to come up with new ideas and ways of working.'
134 See e.g. NE/ALGA 2014, p. 105 for coverage map. Some regional areas are able to access high-speed broadband under the National Broadband Networks, as well as telecommunications infrastructure, but many are not; this report notes that 'the internet is yet to deliver its full potential for rural industries'.
135 A study of small food producers in North West Tasmania found that one of the biggest issues impacting on new businesses' development trajectories was the lack of personal networks and knowing where to go for information when needed (Eversole *et al.* 2015). Another study of manufacturing firms identified that there was a 'lack of formal networks and opportunities to share information within the region,' and also that 'the ability to access market intelligence was identified as an area of constraint' (Enterprise Connect 2013, pp. 26, 32).
136 Sorensen 2015, p. 45. He also notes that: 'Compounding this are innate conservatism, risk avoidance borne of unstable producer environments – especially seasonal conditions and commodity prices, the very small size of many businesses, logistics difficulties resulting from high cost and sometimes second rate transport services, deficiencies in information and communications technology (ICT) infrastructure and considerable absence of venture capital' (p. 45).
137 SGS 2014a observes that in Australia, 'the regions are sourcing more and more of their crucial business inputs from the cities'; there is consequently a need to overcome current disconnects to strengthen ties between cities and the regions.
138 SGS 2014a.
139 Some of these interrelationships were documented recently in a project exploring the value of agriculture in regional development (Bonncy *et al.* 2015).
140 Hogan and Young 2015, p. 10.

3 Regional universities

A story about universities

In a way I became regional completely by accident. My first university job was in a large, Perth-based university. It was only after I applied for it, when I read the fine print, that I realised the job was not based in Perth. The research centre I had applied to work for was located on the university's 'regional campus', two hours south of the capital. And that, to quote Robert Frost, has made all the difference.

From my first days in the Australian university system, I was a regional academic based on a regional campus. That meant certain things. It meant that I would be working in a small and collegial environment, where I would know and drink tea with colleagues in every academic discipline and professional role. In this kind of environment, breadth, flexibility, and relevance were valued above depth and rigour. Academic work per se had no special status; valued academics were those who could explain their work in plain language to local people, attract consultancy money and students, and who were not afraid to fill their own tea urn or set up their own classroom. It also meant that, from the perspective of colleagues in the city, I was probably not a serious academic. Everyone knew that serious, career-focused academics found jobs in the city.

Being regional quickly becomes a self-fulfilling prophesy. Academics based on a regional campus are not necessarily any different from their colleagues in the city – yet it is surprising how often they are. Regional locations leave academics largely isolated from colleagues in their own discipline, yet in close contact with other disciplines and non-academic communities. Regional campuses are often distant from centres of university decision-making and located in environments dominated by non-university institutions and concerns. In the first class I taught, I was faced with a roomful of social service professionals, all older than me. Enthusiastic, I asked my students what they hoped to get out of our semester together studying social research. The answer around the room was consistent: the course was required for their degree, the degree was required for their job, and that was the sum total of their interest in social research. Time and time again, this was the starting point.

On large urban campuses, weighty with professors and crowded with students, universities have no reason to doubt their relevance. Their research is world-class, their classrooms full, their significance unquestioned. But on a regional campus, the university's relevance is continually being questioned. People ask: *Why does this matter? How will it actually help us?* Regional campuses tend to be small – few have more than a couple of thousand students. The bulk of academics are usually junior – PhD candidates and early career lecturers, often local students who have worked their way up. I can count on one hand the number of professors I know on regional campuses. Academic leadership is thin on the ground, as is the local population; yet expectations from local communities are generally high. Regional campuses are established not for academic glory and status, but to serve their regions.

Over 15 years I have worked on three regional university campuses, in three different states. Each belonged to a different university, each was located in a very different setting, and each was a different size. Nevertheless, there were more commonalities than differences. These have been echoed over the years by other colleagues working on other regional campuses. Regional campuses are wonderful places to work: they generally develop a reputation as friendly communities where students feel supported and everyone knows everyone by name. They tend to avoid the bulk of the internal politics that can be observed in large city-based academic departments. The culture is highly egalitarian; it is not unusual for academics and non-academic staff to lunch and socialise together, or for academics and their students to meet over a coffee. At the same time, regional campuses can be incredibly difficult places to work. The power plays that barely manifest at the local level emerge with a vengeance in the relationships between regional campuses and capital cities. In some cases, even the campus heating is controlled from a city several hours away.

The following story from Victoria is, therefore, illustrative, and by no means unique. In 2003 I arrived in a wealthy area of regional Victoria to take up a position at a newly established university-based centre for regional development – one of nearly half a dozen that were functioning in Victoria at that time. This one was owned by a large Melbourne-based university. The campus had been established through the efforts of a segment of the local farming community, which had lobbied to secure a university presence in their region. The metropolitan university had come to the party on the back of a significant government grant and local philanthropic support. The university purchased and refurbished a piece of existing government infrastructure to serve as their new regional campus. They established a nursing program in partnership with the local hospital, a small research programme, a few short courses, and then a centre for regional development.

As regional campuses go, this one was at the small end of the spectrum: less than a hundred students, and about a dozen staff. The most senior academic led the regional development centre and was charged with building research partnerships and related opportunities for the university in the region. As a research fellow, my role was to help identify and deliver community-relevant research projects. Besides us, only one staff member had a PhD – and she was not academic staff. Most of the staff were from the local area, and nearly all – with the exception of the senior academic – were female.

Every day, we had morning tea in the staff room at 10:30 and shared what was going on in our respective areas. There were research projects on local festivals and short courses on coffee-making. There were public events and other initiatives to engage the local community and the schools. There was the nursing program, and every so often, there were concerted efforts to establish another academic program on the regional campus. An area of demand was identified in the local community. Conversations were held with locals and with the relevant department back in Melbourne. And regularly, those in Melbourne said *no*.

This was a small campus in a small market – indeed, as time went on, those in Melbourne emphasised that we should not call it a campus at all; it was not large enough. Yet the small group of local staff kept trying to expand it. People in the region wanted courses. Most did not distinguish between the university and the local technical and further education centre – the 'TAFE'. The TAFE had courses. Didn't we have courses? Locals didn't really see the point of *research*, it was a generally foreign concept: probably something to do with the old government laboratories we occupied, but nothing to do with the day-to-day concerns of businesses and organisations. In the end we attracted three PhD candidates and a handful of local projects, most with the health service. Our significant research projects were elsewhere. Most local people still asked me what I did at the TAFE.

Over time, frustration among colleagues on the campus grew. Sometimes I saw tears. Life on a regional campus was not easy. The organisational structure kept shifting. We were moved to a new university portfolio and had new reporting lines. The community was disgruntled: it wanted new courses, but we weren't providing them. Local colleagues felt guilty: they were letting the community down. Colleagues in Melbourne said we had to prove the numbers were viable. A sensible management decision in Melbourne sounded like abrupt dismissal on the regional campus. *How can we prove there is demand for a course we don't offer?* staff asked. No one explained what we needed to do. For a long time, no one from the city even came.

I do not recall anyone explicitly threatening to close the campus. The spate of Australian regional campus closures was still to come. But it was becoming abundantly clear that the university – the centre in Melbourne – had lost interest in us, to the extent that they had ever been interested. We generated research projects, but they were worth thousands of dollars, not millions. We had a sound nursing programme, but no other courses – yet. We were building good relationships across the region, but these relationships were not converting quickly into things that made money for universities. And in the absence of ongoing funding support, we were both a cost item and an inconvenience. More often than not, we were forgotten.

Despite frequent trips to Melbourne, I found it hard to develop rapport with city-based colleagues. We worked in places four hours apart. We did not share a tea room. Visiting colleagues in Melbourne was not unlike my experience in Perth: mild surprise that I was even there. Often, I joked that I felt like a Bolivian *campesino* coming into the city from the mountains. While I did not wear dusty tyre-rubber sandals or carry a striped *q'epi* bundle on my back, I clearly did not fit. I did not know the city campus language, the gossip, who was who. And I was from the regional campus. Many colleagues didn't even know they had one. In the end, we established a few research relationships with city-based colleagues. But regional staff were the ones who travelled. It is a truism on every regional campus: no matter how far it is to the city, it is twice as far to the region.

Us and *them* quickly became entrenched in the campus culture, particularly as the heating was controlled from Melbourne. Nevertheless, the *us* on the regional campus was a complex identity. Informal conversations with colleagues revealed the lines of tension. They felt a part of the university, but they were also part of the local community. They had an identity and responsibility within the university, and also identities and responsibilities to friends, family, and non-university colleagues in the local community. I was new in town and had few networks, but I could see that colleagues who had strong networks locally were struggling to mediate between 'community' and 'university' identities and expectations.

I saw these tensions, but did not feel them – until a team of colleagues arrived from the city to do a research project in our town. I knew little about the project, but I went to hear the team present their findings. The project was on rural communities; they had done a number of interviews in our town, and another set of interviews in a town in South East Asia. They concluded, they told us, that by comparison we had *no culture*. I did not hear this as an anthropologist; rather, I heard it as a member of the local community, surrounded by local friends and colleagues. The room sat in shock. This was the *university* telling our community that we had no culture.

The research team went home to Melbourne. Over the next few days, in local conversations, rebuttals started to form. *What about the footy clubs* – both of them, each with a proud history and plenty of rituals to prove it? *What about the churches?* The weekly congregations, the choirs, the annual Good Friday procession through town? *What about the men's shed?* The beautiful things they were making, the supportive community they were building? How could these people from Melbourne come here and say we had no culture? Because we do not wear costumes and masks? Because you cannot put us on a postcard?

Back in my day job, my attempts to convince locals of the value of social research began to sound even more hollow. If this was university *research*, local people had no time for it. Not only did it not tell them anything they needed to know, it misrepresented them, it offended them, it was an excuse for outsiders to come in and once again, misunderstand them. I carefully pointed out that our local research centre had nothing to do with *that* project.

At the same time, I retained a cordial relationship with the research team. They were, after all, colleagues – I had so few – and they had, at least, tried. They had travelled the double distance: they had come out to the region. They had tried to work with regional communities. Now they were receiving academic kudos from the university for a successful research project that delivered exactly what the university wanted. For me, however, a successful project had to be much more.

If I were to stand up in front of a roomful of my neighbours, I wanted to tell them something that was true, and useful for them.

In the end, I never did. I tried for three years in that region but never found a significant local need that my social research skills could answer. I did small projects, of course, helping specific local organisations with their specific research problems. I even published the results with non-academic colleagues in academic journals, proving that it is possible to be both scholarly and relevant. But the truth is, my big projects were elsewhere. I led an international research team on a major Australian Research Council funded project. I published two books with international publishers. I ticked all the right scholarly boxes. But when I left town, most people still thought I worked for the TAFE.

From there, I was recruited to the next regional campus that landed government funding for regional development. This time I checked the fine print and consulted the map. This time, I knew I needed to be regional. On the phone to the regional campus director I asked only one question: *This new regional development institute – are they serious?* I did not need to explain who *they* were. She assured me they were, indeed, serious, from the vice-chancellor down: they wanted relevant regional research, they wanted regional development, they wanted the university to play a significant role in regional communities. So I left the little town in regional Victoria with my husband and our new daughter to try again.

Regional university campuses

> More than 70% of Australia's 39 universities are either headquartered in a regional city or have a regional campus.[1]

The terminology of 'regional campus' describes a key distinction in the Australian university system. In Australia the most significant distinction is not between public and private universities (most universities are public), or between research and teaching institutions (all Australian universities, by definition, do both).[2] In Australia the main differences among universities revolve around their age, reputation, and physical location.

Age is embodied in the 'Sandstone' universities: the original Australian universities that were founded in the 1800s and very early 1900s. Reputation is reflected in the 'Group of Eight' universities, those with the strongest research performance and so deemed most prestigious. With few exceptions, the Group of Eight are synonymous with the Sandstone universities.[3] All Sandstone and Group of Eight universities are headquartered in capital cities.

A key feature of the Australian university system is its strong metropolitan focus. In a nation where the bulk of the population lives in the capital cities, the great majority of universities – about two-thirds – are based there as well. So are most Australian university students: in 2011, over three-quarters lived in a capital city.[4] Thus, along with age and reputation, the key distinguishing feature of an Australian university is location.

While metropolitan campuses dominate the numbers, some university sites are intentionally located elsewhere. These are the *regional campuses*, positioned outside the capitals, in a regional city or town. Regional campuses are not only non-metropolitan; they are established with a particular set of place-based aims and expectations. These place-based campuses have been a common policy response to the challenge to skill up Australia's regions for the knowledge economy.

Regional university campuses are intended to play an explicit role in the development of their surrounding region. But how common are they? It is difficult to calculate the exact number of regional campuses in Australia: there is no official list. Calculating the number of regional campuses is complicated by the fact that *regional* can be defined in different ways, as can *campus*.

First, there is no single agreed definition of *campus*, as universities vary in their terminology. In some cases, the simple existence of local activities or partnerships gives rise to the claim of a 'campus'; in other cases, even a set of buildings and local courses is not deemed sufficient for campus status. Many universities distinguish between 'campuses' that offer courses and smaller 'study centres' or 'sites' where students can access computing facilities and local support. For the purposes of this chapter, a *campus* is defined according to: 1) whether the university itself deems the site a 'campus' and 2) whether the university maintains a physical presence where staff and students are present and university-level coursework options are available.[5]

There is also the question of when is a campus truly *regional*? While the term 'regional' refers to non-metropolitan areas, there are some grey areas. Some regional cities – such as Newcastle and Wollongong – do not meet remoteness criteria, so they are not considered 'regional' for the purposes of certain government funding schemes. Nevertheless, the University of Wollongong and the University of Newcastle are widely recognised as regional universities.[6]

Capital cities such as Hobart (Tasmania) and Darwin (Northern Territory) are comparatively small and remote, so universities based there often argue that they should be considered 'regional' too. Equally, some suburban campuses that sit within the metropolitan footprint of capital cities have a place-based mandate to serve their local metropolitan region. For the purposes of this chapter, however, *regional* is defined as per common usage in Australia as areas outside the capital cities. This includes all regional cities, but excludes capital cities and their suburbs.

Armed with a working definition of regional university campuses, it is possible to pose the question: *How many regional campuses are there in Australia?* Popular perception in the university sector is that regional campuses are relatively few, and rapidly becoming an endangered species. Threats of closure to regional campuses, like threats affecting regional industries, quickly make front-page news in the regions. Nevertheless, despite the current funding pressures on universities, only a few regional campuses have actually closed. Some have changed hands, and many have downsized. Others, however, have attracted new investment, and some new regional campuses have opened in growth areas. A closer look at regional campuses reveals they are highly diverse, and yet have some common challenges.

One way to describe the landscape of regional university provision in Australia is to observe that Australia has 40 universities: 27 are based in capital cities and 13 – about a third – are headquartered in regional Australia. There are five regional universities based in New South Wales (Charles Sturt University, University of New England, the University of Wollongong, the University of Newcastle, and Southern Cross University), five in Queensland (James Cook University, Central Queensland University, the University of Southern Queensland, the University of the Sunshine Coast, and Gold-Coast-based Bond University), but only two in Victoria (Deakin University and Federation University Australia), and one in Western Australia (the University of Notre Dame).[7]

At the same time, categorising universities on the basis of their headquarters overlooks the fact that most Australian universities are now multi-campus institutions. Given the multi-campus nature of many universities, there are many more regional campuses than these numbers would suggest.

In total, there are over 70 regional university campuses in Australia. The Australian Regional Universities Network (RUN) brings together 23 of these, run by six different regionally based universities.[8] The other seven regionally based universities do not belong to the network; between them, they have another 25 regional campuses. Furthermore, about half of Australia's capital-city-based universities have at least one regional campus.[9] Together, these comprise 25 additional regional campuses around the country. The breakdown of Australia's regional campuses by state is shown in Table 3.1.

In Western Australia, there are seven regional campuses. Four out of the state's five universities are metropolitan based, but all five have regional campuses. The Perth-based University of Western Australia has a campus at Albany, four hours south of Perth; Curtin University has a School of Mines in the mining town of Kalgoorlie, about six and a half hours from Perth; Edith Cowan University has a campus in Bunbury, about two hours south of Perth, and Murdoch University has campuses in the regional cities of Rockingham and Mandurah (Peel campus), both less than an hour from the city. Western Australia's only regionally based university, the University of Notre Dame, is based in the port city of Fremantle, only a half-hour from Perth; it also maintains a regional campus in Broome, over 23 hours away by road. Western Australia thus has university campuses in seven different regional towns and cities, yet most (with two exceptions – Broome and Kalgoorlie) are located in the south-west of the state, within 400 kilometres of the capital.

South Australia has four universities, and two regional campuses.[10] The University of Adelaide has a campus in the town of Roseworthy, about an hour north of Adelaide, formerly the Roseworthy Agricultural College.[11] The University of South Australia – a new-generation university established in 1991 – has a regional campus at Whyalla (about four hours to the north-west of Adelaide), as well as a 'centre' at Mount Gambier (about four and a half hours to the east), both run under the banner of the Centre for Regional Engagement (CRE) established in 2005. Adelaide-based Flinders University has no regional campuses, but it does have a large number of 'regional locations', primarily rural clinical schools and

Table 3.1 Australian regional university campuses by state

	Regional campuses of regional universities	Regional campuses of metropolitan universities	Total number of regional campuses
Western Australia	2	5	7
South Australia	0	2	2
Victoria	8	8	16
New South Wales	19	1	20
Queensland	19	4	23
Tasmania	0	3	3
Northern Territory	0	2	2
Total Australia	48	25	73

centres for remote health, as far afield as the Northern Territory and Victoria.[12] The private Adelaide-based Torrens University has no regional campuses.

Eight universities are based in Victoria, and there are a total of 16 regional campuses across the state. There are two regionally based universities. Federation University Australia was founded in 2014 as a merger between the University of Ballarat and Monash University's Gippsland campus. Deakin University, Victoria's first regional university, was established in 1974 in the port city of Geelong. Victoria's other six universities are Melbourne-based, and two have regional campuses. The state's 16 regional campuses are located in 11 different cities and towns.

Federation University has three campuses in and around Ballarat, one in the town of Churchill in Gippsland, and one in Horsham in the Wimmera region.[13] Deakin has two campuses in Geelong and a campus at Warrnambool in Victoria's Western District.[14] Melbourne-based La Trobe University has a campus in each of four regional cities: Bendigo, Shepparton, Albury-Wodonga (on the New South Wales border), and Mildura.[15] The University of Melbourne retains an agricultural college at Dookie in the Goulburn Valley, about two and a half hours from Melbourne; a rural health campus in Shepparton, and a campus at Creswick in Western Victoria, about an hour and a half from the city. RMIT University (Royal Melbourne Institute of Technology) has no regional campuses but does have a regional centre in Hamilton in the Western District. Monash University, Victoria University, and Swinburne University all have suburban campuses but no regional campuses.[16] Regional provision can also cross state borders: Sydney-based Australian Catholic University has a campus in Ballarat.

New South Wales is home to 11 universities, five of which are regionally based. Altogether, there are 20 regional campuses in New South Wales, spread across 18 different cities and towns. Of the six Sydney based universities, only one has a regional campus in New South Wales: the University of Western Sydney's Lithgow campus in the Central Tablelands.[17]

Charles Sturt University is headquartered in the inland town of Bathurst, about three hours from Sydney, and has campuses in six other regional locations: Albury–Wodonga, Dubbo, Orange, Port Macquarie, Wagga Wagga, and Goulburn.[18] The University of New England, Australia's oldest regional university (founded in 1938) is based in Armidale in the Northern Tablelands of New South Wales.[19] The University of Wollongong is headquartered in the seaside city of Wollongong and also has satellite regional campuses in the towns of Bega, Bateman's Bay, Nowra (Shoalhaven campus) and Moss Vale (Southern Highlands campus).[20] The University of Newcastle has two campuses in the large regional city of Newcastle, a campus at Ourimbah on New South Wales' Central Coast, and a dual-sector campus at Port Macquarie on the mid north coast, about four hours from Sydney.[21] Finally, Southern Cross University is a regional university with campuses at Lismore in the Northern Rivers region, about eight hours from Sydney, and coastal Coffs Harbour, as well as Coolangatta on Queensland's Gold Coast.[22]

Queensland has five regionally based universities, and three Brisbane-based universities. Including the Gold Coast campus of Southern Cross University, there are 23 regional campuses in Queensland, the largest number of any state.

Central Queensland University has nine regional campuses spread along the central Queensland coast, ranging between 2 and 11 hours by road from Brisbane: one at Noosa, one at Bundaberg, two at Gladstone, two at Rockhampton, one in the inland town of Emerald, and two campuses in Mackay.[23] The University of Southern Queensland has campuses in the inland city of Toowoomba, the coastal city of Hervey Bay (Fraser Coast campus), and the South East Queensland cities of Springfield and Ipswich, less than an hour's drive from Brisbane.[24] The University of the Sunshine Coast has its main campus at Sippy Downs as well as a number of other study locations and centres.[25] James Cook University is based in Far North Queensland with two campuses in the regional city of Townsville and one further north in the city of Cairns.[26] Private university Bond University is based in the Gold Coast town of Robina.

Of the three Brisbane-based universities, all have regional campuses located within an hour of Brisbane. The University of Queensland has a regional campus at Gatton, about an hour west of Brisbane.[27] Griffith University has a campus at Southport on the Gold Coast and one at Logan between the Gold Coast and Brisbane. And the Queensland University of Technology has a campus at Caboolture in the Moreton Bay region.

Tasmania has only one university, the University of Tasmania. In addition to its campuses in Hobart and Sydney, the University of Tasmania has three regional campuses: two in the regional city of Launceston and one in Burnie. Similarly, the Northern Territory has one university, Charles Darwin University, with two campuses in the remote capital city of Darwin and two regional campuses: one in Alice Springs and one in Katherine.[28] Finally, the Australian Capital Territory is home to two universities based in Canberra: the Australian National University and the University of Canberra, neither of which have regional campuses.[29]

These numbers show a large and diverse cohort of Australian regional university campuses – 73 in total, spread across 60 different regional towns and cities, large and small, coastal and inland. Queensland has the largest number of regional campuses, with 23. These are heavily concentrated along the coast and in the populated South East of the state, but they are also scattered over a huge geographic distance from south to north. South Australia and the Northern Territory have the fewest number of regional campuses, with two each, reflecting their thinly spread inland populations. In the face of these vast distances, universities have tended to set up study centres and small sites rather than full campuses.

These numbers also reflect unevenness in the provision of regional campuses. Victoria and New South Wales are relatively well serviced by university campuses in both inland and coastal regions. Most places in Victoria, for instance, would be within a two-hour drive of a campus. In South Australia, the Northern Territory, or the inland areas of Queensland and Western Australia, however, one could easily drive for a day and not find a university presence.

Thus, despite the Australian university system's strong metropolitan focus, regional campuses are a significant presence on the landscape. A total of 27 of Australia's 40 universities have at least one regional campus. While some regional campuses are small and specialised, with only a few hundred students, others have thousands of students, a wide range of course offerings, and significant research programmes. In addition, many regionally based universities also offer capital-city-based, offshore, and online programmes.

While there is often a perception that regional university campuses are disappearing, 73 regional campuses are evident across Australia as at 2015. This number does not take into account the smaller university study centres and sites, which would add several dozen towns and regions to the list of those that host a university presence.[30] The strongest commitment to regional Australia is from regionally based universities themselves; they run nearly two-thirds of regional campuses. Nevertheless, about half of Australia's metropolitan universities have a campus in regional Australia.

Regional campus roles

> We unlock the creativity, talent and potential of regional communities by making higher education fully accessible and achievable … conduct world standard research that matters to regional communities … (and) play a lead role in enriching the social, cultural and environmental quality of life in regional Australia.[31]

Regional university campuses in Australia play multiple roles. As universities, they are expected to generate the same quality of teaching and research as metropolitan campuses. Staff and students must meet the same performance expectations, and the business and funding models are virtually identical. At the same time, regional university campuses play additional roles beyond mainstream academic work.

Establishing a university presence in a regional setting implies a strong place-based commitment. While all universities are to some degree expected to engage with society and provide public benefits, for regional campuses this expectation is central. Regional campuses imply a commitment to a particular place and a particular regional community. The relationship with the region is fundamental and central to everything the regional campus does.

Regional university campuses are therefore established from day one with a dual set of commitments. They have a responsibility to the university institution and the formal systems by which universities are assessed and funded. And they simultaneously have commitments to communities in their local region.

These dual commitments can quickly create tensions, because community and university expectations of what a regional campus should do are often vastly different. A 2008 paper on the role of universities in regional development in Australia highlighted this tension between these different roles: on the one hand, campuses need to ensure their viability within the Australian university system, and on the other hand, they need to be relevant for regional communities.[32]

First, regional campuses are part of university institutions, and so ultimately assessed on their academic reputation. Academic reputation in turn translates as research reputation, measured primarily by disciplinary esteem indicators – what other academics think – rather than the on-the-ground usefulness of the research. Overwhelmingly, the ability to attract grant money and publish in high-status academic journals determines a university's research rankings and thus, in large part, its reputation. Generating research is thus a key part of a regional campus's role.

University campuses must also be financially viable. Financial viability in the Australian public-funded university system in turn depends heavily on 'load', or the number of funded students. Australian university students attract government funding at varying levels depending on their course of study.[33] International students and, now, most domestic postgraduates, receive no subsidy but pay student fees. While many regional campuses also attract research funding, a sustainable business model for a regional campus, as elsewhere, depends heavily on the ability to attract students: preferably a lot of them. Teaching is thus also a key part of a regional campus's role.

As university bodies regional campuses do research and teach, to meet university targets for reputation and load. These are not, however, the concerns of the regions where universities work. Regional communities assess their university campuses according to different metrics: generally, the relevance of the campus and the quality of its relationships with regional communities and industries.

Relevance is typically assessed by the range, accessibility, and quality of courses that are taught locally, as well as the practical usefulness of the research that the campus generates. Relevant campuses offer a range of courses and conduct research on topics that matter to the region: such as Charles Darwin University's work in tropical agriculture, or the University of Tasmania's work on lean and advanced manufacturing.[34] Creating regionally relevant coursework and research, often in partnership with local organisations, is thus another key part of a regional campus's role. This can imply a stretch beyond the traditional (often supply-driven) shape of university institutions to respond to particular areas of local demand.[35]

Regional communities also value the quality of relationships with the local campus. A number of studies have explored universities' regional engagement in the Australian context.[36] These studies emphasise the importance of crafting strong relationships between regional communities and universities – as well as the need for these relationships to be underpinned by institutional commitment, respect, and agreed purpose.[37] Often, a key consideration is the amount of flexibility the campus has to make commitments in the local region.

Regional university campuses exist at the meeting point of a university with a region.[38] As university institutions, they are expected to generate high-quality, status-building research, and to achieve financial viability. As regional institutions, they are expected to be regionally committed, responsive, and contribute courses and research that make a difference to the region. Furthermore, as part of their mandate to *make a difference*, regional campuses are expected to deliver against three distinct regional development policy goals.

First, regional campuses are expected to increase the levels of education in the local region. This is sometimes referred to as 'raising educational attainment' or 'increasing participation in higher education'. Second, regional campuses contribute to the goal of service equity, by providing a visible and active university presence in communities beyond the capital cities. Finally, regional campuses are expected to contribute to regional development by growing the knowledge base about specific regional industries, communities, and environments. Each of these roles is discussed below.

1. Raising educational attainment

> Young people aged 15–24 years from rural and regional Australia are almost half as likely to be attending university as young people from metropolitan areas.[39]

Ever since the 2008 *Australian Review of Higher Education* drove home the point that 'People from regional and remote parts of Australia remain seriously under-represented in higher education,'[40] regional university campuses have been recognised as a key policy instrument for raising educational levels in regional Australia. While this role is not new, it was previously articulated in terms of providing local study opportunities. The more recent policy language of widening 'participation in higher education' has provided a convenient way for regional university campuses to talk about what they have always done: create opportunities for people in regional locations to study at university.

In regional Australia, the statistics on both educational attainment and university participation are generally poor. They consistently show regional Australia to be 'lagging', 'underrepresented', or 'behind' metropolitan Australia. Educational *attainment* refers to the number of people living in regional Australia who hold a university qualification. On average about 27 per cent of Australians living in capital cities have a university qualification, compared with less than 15 per cent of people in the regions.[41] Educational *participation* specifically refers to the number of people who are studying at university. In 2011, more than three-quarters (78 per cent) of all Australian higher education students were in capital cities – less than a quarter in the regions.[42]

There are several reasons why people from regional Australia are less likely to attend, or to have attended, university. The most obvious reason is distance. Across the board, regions more distant from metropolitan centres tend to demonstrate lower university participation and attainment.[43] People who live outside capital cities are less likely to live within commuting distance of a university campus. As a result, attending university requires physically relocating to another area – bringing a range of other financial and personal constraints into play.

While the growing number of fully online courses may be making distance less relevant, slow Internet speeds complicate distance study for many regional Australians. Furthermore, independent, long-distance study is often challenging, particularly for new university students.[44] Distance from secondary school facilities also affects regional participation and attainment; often, students in more remote regions do not finish secondary school, creating a smaller flow-on of students to university.[45]

While distance is the most obvious constraint to university participation and attainment in regional Australia, it is not the only constraint.[46] Socio-economic status and related cost considerations also affect the likelihood that regionally based students will attend university. Cost considerations can be a function of distance – directly related to the need to travel or relocate to study – but they also reflect lower average household incomes in many regional areas.

Furthermore, young people in regional Australia and their parents have historically been less likely than their metropolitan counterparts to even consider university as an option. Many students in regional Australia are the 'first in family' to attend university. Students who have no close role models with university experience are less likely to attend university.[47] They may struggle to see themselves as potential university students, and may lack confidence navigating higher education systems.[48]

Socio-economic constraints are in turn linked to another frequently cited constraint to university study for regional Australians: attitudes to higher education in regional areas. A number of studies have documented 'low' aspirations for university study in regional Australia and attitudes suggesting that higher education is not necessary.[49] Often, there is a marked preference in regional communities for practical trade-based qualifications, seen to be more aligned with industry needs and job opportunities.[50] It is notable that the apparent low attainment of regional students in higher education is often reversed when the focus turns to trade-based qualifications; regional areas tend to have more trade qualifications per capita than capital cities.[51] Nevertheless, there is some evidence that attitudes to university study are changing, as regional young people increasingly see that they need a university education to achieve their career goals.[52]

While more students from regional Australia may be aspiring to higher education in the twenty-first century, there are still questions about whether their aspirations can be achieved. Significant obstacles still prevent many regional Australians from attending university. Distance, cost of study, and the often foreign culture of university education continue to limit participation. A 2011 study found that only about half of parents in regional areas expected their young sons or daughters to someday attend university; in capital cities the figure was much higher.[53] Not only do fewer regional students apply to university, but a large number of those who are accepted into university ultimately do not attend, often for financial reasons.[54]

Furthermore, while most studies of university participation focus on young people, a large proportion of Australian university students are not young. So-called 'mature-age' students – students aged 25 or older who are returning to study – comprised over 40 per cent of Australia's university students in 2011.[55] Mature-age students in regional areas often face even greater obstacles to accessing a university education than young people: they typically have families, jobs, and other commitments that make it difficult or impossible for them to relocate or undertake long commutes. Many mature-age students study part-time while working and caring for their family.[56] Regional university campuses play an important role for these students, providing study options that would otherwise be inaccessible to them.[57]

In 2013, 40 of Australia's 55 Regional Development Australia committees reported low levels of educational participation and attainment in their regions, lack of educational opportunities, and the need to travel long distances for education.[58] In a policy context that aims to increase the participation of all Australians in higher education, regional campuses have particular salience. One recent study noted that 'the existence of a university campus within the region changed the way the community viewed further education.'[59] Regional campuses provide accessible study options for those of all ages who cannot, or choose not to, relocate to capital cities to study. In doing so, they make university study a more achievable option for students in Australia's regions.

2. Promoting regional equity

> Once students reach the tertiary level, the current education system does not provide the same opportunities to students from regional areas.[60]

While regional university campuses support the policy goals of educational participation and attainment, they also play an equity role. Regional campuses are intentional counterpoints to the metropolitan-dominated Australian university sector. They are concrete efforts to bring a university institution – all that a university is and does – into a regional setting. Locating a campus in a regional area means giving regional communities access to university services that would otherwise only be available in capital cities.

Regional campuses extend the benefits of 'university' into regional Australia.[61] Charles Sturt University has captured a snapshot of the range of services a regional university campus provides to its region:

> In addition to their role in educating future professionals and conducting research, universities have a direct social, cultural, environmental and economic impact on their surrounding communities. While this is true of all universities, it is also true that universities in regional locations have a proportionally greater impact on their immediate regions because they are often the largest employer, economic player and cultural institution in the area.[62]

Having a university institution in the local area thus leads to a range of flow-on impacts for regional communities.

Australian regional university campuses are spread across a number of different regional towns and cities. Overall, they tend to cluster roughly where the population clusters: along the coast, within two hours' drive of capital cities and in larger, inland regional centres. There are many more in some states (New South Wales, Queensland, Victoria) than others (South Australia, Western Australia, Tasmania); regional campuses are far from evenly distributed.

Nevertheless, it is notable that there is relatively little overlap in the location of regional university campuses. Seventy-three Australian regional campuses are spread across 60 different towns and cities. No town or city has more than two. South East Queensland has the largest number of campuses, but even these are spaced across local regions (e.g. Gold Coast, Sunshine Coast, Moreton Bay). In general, therefore, there has been an effort to spread the benefits of university services across a large number of towns and regions, rather than just focusing on a few regional cities.

At the same time, the overall distribution of regional university campuses across Australia is not particularly strategic; like other services in thin regional markets, the location of regional campuses results from a mix of overtly political acts, community passion and activism, and opportunistic leveraging of resources. Many campuses were established as mergers between universities and other, existing educational institutions.[63] Others were specific efforts to extend a university presence into particular markets, particularly those with growing populations.[64] Many campuses have received some level of government funding for providing educational services to regions.

While regional university campuses provide a range of services to their local communities, their core role is to provide educational services: in particular, courses.[65] It has been observed that: 'The existence of regional universities offers students in the regions the opportunity to study within easy access of their families and support structures.'[66] Furthermore, many regional university campuses intentionally specialise in providing learning opportunities for so-called 'equity groups': students of low socio-economic status, those that are first in their family to attend university, and mature-age students.[67] Compared with metropolitan campuses, regional campuses tend to have higher proportions of students in these equity groups.[68]

For many regional campuses, providing equal educational opportunity for 'non-traditional' and disadvantaged students is a central part of their role. As a result, regional university campuses in Australia have been pioneers in developing preparation and enabling programmes and other support mechanisms to facilitate students' transition into university. A recent evaluation of one such programme, the University Preparation Program (UPP) on the Cradle Coast campus of the University of Tasmania, concluded:

> At a regional level, UPP was a key university strategy in meeting the educational needs of a large number of people who had left school early. It provided an accessible option for those who wished to remain in their local area, paving the way for further study and opening up employment opportunities not previously available to them.[69]

This study also found that the programme increased the confidence of non-traditional students, their understanding of university culture, and their appreciation of different perspectives and worldviews.[70] Similarly, a study of an enabling programme at Central Queensland University found that it provided a 'transformative experience' for learners as they learned to challenge long-held assumptions about themselves, others, and the world in general.[71]

Regional university campuses have also pioneered a number of innovative programmes working with Indigenous Australian students – arguably the most disadvantaged group in Australia in terms of access to educational services.[72] Indigenous Australians' university participation and attainment is low compared with Australian averages, but it has been growing significantly in recent years, including increased participation in postgraduate programmes.[73] Many Indigenous Australians who study at university are mature-age students, and they are more likely to study on a regional campus than in a capital city.[74]

Overall, regional campuses play an important role in facilitating equitable access to services in regional settings. They not only provide a range of services to communities, but their services are often focused on meeting the needs of particular equity groups.

3. Driving regional development

> Around the world, regional campuses have been established as policy instruments for regional development ... universities possess a range of institutional features and characteristics that position them well to act as regional development catalysts.[75]

In addition to regional university campuses' roles supporting educational attainment and regional equity, regional campuses also have an explicit role in driving regional development. The role that regional campuses can play in regional development is acknowledged internationally, particularly with reference to their role in regional economic development.[76] Broadly, regional campuses contribute to regional development in three ways: through their organisational contributions, their human capital contributions, and their knowledge-generating and knowledge-catalysing contributions.

The organisational contributions of a university campus include all of the benefits that an additional, often large, organisation can make to the economic, social, and cultural life of a region. This includes the university's economic contributions as a significant local employer and purchaser of local services.[77] It also includes its social and cultural contributions to the region, including as a venue that brings together a diverse range of people. Universities provide a significant organisational presence in a region and may become part of regional leadership groups.[78] Overall, the organisational contributions of a university are important, though not dissimilar to the contributions that any large, professional organisation might make to a region.

More specific to universities are human capital contributions: their contributions to raising the overall educational levels in a region. Students who study at regional campuses in Australia are predominantly from the surrounding regional area, and they tend to stay in regional areas after they complete their study – thus contributing to human capital over the long term.[79] In Australia and internationally, local universities are the main providers of skilled workers for many regions, and many work closely with local employers to ensure that graduates have the skills that industries require.[80] Furthermore, regional campuses often attract highly educated people as PhD candidates and academic staff, raising the overall availability of human capital in the region.

Perhaps of most interest, however, is the regional development role that regional campuses play as knowledge-generating and knowledge-catalysing institutions. Many regional campuses have research centres and programmes on topics of direct relevance to their home region. Local organisations and industries are often involved in the research, creating opportunities to combine academic and non-academic forms of knowledge.[81] Furthermore, some campuses are highly embedded in their region and play an important role in knowledge networks. The resulting 'spillovers' of university research activity have been shown to increase local innovation.[82] Finally, universities working in regions can broker knowledge across traditional boundaries to catalyse development outcomes.[83] Brokerage activities can intentionally create knowledge spillovers by providing opportunities for different organisations and sectors to communicate, share knowledge, and generate joint solutions.[84]

In all of these ways, regional university campuses contribute to regional development. As observed in one federal government policy document:

> The impact of universities with campuses in regional Australia … often extends far beyond traditional educational and research activities. They play a crucial role in regional economic growth and development and in the social and cultural life of their communities. They are often central to regional economic and labour force benefits, including retaining graduates and professionals in the regions, generating diverse employment opportunities, and promoting regional research and investment.[85]

Despite their broadly recognised benefits, however, regional university campuses in Australia face a range of challenges which are directly related to these multiple roles and expectations.

Regional campuses: grounded but peripheral

A downgrading by stealth or neglect of universities in regional and rural Australia would be economically disastrous, politically problematic ... and counter the bipartisan pursuit of equity through education that has traditionally characterised and inspired Australian advances.[86]

Regional university campuses play important roles on the ground in regional communities. In many ways, they epitomise an ideal of higher education in dialogue with place. In a regional campus, the knowledge and resources of a powerful university institution come into dialogue with the knowledge and resources of a region. The meeting points between university and region support a range of educational, equity, and regional development outcomes.

At the same time, the impacts of Australian regional campuses are limited. They face a number of issues related to their status and financial viability as part of the Australian university system, and their ultimate ability to generate real impacts in regional communities. Critics claim that regional university campuses make comparatively little impact in regions compared with the cost to run them.[87] It is observed that many young people from regional Australia still travel to the capital cities to study at their preferred university – yet few students from the capitals choose regional campuses.[88] Experience has shown that 'young people will always leave regions even if there is a local campus', because regional campuses can never provide the full range of programs that people want.[89] Furthermore, there is limited evidence of big economic innovations being generated from regional campuses.[90]

From a university perspective, as well, regional university campuses have issues. Student numbers tend to be lower, and cumulative research outputs lower, than large capital-city campuses. Financial viability becomes questionable. Regional campuses are portrayed as a luxury that the sector cannot afford. Thus, in recent years a number have been actively downsized or even closed. Regional university campuses have lost research centres, teaching programmes, and resident professors. There is evidence of a strong push to re-centralise university provision in the nation's capital cities.

The challenges faced by regional university campuses are the direct result of being regional. They serve thin markets with lower populations and thus have a smaller pool of potential students and research partners to draw on. Financially, it costs more to provide university services in regions, and the income-generating opportunities are much more limited than in the capital cities. Some estimates place the cost of service delivery in regional Australia as 30–40 per cent higher than in metropolitan areas.[91] A 2010 study notes that: 'Regional campuses may have less potential than their metropolitan-based counterparts to diversify revenue sources, including less capacity to attract fee paying students and fewer opportunities for commercial partnerships.'[92]

The Business Higher Education Roundtable has similarly observed that: 'Many of the universities in the regions have been created only in the relatively recent past, they lack substantial endowments, (and) their industry base is frequently small.'[93]

These challenges are exacerbated by the perception that regional campuses are – by virtue of being regional – lower-quality institutions. Despite the quality outputs of many regional campuses, they are still widely viewed as second-class when compared with campuses in capital cities. Research reputation is an area where many regional campuses struggle. They tend to have fewer, and relatively junior, staff, often in teaching-intensive roles. This limits the campuses' research outputs and their ability to build a strong academic reputation. While some regional campuses have developed areas of research specialisation and reputation, most do not have the critical mass – in people or dollars – to compete with large, well-established and well-endowed metropolitan universities. Regional campuses generally lack 'big names' and have few academic leaders.

And there are deeper issues. On a regional campus, the difference between the kind of research that matters to academics and the needs of industries and communities is cast in sharp relief. Universities create and value knowledge in disciplines for the purposes of theory-building; regions grapple with practical problems and opportunities that cross disciplines and sectors.[94] Many academics who are highly knowledgeable in their field are uncomfortable crossing into areas where they know little. Furthermore, there is little incentive to do so: applied and cross-disciplinary research is poorly rewarded in the academy.[95] High-quality, grounded 'regional research' is both harder to do than traditional research, and less valued by university institutions.

As the story at the start of the chapter illustrated, regional campuses and their staff tend to experience marginalisation in the Australian university system: they work from the periphery.[96] Staff often find themselves caught in the gap between what regional communities want, and what the university system can feasibly provide. Regional campuses have limited influence and resources. Economically marginal regional courses and activities are frequently closed, engendering a 'loss of confidence' from communities.[97] While regional university campuses are often heavily dependent on government funding, they are distant from the centres of government decision-making.[98] This makes it difficult for them to communicate the value they provide and make a case for support.

Yet even as they face these issues, regional campuses in Australia are tackling many of the important challenges that face the university sector as a whole. Working from the periphery, regional campuses stand at the fault lines of discovering what it means, in practice, to be relevant as a university in the twenty-first century.

Currently, universities and other research organisations – even those in the capital cities – are assessed as making minimal contributions to business or policy innovation in Australia.[99] Regional campuses grapple every day with this central question of how to make the work of a university relevant to the real needs of people and industries on the ground. To this question, they bring a 'deep under-standing of regional contexts and issues'.[100] Academics on regional campuses tend to respect and integrate local knowledge into research and teaching, to work with non-university partners, and to focus on practical problems alongside theo-retical considerations. This creates opportunities for new kinds of cross-boundary knowledge production.[101]

Furthermore, regional university campuses are accessible to a wide range of people. They are often perceived as friendly options for students dipping their toe into university study for the first time. Some have partnered with vocational training (VET) providers such as TAFEs to offer students in the region a more seamless pathway between vocational and higher education. Many have devel-oped specific initiatives to support non-traditional students and equity groups. Thus, regional campuses become useful sites for challenging and changing cul-tural perceptions about the relevance of a university education – and about who is 'smart enough' to be a university student.

In the end, the story of regional university campuses illustrates both the con-tradictions and opportunities of being regional in Australia. On the one hand, regional campuses and their staff have deep insights into the on-the-ground needs and opportunities of communities and industries. They are in a key posi-tion to create more inclusive, innovative, and relevant university institutions. Nevertheless, regional campuses in Australia remain culturally and politically peripheral. They are still regularly cast as regionalist service-delivery mecha-nisms of questionable quality and viability, rather than high-potential regional development catalysts.

Notes

1 Daley and Lancy 2011, p. 30. Australia now has 40 universities, as Torrens University was founded in late 2011. Despite recent closures and downsizing of regional cam-puses, this chapter calculates the current figure at 68 per cent.
2 Thirty-seven out of Australia's 40 universities are public (Norton and Cherastidtham 2014, p. 65), though the public–private distinction is not always clear in the Australian system, where private universities may receive public funding, and vice versa.
3 The University of Sydney was founded in 1850, the University of Melbourne in 1853, the University of Adelaide in 1874, the University of Queensland in 1909, and the University of Western Australia in 1911; all are both 'Sandstone' and 'Group of Eight' universities, and all were the first university to be established in their respective states. The other Group of Eight universities (Monash University in Victoria, the University of New South Wales and the Australian National University in Canberra) were established in the mid-twentieth century. Norton and Cherastidtham 2014, p. 85 note that: 'On all three prestige metrics, Group of Eight universities outperform the other university groups.' The University of Tasmania, founded in 1890 as the first and only university in the island state of Tasmania, is the only Sandstone university not part of the Group of Eight.
4 Seventy-eight per cent (ABS 2013c).
5 Most regional campuses also conduct research. This definition excludes research-only sites, however, as these are often used simply as field outposts for students and staff based elsewhere.

6 UA 2009, p. 3 notes that government definitions for 'students studying in regional areas', based on remoteness category, 'excludes a number of major institutions (such as the University of Newcastle and James Cook University) that would generally be considered to be regional universities in popular usage of the term'.

7 There are no regionally based universities in South Australia, Tasmania, or the Northern Territory, though there are regional campuses of capital-city-based universities. Federation University formed through a merger of the University of Ballarat with Monash University's Gippsland campus. Southern Cross University, though based in New South Wales, also has a regional campus on the Gold Coast in Queensland. It is notable that two of Australia's three private universities – Bond University and the University of Notre Dame – have chosen to base themselves in a regional city.

8 Central Queensland University, the University of Southern Queensland, the University of the Sunshine Coast, Southern Cross University, Federation University Australia, and the University of New England.

9 According to the author's calculations, 14 of Australia's 27 capital-city-based universities have at least one regional campus. Universities Australia (UA 2009, p. 6) put the number at 12 'major capital city' universities with regional campuses, excluding Hobart and Darwin. It is notable that such lists can quickly become out of date: the UA list included Monash University, which subsequently divested itself of its Gippsland campus, and RMIT, which now lists its Hamilton campus as a 'site', not a campus. The 2009 list did not, however, include the University of Western Sydney's Lithgow campus in the Central Tablelands, opened in 2014; the Queensland University of Technology campus at Caboolture, which offers eight courses onsite in the Moreton Bay region; or Griffith University's campuses at Southport and Logan.

10 Four universities based in South Australia; not counting Sydney-based Australian Catholic University's Adelaide campus.

11 As agricultural colleges are specialised, they are often overlooked in discussions of regional campuses, particularly as most universities have withdrawn from rural agricultural campuses. Roseworthy, suburban Waite campus in the Adelaide foothills, and the University of Melbourne's Dookie campus are exceptions.

12 Flinders University and Victoria-based Deakin University have formed a partnership to promote rural and remote health education training and research in western Victoria and eastern South Australia. See: http://www.greaterhealth.org/ (viewed 1 June 2015).

13 Federation University also has partnership arrangements for vocational course delivery in Stawell and partnerships for student placements and occasional health-related courses in Ararat.

14 Deakin also has a city campus in Melbourne itself, at Burwood.

15 La Trobe previously had a campus in the smaller town of Beechworth, but this site has been sold.

16 Monash divested itself of its Gippsland campus in 2014, which merged with the University of Ballarat to form Federation University Australia. Melbourne-based Swinburne University had a 'regional campus' in the suburb of Lilydale, which closed in 2013.

17 The University of Western Sydney is metropolitan based, but it has a specific mandate to serve the greater western Sydney metropolitan region, via seven suburban campuses. The University of New South Wales, the University of Sydney, Macquarie University, and the University of Technology Sydney have no regional campuses. The Australian Catholic University has only one regional campus, which is in Victoria (Ballarat).

18 Charles Sturt University also has regional study centres in Griffith, Parkes, and Wangaratta, Victoria, as well as several metropolitan and international campuses and centres.

19 Originally the University of New England was a college of the University of Sydney; it became an independent university in 1954. See http://www.une.edu.au/ about-une/a-world-of-learning/the-une-story (viewed 1 June 2015). UNE has several regional study centres, but no additional campuses.
20 The University of Wollongong also has campuses in Sydney and overseas.
21 In addition, the University of Newcastle has campuses in Sydney and overseas, and several rural health centres in Orange and elsewhere. The Centre for Rural and Remote Mental Health is located in Orange (http://www.crrmh.com.au/ [viewed 1 June 2015]) and the University Department of Rural Health works across several towns.
22 Southern Cross University also has Sydney and Melbourne branch campuses and a study centre in Grafton.
23 Central Queensland University also has capital city campuses and various study centres and sites.
24 The University of Southern Queensland is also a partner in the College of Wine Tourism in Stanthorpe and has additional 'hubs' in Maryborough and Stanthorpe.
25 These are not called campuses, though some may function as such.
26 James Cook University also has a hospital-based education centre in Mackay, a Centre for Rural and Remote Health in Mount Isa, and a teacher education focused study centre on Thursday Island, as well as campuses in Singapore and Brisbane.
27 The University of Queensland also formerly had a campus at Ipswich, but this was transferred to the University of Southern Queensland in 2015.
28 Charles Darwin University also has Melbourne and Sydney sites, as well as vocational training campuses and study centres in various, often remote, locations.
29 The Australian National University does have research bases and field sites located at various places around the country.
30 Nor does this calculation take into account the numerous suburban campuses of Australian universities, which often have a close relationship with their local regions. The University of Western Sydney is an oft-cited example of a suburban university with a strong regional mandate.
31 Quoted from the Regional Universities Network (RUN 2015a). Interestingly, 'Unlocking Talent' was previously the title of a regional campus development project in Tasmania funded by the Diversity and Structural Adjustment Fund; the term was borrowed from a UK policy document on place-based approaches to widening participation in university study (DIUS 2008).
32 Allison and Eversole 2008, pp. 98–101.
33 This funding comprises a direct grant component, known as CGS, and a student loan component, formerly HECS (Higher Education Contribution Scheme) and now known as HELP (the Higher Education Loan Program). Norton and Cherastidtham 2014, p. 43 explain that 'the single largest source of public funds for higher education is the Commonwealth Grant Scheme (CGS). $6.4 billion was distributed through the CGS in 2014.' They also note that this funding has declined steadily in real terms since the mid-1990s (p. 44).
34 Harding 2007 gives some examples.
35 See Allison and Eversole 2008, pp. 99–100.
36 Australia has a network for promoting university–community engagement (Engagement Australia) which sponsors the *Australasian Journal of University-Community Engagement* and an annual conference which have produced considerable research on university–community engagement in the Australian context.
37 See e.g. Garlick and Pryor 2002; Scholfield 2005; Winter *et al.* 2006, p. 221.
38 See Allison and Eversole, 2008.
39 CSU 2009, p. 6.
40 Bradley 2008, p. 31.
41 ABS 2013d.

42 ABS 2013c. While it is true that students move in from the regions to study in the capitals, this study notes that 'for the most part, students from capital cities tended to study in capital cities, and those who lived outside capital cities tended to study in regional areas' with 91 per cent of capital-city based students stating that they had lived in that capital city five years previously (ABS 2013c, np).

43 DEEWR 2010, p. 4, notes that: 'There is considerable research evidence showing that regional areas located further away from metropolitan centres are more likely to have lower participation rates.' ABS 2013d, np notes that: 'In 2011, the regions with the highest rates of attainment of non-school qualifications were all in or near greater capital cities' while 'the regions with the lowest rates of attainment of non-school qualifications tended to be in rural and remote areas.'

44 Eversole's 2000 study of university training needs in South Western Australia, for instance, identified that distance and travel were often reasons for discontinuing university study, while isolation and motivational problems were obstacles to external study.

45 For instance, Alston 2002, p. 8 observes that: 'Higher numbers of rural children drop out before they finish high school. For example, in Western Australia, drop out rates vary from 25% in the capital city to between 50% and 75% in rural schools with much higher rates among Aboriginal students.'

46 DEEWR 2010, p. 3 provides a brief summary of the research on constraints to university participation in regional Australia, observing that: 'There is a considerable research literature examining the lower participation rates of people from regional, rural and remote areas … Most of the research in this area acknowledges the complex variety of factors that lead to differing participation rates across regions. These include distance from a university campus; the socioeconomic status of people living in regional and remote areas; differences in aspirations and attitudes of regional students; Year 12 retention and completion, and the cost of university study.'

47 ABS 2013c cite a study that found that students were more likely to be enrolled at a higher education institution when at least one (40 per cent) or both (65 per cent) of their parents had completed a Bachelor Degree or above.

48 Hawkins 2014 discusses this in terms of a lack of 'cultural capital' for university study.

49 DEEWR 2010, p. 8, notes that: 'Many studies have found that students in non-metropolitan areas are less likely to aspire to university study than their metropolitan counterparts…. In many studies, the development of aspirations has been linked to family and community attitudes towards further study.'

50 This observation is reflected in educational attainment data, which show a much higher propensity for people located outside of capital cities to hold trade rather than university qualifications. ABS 2013d, np observes that: 'In the greater capital cities combined, there was little difference between the proportions of people with higher education and vocational qualifications (27.3% and 25.1% respectively). In contrast, people living in the rest of the states and territories were twice as likely to have vocational qualifications (30.0%) than higher education qualifications (14.8%) as their highest qualification.'

51 See ABS 2013d for an overall comparison of capital cities and other areas, as well as a list of the ten Australian regions with the highest level of vocational qualifications: topped by the Hunter Valley, and including only one capital-city region. IRD 2007 conducted this analysis specifically with reference to North West Tasmania, a region known for low educational attainment, and found that this region outperforms national averages in trades-based qualifications.

52 Hawkins 2014 found that the young rural girls in her study did not have 'low aspirations', as policy makers claim; rather, many aspired to university study. The research did, however, raise concerns about whether these girls will actually be able to achieve their aspirations.

53 Baxter *et al.* 2011, p. 5: 78 per cent of parents in major cities expected their daughter to obtain a university-level qualification, compared with only 59 per cent of parents in outer regional areas; for sons, the figures were 62 per cent in the cities and only 40 per cent in the regions.

54 Parliament of Victoria 2009, p. xiv documented that regional students in Victoria were less likely to apply to university (in all but one region), and more likely than Melbourne-based students to reject an offer of university study; furthermore, one in three students from regional Victoria who accepted their offer did not commence study. Richardson and Friedman 2010, np documented that: 'Students from regional areas who wish to attend HEIs are often prevented from doing so by the costs associated with study, and are highly likely to defer the commencement of their courses for financial reasons.'

55 ABS 2013c gives the figure of 41 per cent of Australian university students aged 25–64; on our own regional campus, we have had students as old as 90.

56 ABS 2013c documents that while only 10 per cent of younger students were studying part-time in 2012, 58 per cent of older students were studying part-time.

57 Regional campuses generally have a much higher proportion of mature-age students than capital-city campuses. The Regional Universities Network has calculated that its member universities average 50 per cent mature-age students, compared with an average of 24 per cent in the higher education sector as a whole (RUN, 2014, p. 9).

58 Faulkner *et al.* 2013, p. 17.

59 Johns *et al.* 2014, p. 55.

60 The Nationals 2013, p. 17.

61 As part of the broader quest for service equity discussed in Chapter 1, regional campuses thus represent an intentionally 'regionalist' approach to service provision.

62 CSU 2009, p. 11.

63 It is notable that a number of these institutions have struggled with their transition into the university sector.

64 Burnley and Murphy note a tendency for the 'establishment of university branches in turnaround localities, such as at Gatton in Queensland, and at Lismore and Coffs Harbour in NSW' (Burnley and Murphy 2004, p. 103).

65 For instance, Parliament of Victoria 2009, p. xix notes that: 'Participants in the inquiry emphasised the importance not only of a local university presence, but of the quality and range of courses available.'

66 BHERT nd, p. 3.

67 Many students on regional campuses fit all three categories.

68 The Regional Universities Network estimates that 32 per cent of their commencing, domestic undergraduate students were from low-SES (socio-economic status) backgrounds and these numbers are growing (RUN 2015b, p. 7). RUN 2014, p.11 presents a table showing the proportion of low-SES domestic undergraduates in different Australian universities; if the University of Western Sydney is included, then the ten Australian universities with the highest percentage of low-SES students are all regional universities.

69 Johns *et al.* 2014, p. 7.

70 Johns *et al.* 2014, pp. 28–30 and 43–44.

71 Quoted in Johns *et al.* 2014, p. 11.

72 Parliament of Victoria 2009, p xxiii observes that 'Indigenous Australians are the most under-represented group in higher education.' ABS 2013c, np quantifies this: 'In 2011, Aboriginal and Torres Strait Islander people accounted for around 2% of the entire population of 15–64 year olds but only 1% of all higher education students in this age group.'

73 'The number of Indigenous people enrolled in higher education Australia-wide is increasing. There has also been a shift in enrolments, with a reduced proportion of Indigenous students enrolling in sub-degree programs and an increased proportion

enrolling in bachelor and postgraduate programs' (Parliament of Victoria 2009, p. xxiii). According to ABS 2013c, np: 'The rate of Aboriginal and Torres Strait Islander people aged 15–24 attending a higher education institution more than tripled in the 25 years between 1986 and 2011 (1.4% to 4.9%).'

74 'In 2006, the average age of a commencing Indigenous undergraduate student in Australia was 29 years, compared to 22 years for other students' (Parliament of Victoria 2009, p. xxiii). Richardson and Friedman 2010 documented that students studying on regional campuses were more likely to be Indigenous than those studying in capital cities.

75 Allison and Eversole 2008, pp. 98, 103.

76 See e.g. Allison and Eversole 2008; Charles 2006; Goddard and Kempton 2011; Goddard and Vallance 2013; Huggins *et al.* 2012; OECD 2007b; Uyarra 2010. Goddard and Kempton 2011, p. viii observe that: 'Universities in the round have potentially a pivotal role to play in the social and economic development of their regions. They are a critical "asset" of the region; even more so in less favoured regions where the private sector may be weak or relatively small, with low levels of research and development activity. Successful mobilisation of the resources of the university can have a disproportionately positive effect on their regional economies and achievement of comprehensive regional strategies.'

77 Numerous studies have been conducted internationally and in Australia; see e.g. Dalziel *et al.* 2009, pp. 204–205, and Drucker and Goldstein 2007, among others. Daley and Lancy 2011, p. 33 note that Australian studies show that the direct economic impact of a university in a region can be significant.

78 See, for instance, Garlick 2000, p. 89.

79 Richardson and Friedman 2010. RUN 2014, pp. 3–4 notes that: 'Between 60 to over 80 per cent of graduates from RUN universities stay in the regions to work after graduation.' CSU 2009, p. 15 documented that, of their regionally based on-campus graduate students, 73 per cent went on to take jobs in a regional location.

80 See OECD 2009, pp. 73–74. In Australia, the strongest examples of engagement to grow workplace skills have been in public-sector organisations such as hospitals and schools, but there are also examples of engagement with private industry.

81 The Institute for Regional Development at the University of Tasmania uses the concept of *knowledge partnering* to describe the intentional combination of different forms of academic and non-academic knowledge to address development issues. See Eversole 2015; Eversole and McCall 2014.

82 See e.g. Drucker and Goldstein 2007; Dalziel *et al.* 2009.

83 Allison and Eversole 2008, p. 107 propose that 'a place-based university that is capable of catalysing regional development outcomes' would involve 'a new approach to knowledge and learning, characterized by interaction, participation, and inclusivity; capable of mobilizing both formal and informal knowledge together across traditional boundaries' using 'strategic capability-building and brokering, to enable innovation within and across institutions'.

84 See for instance, examples in Eversole and McCall 2014.

85 DEEWR 2010, p. 2.

86 BHERT nd, p. 3.

87 See e.g. Daley and Lancy 2011.

88 Hillman and Rothman write that: 'Despite the presence of rural universities and the general widespread availability of VET programs and public facilities in rural centres, many young people are leaving non-metropolitan areas in pursuit of further education. A recent publication from the Department of Education, Science and Training has found that around 40 per cent of country-based students (those whose permanent home address was in a non-metropolitan area) had moved to attend university, compared to only 4 per cent of metropolitan or city-based students.... Much of the movement of non-metropolitan students was not necessarily related to lack of access

to a tertiary campus in their local area, but to subject and course choice' (Hillman and Rothman 2007, p. 3).

89 Collits and Rowe 2015, p. 90.

90 Daley and Lancy 2011, pp. 33–35.

91 House of Representatives 2000, cited in BHERT nd, p. 3.

92 DEEWR 2010, pp. 2–3.

93 BHERT nd, p. 2.

94 Allison and Eversole 2008, p. 103 make this observation, writing that: 'Disciplines, grouped into schools and faculties, are the basic building-blocks of the university. "Knowledge" in universities is codified knowledge, often highly specialized. Delivery of courses and R&D into a region, in turn, is often discipline-based. Regions, on the other hand, are complex, multidimensional landscapes. Tacit and relational forms of knowledge are hard to see. Multiple perspectives jostle for prominence. Academic expertise is needed, but to be effective it must have an appreciation of spatiality and interconnectedness.'

95 See e.g. Gunasekara 2006.

96 Few have documented this. An exception is Baguley 2009, p. 1 who explicitly remarks on her 'sense of marginalisation which continues to affect, but also enrich, my current and complex position as an academic and researcher in a regional area'.

97 BHERT nd, pp. 3–4.

98 RUN 2014, p. 4 notes that: 'Regional universities are particularly dependent on Government funding e.g. the RUN universities, on average, rely on Government funding for 67 per cent of their revenue, whereas it is 56 per cent for the Group of Eight (Go8) universities.' One reason for this is the young age of many regional universities.

99 On limited contribution of universities and other research organisations to business innovation, see Commonwealth of Australia 2014b, p. 61. On limited contributions to policy innovation, see Norton and Cherastidtham 2014, p. 17.

100 RUN 2013, p. 1.

101 See e.g. Eversole 2015 on knowledge partnering, a methodology developed on a regional university campus. In the United States it has been observed that: 'Partnerships with community organizations expose (university) faculty to here-and-now research challenges that resist the controlled environment of typical academic research projects' and that there is potential to 'create a powerful hybrid of knowledge that blends practitioners' "on-the-ground knowledge" with the objective "outsider" perspective of the researcher' (Pew Partnership 2003, pp. 23, 35).

4   Institutions and communities

A story about communities

In Western Australia, I quickly discovered that regional towns contained multiple communities: interest groups, town committees, industry groups, professional networks, sports teams, service clubs, churches, Indigenous groups. On the ground, it was easy to see that town 'communities' were in fact multiple, diverse communities: people with a range of identities, affiliations, and organisations that represented them. Some of these community organisations were concerned with development issues; others were not. All, however were active in, and deeply knowledgeable about, local contexts.

When I moved to Victoria, and later to Tasmania, I observed the same: regional communities are socially heterogeneous and institutionally thick. Despite having small populations by international standards, regional communities have an enormous range of organisations present and active at the local level. These organisations look after everything from local reserves to community festivals. They fight bushfires and serve school lunches. Many have a strong volunteer base. They include sports teams and clubs, churches and church groups, service clubs, schools, health services, and a range of other clubs, committees, action groups, progress associations, chambers of commerce – and the list goes on. In any town, an attempt to list the locally active organisations quickly runs into multiple pages. Any one person is unlikely to know them all.

Over the past 15 years, across three states, I have worked with many dozens of regional communities and their organisations. Some organisations represent communities of affiliation: such as professional or business networks or Returned and Services League (RSL) clubs. Some are communities of interest: such as interest-based clubs or organisations that promote and support education, tourism, agriculture, the arts, or the natural environment. There are organisations that look after infrastructure and services: from local government councils to voluntary committees. Other organisations serve as a centre for communities of identity: ethnic, cultural, religious. Organisations in regional Australia play multiple roles – and there are a lot of them.

On the ground, being regional means being part of a landscape of many diverse communities, each with specialised knowledge, and with particular interests and agendas. No master-list of community groups and organisations exists; despite many efforts by local councils to assemble directories, these lists are never complete, and date quickly. Yet any effort to tackle regional development issues on the ground means entering the institutional turf of these multiple communities and their organisations.

In 15 years of working in regional Australian research centres, I have learned that for any given regional development issue, initiative, or project idea, there are a wide range of communities who will have ideas, insights, and knowledge about it. Key resources – infrastructure, time, skills, dollars, governance mechanisms, and so forth – are also usually located across multiple communities and organisations. Early-stage discussions of new initiatives or project ideas immediately raise questions like: *Who is involved? Have you talked to Group X? Have you run this by Y?*

These questions are a central part of how things are done in regional Australia. It is not enough to propose a project on rural education, even if all the desktop data support the need for the project. It is necessary, first, to talk with the community: from the Department of Education to local schools, NGOs (non-governmental organisations), literacy programmes, online centres, pro-education committees, and any other community organisation whose interests and agendas might relate to the proposed initiative. Project conversations in regional Australia are a kind of stakeholder mapping on the fly.

Someone new in town can be quickly overwhelmed: *Which education committee was that?* Those with experience in a region, however, can usually recite a list of go-to people and organisations for any given topic. Those who live and work in regional communities seem to have an internal running list of contacts. Of course, no one's list is exhaustive. Even after eight years based in a regional research centre in a region of only 100,000 people, having managed community-based research projects on topics as diverse as retirement living, social enterprise, and food security, I still find organisations and groups that I have never heard of.

Everyone's list of local organisations is a work in process, an incomplete map of a complex social landscape. Organisations don't necessarily work together, but at the local level they at least know broadly who other key organisations are. When an issue or idea is tabled, the most appropriate response is a suggestion of who to talk to, or a friendly warning about who should not be left out of the loop. Project ideas are never entirely new; there is usually someone who is doing, or has previously done, something similar. There is nearly always a body of acquired knowledge, networks, and resources that can ease new initiatives into being.

People who live and work in the regions understand the complexity of local social landscapes. Those who arrive to consult with the community or to conduct research on it, however, frequently do not. They tend to assume that the local community is simple, easy to observe, and that – being regional – there is not much going on. The practice of responding to ideas and initiatives with an impromptu list of contacts and go-to resource people has a subtext in regional Australia. That subtext is: *Do not overlook what we know.*

Most regional community organisations have stories of being left out of the loop: of learning only later of initiatives that were designed and delivered without them, in spite of their experience and their previous work. This is perhaps the most frequent complaint one hears when working in regional Australia. The people who overlook the knowledge and experience of local communities typically come from somewhere else. They are also often the people with the power to make decisions.

In Australia, despite the institutional thickness of regional communities, decision-making of any consequence is still based in capital cities. This was not immediately apparent to me when I arrived in Australia. Government departments and other major institutions were, of course, all located in the capitals. Yet at the same time, there were plenty of regional and local institutions. There were abundant regional development bodies – often, more than one per region – as well as regional catchment authorities, local government councils, and local community development groups. All appeared to have decision-making power.

Over time, however, the dynamics of institutions and communities in regional Australia became more visible. Regional communities' own organisations and their own ways of working – their institutions – tended to interact in certain ways with decision makers in the capital cities. These meeting points nearly always generated tension. Over and over in the regions where I worked, decisions from the capital cities were imposed on regional communities in the absence of local input. In some cases, this simply fed a cycle of complaint and suspicion. In other cases, organisations based in regions made the effort to try to have a say in the decisions that affected them.

One example of decision-making in the regions was a regional planning exercise I observed not long after I arrived in Western Australia. The framing of the exercise – as regional planning, in a region where people's alliances were strongly to their local towns – was determined by government employees from Perth. So was the format: an all-day planning workshop inaccessible to most working people who were not attending as part of their job. In the meeting itself there was, unsurprisingly, very little local participation. A range of relevant organisations that worked in the region were visible around the room. Yet over three-quarters of the people present had driven down from Perth. The regional plan that was generated had very little of the knowledge or aspirations of the region itself.

Of course, local people were encouraged to participate – consultation at a basic level is nearly always a feature of Australian policy efforts. Nevertheless, most people chose not to spend a day in a long meeting, even if they were in a position to do so. Furthermore, the track record for community consultation did not suggest their time would have been well spent. Over and over in the following years I was told: participation in consultation exercises is generally a waste of time. Input is fed in to decision makers from the capital cities, but very little ever comes back.

In theory, state and federal governments claim to coordinate and facilitate community action; in practice, they dominate. To have any input into decisions, community organisations must venture onto the institutional turf of capital-city-based governments – directly, or indirectly. In the end, even 'local' and 'regional' bodies sit in a direct relationship of dependency to the capital cities. Thus, local progress associations and festival committees regularly affiliate themselves with local councils, believing that they are working with a local organisation. Yet despite their local representatives, councils ultimately function as an administrative arm of state government. Similarly, local environmental groups work with their regional natural resource bodies – whose work in turn is defined by legislation and funding decisions made in capital cities.

Engaging decision makers on their own institutional turf does not, however, guarantee regional communities a voice in decision-making. Often, community organisations are simply learning skills in compliance. By learning the language and practices of bureaucratic institutions, they learn to work within institutional frameworks controlling what can be done and how it can be done. There is generally little scope to change either. As expressed in one study of local environmental groups, volunteers felt they had little influence on decision-making, but they were burdened with a large weight of externally imposed paperwork.[1]

Thus, while regional Australia is full of local organisations, they have little actual voice in decision-making. Community organisations that seek to work with powerful institutions – or increasingly, those that seek simply to exist – are subjected to a raft of legislation, processes, protocols, and institutional expectations, either directly imposed from the capitals, or mediated through local or regional organisations that ultimately answer to the capital cities. All insist that community organisations speak the language of bureaucracy and mimic its practices. Thus, in twenty-first century Australia, volunteers must complete reams of paperwork in exchange for the continued existence of their organisations, while parents who want to help coach their child's sports team or work with the elderly are required to acquire a range of police checks and training and competency certificates.

On the ground in regions, it is clear that these instruments of bureaucratic control are not needed – other forms of community-based knowledge and control are much more effective and efficient. But community-based ways of working go unnoticed, and new processes are continually imposed from afar. Sometimes people laugh: *They want us to get a ladder licence!* Often, they mutter in frustration at the waste of time and the illogic of what is required. In some cases local organisations forego applying for funding as the complex accountability processes cost more than the value of the funds. Rules arrive from the capitals, ranging from the inconvenient to the patently ridiculous, and community organisations comply. They are afraid not to.

Of course, the bureaucratisation of Australian society affects communities in metropolitan centres too. The larger forces that drive – and allow – these processes are outside the scope of this book. The point here is that in regional Australia, these processes have a geography. Control is imposed on regional communities, and it comes from the metropolitan capitals. Organisations in the regions – even local government and regional governance organisations – are structurally positioned to always be on the receiving end of capital-city decisions. Despite the institutional thickness and dynamism in the regions, community organisations actually have very little room to manoeuvre.[2]

In regional Australia, people chaff against decisions imposed from capital cities, and they contrast the importance of local knowledge, local experiences, and local characteristics. It is frequently observed that communities on the ground in regional Australia work differently than the capital-city decision makers assume. This is the case even when decision makers and local communities share surface cultural similarities. It is even more the case when the communities in question are culturally distinctive. These communities' ways of working are different again, and the gulf between their institutions and those that dominate decision-making, even more marked.

Indigenous communities are one key example. Aboriginal Australians have long struggled to maintain their own local ways of working in their own country, in unequal dialogue with decision makers far away. When I worked in Western Australia, for instance, I was regularly made aware of a range of initiatives being designed and implemented by Noongar community leaders and organisations: initiatives to support young people, enable cross-cultural dialogue, and create jobs and income-earning opportunities.[3] Community-based initiatives were, however, regularly overlooked – and even, inadvertently squashed – by government decision makers seeking to design and implement their own programmes.

Over the years I have observed the on-the-ground knowledge of Aboriginal communities regularly ignored and overlooked, by both local and capital-city decision makers. Equally, I have observed serious efforts by decision makers to engage with Aboriginal communities to offer useful services, inclusive planning, and more equitable partnerships. Yet such attempts can easily be undermined: on the one hand, by accumulated mistrust of government, and on the other hand, by failure to engage respectfully with Aboriginal communities' distinctive knowledge and institutions. The Western Australian initiatives I documented in my 2003 article on 'managing the pitfalls of participatory development' give some examples of the latter.[4]

For the most part, non-Indigenous ways of working are still imposed on Aboriginal communities. Decisions emanate from non-Indigenous organisations based in the capital cities. Recent examples include the federal government's Northern Territory Emergency Response in 2007 – which imposed a range of centrally mandated controls on Indigenous communities deemed to be child-abuse hotspots – and the proposed closure of remote Aboriginal settlements on traditional country announced early in 2015.[5] When it comes to service delivery for remote communities, powerful external organisations can easily win out over local organisations in bids for funding; these services are then delivered on a drive-in–drive-out basis from afar. All are dramatic examples of the ways that metropolitan institutions dominate – and sometimes actively destroy – local organisations and institutions, especially those that are culturally different.

I often have a sense that regional Australians are foreigners in their own institutions. Decisions are regularly imposed from afar, while the knowledge and practices of community organisations are overlooked. When John Martin and I drew together a group of colleagues in 2004 to write about 'participation and governance in regional development' in Australia, study after study raised the question, 'How much control do local communities really have?' Government policies were ostensibly promoting decentralisation, but the over-all conclusion was that 'creating governance structures that will assure excluded groups a voice remains a serious challenge'.[6] Since then, I continue to observe capital-city-based decision makers engaging non-metropolitan communities in ways of working that ignore, devalue and/or actively colonise their knowledge and institutions.[7]

I have seen diverse regional towns and industries painted from afar as an undif-ferentiated landscape in decline. I have seen entrepreneurial regional university campuses dismissed as irrelevant outposts, and complex regional communities approached as blank slates for externally decreed plans. I have seen regional com-munities, in their rich social and physical landscapes, portrayed as deficits to be remedied and problems to be solved. I have seen their distinctive ways of work-ing and their rich local knowledge ignored and undermined, over and over, until I am convinced: being regional means being on the inside of every on-the-ground process – and on the outside of every significant decision.

Communities and their institutions

> People living in rural and regional areas frequently feel that their perspectives and interests are neither understood nor valued by central policy-makers or decision-makers.[8]

Australia as a nation has a complex institutional fabric. Institutions can be defined as ways of working: how things are done in a given social setting.[9] Institutions are sometimes manifested visibly in the form of organisations. In Australia, government institutions are important: Australia has a large govern-ment that operates across three levels – federal, state, and local. Private sector institutions are important, too; Australia has a diverse private sector, with a range of industry-level governance bodies. Civil society institutions are also important; they form organisations ranging from local clubs to large not-for-profits. Australia also has institutions and organisational forms that do not easily fit into these categories – such as social and community enterprises and quasi-governmental governance bodies.

Much of this complexity is replicated in any particular non-metropolitan region, with one key difference: the level of decision-making power. In any strand of the Australian institutional fabric, the highest level of decision-making is almost without exception located in the capital cities. Whether it is the head office of an NGO or industry body, or the departments of state and federal government, the bulk of real decision-making power is located in the central business districts of Australia's capital cities.[10]

Regional Australia, meanwhile, is rich in local institutions. These are visible in local organisations such as the football ('footy') club, the RSL club, the progress association, the school committee, and the local council. Organisations operating at the local level attract local loyalty, contain a wealth of local knowledge, create and strengthen local networks, and operate according to certain unwritten rules. They are characterised by their awareness of on-the-ground circumstances – needs and opportunities – and their familiarity with local ways of working. They are part of a universe of local institutions.

In regional Australia, the institutional fabric has both warp and weft: there are local institutions, and then, there are central institutions. Central institutions are high-level ways of working. Though based in capital cities, they may have local or regional offices. They are mechanisms of coordination, support, advocacy, and control. Thus, schools and hospitals are local institutions; Departments of Education and Health are central institutions. Sports clubs and shops are local institutions; league associations and head offices are central institutions. Local and central institutions represent distinct ways of working. Both are visible day-to-day on the landscape in regional Australia.

It is generally recognised that Australia needs strong *regional-scale institutions* equipped with both in-depth place-based knowledge and higher-level decision-making clout. Building governance institutions at regional scale has been attempted for many decades in Australia.[11] Yet despite the large number of regional organisations on the landscape, true regional institutions are hard to find. Regional organisations are layered onto an institutional landscape characterised on the one hand, by embedded local institutions, and on the other hand, by powerful central institutions. Caught in the gap between the two, regional organisations struggle.

1. Regional organisations

> Consistently with international theories of 'new regionalism', in Australia regional development agencies are now seen as a vital link in the matrix of institutions needed for more participative, entrepreneurial, and collaborative styles of development.[12]

Regional Australia has very few regional institutions: that is, embedded ways of working at regional scale. Australia does, however, have a large number of regional *organisations*. These are formal bodies that aim to promote and support regional-scale work. These organisations, on first look, suggest a rich landscape of regional-scale governance arrangements in Australia. On closer examination, however, it becomes apparent that these are organisational frameworks with little in the way of institutional substance.

There are four broad types of regional organisations in Australia: *regional development organisations, regional-scale local government bodies, regional natural resource bodies,* and *regional branch offices* of larger organisations.[13] Though their roles are different, all are designed to facilitate regional-scale action. While examples of regional organisations date back at least to the Regional Development Committees of the 1940s, since the mid-1990s there has been an 'explosion' of regional scale organisations.[14] These organisations aim to bridge the wide divide between local and central institutions by mobilising knowledge, networks, and decision-making at regional scale. All, however, are ultimately caught in the fault lines between local and central institutions.

Regional development organisations are primarily, but not exclusively, concerned with regional economic development. They include regional development committees, agencies, commissions, and regional marketing bodies charged with supporting the development of particular regions.[15] Some of these are state-level quasi-governmental bodies, such as Western Australia's various Development Commissions (Great Southern Development Commission, Wheatbelt Development Commission, etc.). Some are direct arms of the state government, such as the regional offices of Regional Development Victoria. Some are federally sponsored, such as the current national network of Regional Development Committees, which are attached to the federal Department for Infrastructure and Regional Development.

Generally, Australian regional development organisations attempt to generate strategic collaboration in their local region while acting as a conduit for targeted state and federal funding programmes.[16] They thus aim to mobilise place-based networks and create synergies with external resources. Nevertheless, Australia's regional development organisations are 'generally small bodies, with poor and insecure funding' and often not very long-lived.[17] Studies that have been conducted on these organisations generally conclude that they are 'relatively powerless bodies' with limited funding, decision-making clout, or local legitimacy.[18]

Regional-scale local government bodies have a different structure; they are regional organisations formed by local councils. These may take the form of large 'regional councils' formed from the formal amalgamation of local councils; or alternatively, 'regional authorities' or 'regional organisations of councils' formed by a looser alliance of independent councils. Regional councils are a form of local government operating at a regional scale, while regional organisations of councils (ROCs) are voluntary collaborative arrangements among groups of local councils. Examples of the latter are found across Australia; these organisations may pursue cross-council resource sharing and other forms of regional-scale action.[19]

Regional-scale local government bodies represent interesting attempts to move local government beyond the parochialism of the local scale. Many, however, were originally established by either federal or state governments.[20] Today, a number of ROCs continue to collaborate voluntarily on activities such as resource sharing, advocacy, and regional strategy. Some have formed solid collaborative arrangements at regional scale, though the range of activities varies, and many of these organisations are not well resourced.[21] Regional-scale local government bodies typically have a strong interest in the strategic development of their region. They are often layered onto a landscape alongside regional development organisations with similar mandates, and face many of the same issues as these organisations.

Regional natural resource organisations are a third type of regional organisation in Australia. They are found in every state and territory – with 56 regional NRM (Natural Resource Management) organisations across Australia.[22] The names of these organisations vary: in Victoria they are Catchment Management Authorities (CMAs), in Tasmania, South Australia and the Northern Territory they are Regional Natural Resources or NRM organisations; in New South Wales they are Local Land Services, and in Queensland and Western Australia they go by a range of names. All aim to facilitate regional-scale management of the environment, including planning and specific funded projects.

The creation of regional, catchment-scale organisations for environmental management would appear to be an important commitment to regional-scale governance. It would appear to have the potential to firmly situate environmental decision-making at the regional level. Yet like other types of regional organisations, regional natural resource bodies are caught in the fault lines between local and central institutions. At the local level, they tend to lack democratic legitimacy as they are not elected bodies.[23] Their role primarily revolves around the administration of federal environmental funding programs, with strong pressures for accountability to central governments.[24]

Finally, *regional branch offices* comprise the regional administrative offices of state and federal government departments and programmes, private firms, non-governmental organisations, service providers, and so forth, all typically found in quantity in any given region. Branch offices are examples of 'regionalised' service delivery, where regional offices are set up to serve a particular, externally defined region.[25] They tend to be administrative arms of central offices rather than independent organisations.

Regional branch offices are usually sectoral (rather than place-based). Their role is to provide services or support to the region in specific sectors such housing, social services, agriculture, finance, and so forth. At the same time, because of their base in the regions, branch offices are also subject to the local institutional environment. Like other regional organisations, they experience place-based demands, and must mediate the tensions between local expectations and central control.

Overall, organisations operating at regional scale are plentiful on the landscape in regional Australia. Any given region will generally have multiple regional organisations, with multiple roles, all aiming to play some kind of role in the well-being of the region. Regional organisations in Australia are present, active, and have been for decades. Yet they are many, and uncoordinated.[26] They are also generally weak: relatively powerless and under-resourced organisations, with limited local buy-in. In many cases they are run directly or indirectly from elsewhere. Regional organisations are plentiful, but regional institutions – embedded ways of working at regional scale – are much rarer in practice.

2. Local and central institutions

> The administrators' forest cannot be the naturalists' forest … Officials of the modern state are, of necessity, at least one step – and often several steps – removed from the society they are charged with governing.[27]

In regional Australia, regional institutions are weak. Regional Australia is dominated, on the one hand, by local organisations and ways of working; and on the other hand, by centralised, 'top-down' administrative organisations. Local institutions and central institutions represent distinct ways of working; both are present on the landscape in regional Australia.

Local institutions are strongly place-based. They are manifested in local organisations and have strong local legitimacy. Thus, people generally know and trust local organisations and are comfortable with their ways of working. As a result, local organisations routinely mobilise place-based networks to get things done. For instance, organisations in regional Australia work together informally across sectors to fill gaps in local service provision.[28] Local firms leverage local relationships to reduce transaction costs and make doing business easier.[29]

Central institutions, meanwhile, work differently. They typically take the form of centrally managed organisations such as government departments, head offices, and other centres of administration and decision-making. These organisations are nearly always located in capital cities. Nevertheless, they tend to be operationally placeless. Their higher-level responsibilities mean that they need to generalise across places, creating 'thin, formulaic simplifications' to replace the complexity of on-the-ground realities.[30]

The tensions between local and central institutions in regional Australia quickly surface in practice. Local institutions are grounded in local contexts. They have strong local knowledge and networks, and they understand the distinctive attributes of particular places. Nevertheless, they have very little ability to influence the broader institutional landscape. They lack decision-making clout. Central institutions, on the other hand, can mobilise higher-level resources and drive decisions. Yet they lack on-the-ground knowledge and networks to inform their decisions.

The differences between central and local institutions can be observed in the workings of any capital-city head office and any regional branch office. Even though 'head office' and 'branch office' belong to the same organisation, they work differently. Head offices prioritise organisational business and processes. Central institutions dominate. Branch offices are embedded in local communities, so workers will generally adopt a place-based focus. Local institutions dominate. Branch office staff recognise that sometimes it is necessary to do *this* (support a local initiative, accommodate a local circumstance) in order to achieve *that* (organisational core business). Head offices are less flexible. Though it may be an oversimplification, it would resonate to say that central institutions make the rules, while local institutions stretch them, massage them, and try to make them fit.

In regional Australia, this bifurcated institutional landscape is echoed in organisations of all kinds, across the public, private, and third sectors. There is always tension between central and local institutions, and a tacit acknowledgement that they work differently. Regional Australia has a long history of grappling with 'top-down' decisions and 'presumption of bureaucratic and technocratic wisdom' delivered from the nation's capital cities.[31] The response is usually highly localist – mobilising resistance at the scale where institutions and community alliances are strongest. This creates a landscape of local institutions and central institutions: each strong in their own way, but separated by a large gap.

3. The institutional gap

> Institutions develop over the long run. The creation of effective institutions might be critical for regional development, but they cannot offer a quick fix.[32]

The institutional landscape in regional Australia is characterised by a broad gap between local institutions – which are deeply grounded in local places – and central institutions, which are powerful seats of resources and influence. Each represents a very different way of working, and these are often in tension.

On this institutional landscape, regional institutions are desperately needed to bridge the gap. Regional institutions could potentially bring together grounded local knowledge at a scale that is powerful enough to mobilise resources and drive region-appropriate decision-making. Nevertheless, in practice, regional organisations are neither grounded nor powerful. They spend much of their time navigating the gap between local and central institutions, never fully accepted by either.

Regional organisations grapple with local cynicism about regional-scale initiatives, coupled with a lack of any real ability to influence policy.[33] Regional institutions do not have the legitimacy of local institutions. At the same time, they are unable to challenge the power of central institutions. They are neither one thing nor the other. Lack of on-the-ground trust and lack of delegation of power from the centre leave regional institutions caught in the middle.

A lack of local legitimacy means that regional organisations struggle to make any real difference to highly localised ways of working. It is no accident that recent writing on regional Australia has described Australian regional policy as *localist*.[34] Local institutions dominate. As described in Chapter 1, forced regionalisation has left scars in local communities. Initiatives are most often implemented at town scale. Furthermore, the structure of regional organisations themselves does not enhance their legitimacy. They are often run by appointed boards and may be perceived as elitist and non-representative.[35] There is a frequent perception that regional organisations are disconnected from on-the-ground concerns in the region.

At the same time, regional organisations lack the ability to shift highly centralised decision-making structures and processes. They generally have no regulatory authority and no independent revenue streams. They are reliant for their resources on state, federal, or local government. As a result, there is very little they can do to create more regionally based ways of working. Rather, centrally imposed agendas tend to dominate; one study documented that regional agencies felt 'micromanaged' by central governments.[36] Ultimately, the actions of regional organisations must orient toward the centre, from whence their resources come. They must lobby for central support, and in many cases they function primarily as delivery mechanisms for centrally determined policies and funding schemes.[37]

Regional organisations sit in the fault lines between local institutions and central institutions. In an institutional context where 'coordination between the three levels of government is characterised by inadequacy, duplication and wastage', regional organisations appear to promise a useful governance solution.[38] They can give central organisations a foothold and source of knowledge about the characteristics, needs and assets of particular places. They can give local organisations a scaled-up voice and opportunity to mobilise resources at regional scale. In theory, regional organisations can bridge the institutional gap.

In practice, however, they fail to do so. Regional organisations lack the institutional groundedness of local organisations, and they lack the resources and influence commanded by central organisations. Regional organisations are therefore unable to challenge the prevailing institutional patterns in regional Australia. Place-based knowledge remains strongly seated in local institutions, and decision-making clout remains entrenched in central institutions. Between the two lies a deep gap that regional institutions have not yet emerged to fill.

Regional communities on the margins

> A crucial element … is the concern with giving voice to groups or individuals hitherto excluded from the processes of formulating and applying development policy and practice.[39]

Local communities and their organisations are part of the local institutional fabric in regional Australia. These communities are, however, far from homogenous. Different communities work differently. Some local institutions are comparatively close to the logics and ways of working of central institutions, others quite far off. Cultural difference and social distance widen the institutional gap.

In regional Australia, there are a range of culturally distinctive communities. The way they work is not just grounded in their local place and community; it is also underpinned by different cultural values and worldviews. For instance, many Indigenous Australians – Aboriginal and Torres Strait Islanders – live in regional Australia. The original inhabitants of the continent have distinctive cultures and ways of working, which are reflected in their organisations at the local level. Refugee and migrant community organisations are another example of communities whose ways of working are underpinned by cultural differences.

For culturally diverse communities in regional Australia, the gap between their own local institutions and the central institutions in capital cities is magnified. These communities and their organisations face the same physical distance from centres of decision-making as other local communities in regional Australia, and the same structural dependence upon those centres. At the same time, they are further distanced by the differences between their languages, values, and ways of working and those of Australia's dominant institutions.

Communities that are socially distant from the mainstream face some similar challenges. The old, the young, or the socio-economically disadvantaged tend to have different concerns and constraints than economically comfortable, working-aged decision makers. Even when not culturally distinctive groups *per se*, they may work differently: preferring informal interactions or locally accessible communication, for instance. These ways of working do not always translate easily into dialogue with powerful central institutions. Thus in regional Australia socially disadvantaged groups are likely to face extra disadvantage, as they are unlikely to be able to craft a government submission or speak confidently at a high-level meeting to defend their interests.

In regional Australia, both culturally and socially distinctive communities are often tagged as 'disadvantaged' or 'marginalised'. As a result, they frequently find themselves on the receiving end of development interventions intended to help them. Yet the people and organisations who propose to help often work in quite unfamiliar ways. This is the case even at the local level, but it is particularly marked when crossing the divide between local communities and central institutions.

1. Indigenous Australian communities

> While Aboriginal people may want to engage with the state, they want to do so on their own terms and in ways that make sense to them.[40]

About 2.5 per cent of Australia's population identify as Aboriginal Australians and Torres Strait Islanders – about 550,000 people – and about two-thirds of these live outside the nation's capital cities.[41] The Australian Bureau of Statistics defines 37 Indigenous Regions for statistical purposes, but these administrative regional groupings do not begin to reflect the diversity of Indigenous Australia, which comprises hundreds of groups, with many different languages and dialects.[42]

Aboriginal and Torres Strait Islander communities are typically organised along kinship lines, as extended families and clans. There are also a range of formally constituted Indigenous community organisations, such as Native Title claimant groups, Aboriginal Land Councils, and community-based NGOs, as well as Aboriginal local governments in remote areas.[43]

The estimated period of cultural continuity for Indigenous peoples in Australia predates European colonisation by at least 40,000 years. Indigenous Australians are thus culturally very distinctive. Yet in the wake of British colonisation they were variously deemed invisible – residents of 'empty lands'[44] – new British subjects, or groups in need of special protection. Over 200 years of close contact with colonial and Australian society and its institutions has somewhat blurred the distinctiveness of Indigenous Australian institutions.

As a result, Indigenous organisations are often hybrids of Indigenous and non-Indigenous ways of working. On the one hand, they are 'embedded in a wider institutional context of Indigenous law, traditions, kinship systems, values and behavioural norms'; at the same time, 'they have been formed under western law', in dialogue with mainstream legal and governance institutions.[45] Thus, Indigenous organisations are institutionally distinctive, but that distinctiveness is not always readily apparent to outsiders, as organisations – such as Aboriginal local governments – may take superficially familiar forms.

Indigenous Australians retain their own identities, worldviews and institutions, but these exist in close and often disadvantageous dialogue with mainstream

Australian institutions. Mainstream institutions in Australia are much more western than Indigenous.[46] The dominance of mainstream ways of working can actively marginalise Indigenous Australian values and institutions, creating the impression that Indigenous Australians are not present, or at least, not a distinctive cultural group. Thus, while few Australians would disagree that remote Aboriginal communities have a distinctive culture, more urbanised Aboriginal communities have often had to battle perceptions that they are no different from other Australians.[47]

Over the years, unequal encounters with non-Indigenous economic, social, and political institutions have created situations of disadvantage for Aboriginal Australians and Torres Strait Islanders. As a demographic category, they remain the nation's most disadvantaged group. They are overwhelmingly over-represented in prisons and the ranks of the unemployed.[48] They are sharply under-represented in institutions of higher education, industry leadership, and government.[49]

The reasons for this can be understood in the ways that colonial and contemporary Australian institutions have interacted with Indigenous Australian institutions. Economically, the colonial positioning of Indigenous people as landless labourers laid the groundwork for future economic disadvantage and unemployment.[50] Socially, past government policies fragmented families and communities, moving communities and forcibly removing children from their families, creating the so-called 'Stolen Generation'.[51] Indigenous communities and their institutions have been repeatedly undermined, both intentionally and unintentionally. Social, cultural, and economic continuity has been lost; many people have had to re-discover and re-establish these connections.

Today, mainstream Australian institutions increasingly acknowledge the need to engage with Indigenous communities and their organisations in a more equitable way. There have been numerous attempts to build partnerships between mainstream institutions and Indigenous communities. On the one hand, working together promises to enable better responses to social and economic disadvantage.[52] On the other, Indigenous Australians are increasingly positioning themselves as important political and economic actors in regional economies, and legal recognition of Indigenous land rights and native title has created a significant asset-base for some communities.[53] This creates strong incentives for mainstream institutions to work with them.

Despite growing interest in partnerships, however, the meeting points between Indigenous and mainstream institutions are often vexed. Indigenous values and ways of working are distinctive, and this often goes unrecognised in attempts at partnership.[54] Indigenous Australian organisations 'often do not intersect well with non-Indigenous systems'.[55] Often, non-Indigenous ways of working dominate the relationships. In her study of three partnerships in regional Australia, Sherry Saggers documented some of the complexities involved in building partnerships involving Indigenous and non-Indigenous communities. The cases included tokenistic Indigenous involvement in a project dominated by non-Indigenous groups, as well as a more successful partnership built upon interpersonal trust between individuals at the local level.[56] Another study of Indigenous-run initiatives in an Australian town documented a wide range of social, economic, cultural, and leadership projects, formal and informal, some undertaken in partnerships with non-Indigenous organisations. Here, as well, informal social networks at the local level played a role in facilitating constructive relationship-building across cultural divides.[57]

Most typically, however, governments, NGOs, and other organisations engage Indigenous communities from the safety of their own institutional turf. Non-Indigenous ways of working take precedence, rendering Indigenous communities' own ways of working invisible. Professionals from outside Indigenous communities often 'struggle to recognise the strengths in unfamiliar Aboriginal organisational forms' and instead 'seek to impose organisational arrangements that are familiar to them.'[58] One recent forum on Indigenous governance noted that the term *Indigenous governance* could itself be questioned, given that many staff in Indigenous organisations felt that they were spending their time 'complying to imposed rules, rather than to their own [Indigenous] rules.'[59] Rigid and elaborate systems of financial accountability required for 'good governance' by external standards place heavy burdens on small organisations, and may ultimately lead them to opt out of partnerships. Meanwhile, external organisations comfortable with these ways of working are more likely to capture resources 'on behalf of' – but ultimately, instead of – Indigenous communities.

When non-Indigenous organisations seek to work with Indigenous communities, the institutional context matters. If non-Indigenous institutions dominate, the partnership is unequal and likely to fail. There are several reasons why. First, non-Indigenous institutional formats may be poorly suited to capturing Indigenous Australian concepts. Complex cultural concepts such as 'country' have been difficult to communicate through western institutional apparatus such as planning reports.[60] Thus, important concepts can easily be misunderstood or misrepresented, and Indigenous worldviews rendered operationally invisible.

Next, the ways of working of bureaucratic institutions – even the language used by their staff – may be uncomfortable or inaccessible to Indigenous communities.[61] Furthermore, based on past experiences, communities simply may not trust outside institutions. Research on Indigenous governance has concluded that, 'the expectations and values imposed by the state for "good governance" are often counterproductive to the establishment of workable forms of Indigenous governance'.[62] In addition, it has recently been observed that government efforts to engage with Indigenous communities often involve significant, unpaid 'governance workloads' for Indigenous people.[63]

Finally, there is the argument that 'the state needs to take more responsibility for working cross-culturally'.[64] This argument recognises that Indigenous Australians have historically borne the burden of bridging the cultural and institutional differences between their communities and mainstream organisations. Acknowledgement and respect for Indigenous institutions begins to put partnerships on a more even footing.

Inside and outside of partnerships, however, a wide gap still remains between the on-the-ground concerns of Indigenous Australian communities and the ways of working of mainstream Australian institutions. Yet mainstream institutions continue to play very important and powerful roles in local communities.[65] Encouragingly, there are examples of Indigenous organisations in Australia that have managed to successfully navigate the gap between local and central ways of working. Yet even successful organisations are vulnerable to sudden government policy shifts that can strip their legitimacy and resourcing.[66] In the end, it is Indigenous organisations that still bear the bulk of responsibility for mediating the gap between local concerns and central institutions.

2. Refugee and migrant communities

> A simple equation is sometimes presented, that regional areas need population and workers and that refugees need jobs and therefore the refugees should go to regional areas.[67]

Like Indigenous communities, migrant communities are culturally distinctive. They have their own community-based organisations, which may be centred on country of origin, ethnicity, or other commonalities, with their own ways of working.[68] Moreover, migrants and refugees, having come to Australia by choice or necessity, often work hard to integrate into mainstream Australian society and make significant economic and social contributions.[69] Yet the experiences of refugee and migrant communities in regional Australia reveal a number of persisting gaps between local-level issues and powerful central institutions.

Contextually, Australia is a nation of migrants; about a third of Australians aged 15 and over were born overseas.[70] Most permanent migrants who enter Australia come as skilled migrants or to join family members who are already in Australia.[71] Humanitarian entrants or refugees are a smaller stream of migrants, who may enter Australia either as temporary or permanent residents.[72] Refugees accepted under permanent humanitarian visas in Australia in recent years come from a number of countries, primarily in Africa and the Middle East as well as Myanmar (Burma).

Historically, many migrants to Australia, particularly those from non-English-speaking backgrounds, have settled in major capital cities with established ethnic communities. Nevertheless, there have been specific government policy initiatives in recent years designed to encourage or direct migrant settlement into regional Australia.[73] The aim has typically been to use migrants to meet particular workforce needs – both skilled and unskilled – in regional areas.[74] In addition, there is also growing evidence of secondary migration to regional Australia; that is, refugees or other migrants who originally settled in the capital cities are independently choosing to move to regional areas, particularly those with established migrant communities and community organisations.[75]

Australian regional towns with significant refugee and migrant communities include the northern Victorian towns of Shepparton, Swan Hill, and Mildura; the Goldfields towns of Bendigo, Ballarat, and Castlemaine; the Western District towns of Warrnambool and Colac; as well as the Gippsland region and the

Latrobe Valley. These regions have attracted concentrations of Iraqi, Sudanese, Burmese, and other migrant groups.[76] In South Australia, the Limestone Coast region, including the major regional town of Mount Gambier, and the smaller towns of Bordertown, Naracoorte, and Murray Bridge all have migrant communities including Burmese, Congolese, Afghan, and Sri Lankan communities.[77] In New South Wales, Coffs Harbour, Wollongong, and Wagga Wagga are among the towns that have been intentionally targeted as regional resettlement areas for refugees; Griffith and Young also have a significant Middle Eastern migrant population, as does Katanning in Western Australia.[78]

For many immigrants, a key attraction of these regional towns has been the accessibility of employment opportunities in regional industries – often industries such as orchards and meatworks that do not require strong English language skills.[79] Migrants who relocate to regional areas can meet important workforce needs, as well as bringing sought after skills. Skilled migrant programmes, for instance, have brought migrants such as doctors into regional areas where their skills are in short supply.[80] Studies of migrant and refugee experiences in regional Australia emphasise the importance of employment – alongside other considerations such as housing, education, and transport – in ensuring successful resettlement in the regions.[81] These studies also highlight that, despite the fact that migrants in some regional areas are more highly educated than the population as a whole, they can face disadvantages in their access to employment.[82]

Migrants, particularly those who arrive as refugees without strong English skills, can find it difficult in regional areas to find employment beyond casual and seasonal manual work.[83] Their qualifications are not necessarily recognised in Australia, so it is not uncommon to find migrants working in jobs well below their actual skills level.[84] Furthermore, migrants who take low skilled casual and/ or seasonal work often find it difficult to transition into more permanent and stable forms of employment.[85] Government funded job-service providers exist, but migrants often assess them as unhelpful.[86] The situation is further complicated for humanitarian migrants on temporary visas that limit the types of employment these migrants can accept. Thus, while migrants and refugees are expected to help build the skills base of regional areas, it can be difficult for regions to take full advantage of their skills.

In regional areas, migrants do join local organisations such as churches and sporting clubs, generally feel welcomed, and may receive support and assistance from members of local communities in regional towns.[87] Nevertheless, they tend to rely heavily on their own community organisations.[88] Migrant community organisations play an important role in helping migrants to regional areas adjust to new contexts, often in a new language. In regional areas where the numbers from any particular country or language group are small, the absence of such organisations is keenly felt.[89] It is thus unsurprising that migrants are more likely to settle in regional areas where community organisations from their country of origin already exist.[90]

Migrant community organisations play an important role in mediating interactions between migrant communities and mainstream Australian institutions such as service providers. Migrants' own community organisations provide social, emotional, and cultural support.[91] These organisations are important, but they tend to be small and work from the margins. It is not always easy for them to access resources for their communities through mainstream institutions: such as venues for community events, accessible educational opportunities, or even permission to operate their community enterprises.[92] As small organisations, they do not usually have the numbers to gain the ear of politicians in order to influence decision-making.[93] Furthermore, they can easily find themselves in dependent relationships with large NGOs. Large, formal NGOs are in a better position to access government settlement resources than small migrant community organisations.[94] Once again, communities can find external organisations capturing resources on their behalf.

Overall, many Australian regions have welcomed migrant communities, and migrant communities have brought considerable benefits to these regions. Yet in many ways, regions are unable to fully benefit from migrants' skills. Ultimately, the main policy decisions affecting migrants are made centrally, by the federal government.[95] These policies affect – often very negatively – migrant communities' access to work opportunities, housing and settlement services.[96] Migrant community organisations have an in-depth understanding of what such policy changes mean on the ground, but they are seldom consulted.[97] In the end, community organisations at the local level have on-the-ground knowledge, but limited ability to drive change.

3. Other groups on the margins

This is the way it is and is gonna be.[98]

Indigenous and migrant community organisations understand the lived experiences of their local communities, but they struggle to communicate what they know into the centres of decision-making. Meanwhile, central institutions – from governments to NGOs – strongly influence what these organisations can accomplish at the local level. This pattern is repeated, if more subtly, with other groups in regional Australia that are socially distant from the mainstream. The young, the old, the unemployed, and otherwise socially disadvantaged are often the objects of policy, but seldom have a voice in it. The social distance between their circumstances and those who make the decisions is often vast.

Groups whose social positioning is labelled 'marginal' or 'vulnerable' have a further disadvantage; in most cases they do not have organisations to speak for their interests. These are thus 'communities' only in name, in the sense of sharing some common experience – and a common label. Often, labels are imposed by others and assume a homogeneity that does not really exist. The framing of policy problems often contains an unspoken assumption that all 'youth', 'unemployed' people, or 'single mothers' have the same experiences and need the same things. This further complicates engagement with policy makers, as at best they seek to speak with 'community representatives' from communities that do not, in fact, exist.

'Marginalised communities' such as unemployed young people and socially isolated old people are a recurring policy topic in regional Australia. Yet the reality is that these are not communities at all, but individuals and families who are not in a position to benefit from mainstream institutions. For them, education is distant and exclusive; jobs are poor-quality or elusive; social networks and access to information are thin on the ground. Being young, old, cash-poor, jobless, in poor health, or outside of familiar social networks can place many resources out of reach. For instance, welfare-dependent families who move to regional Australia in search of affordable housing are often actively marginalised, labelled as 'itinerants', 'transients', or 'blow ins' and excluded from social and economic networks.[99]

When studies are conducted with marginalised groups in regional Australia they typically find the lived experience of these individuals and families to be quite revealing. On-the-ground gaps and needs – in basic areas like accessible transport, fresh food, or simply information about what is available – quickly become visible.[100] The conclusions also remind policy makers that these individuals and families are not all the same. Their situations are different, and they often want different things.[101] One-size-fits-all policy initiatives rarely work in practice.

Most policy makers have little or no understanding of the issues facing people on the margins. And it is hard in turn for people to communicate what they know. Engaging with mainstream organisations to influence decision-making or access resources means entering socially foreign institutional turf. It requires learning the ways of being and speaking that are needed to deal with educational institutions or service providers – and having the required resources, such as money and time, to do so.[102] It means learning the protocols involved in participating in consultations, working groups, committees, government submissions, and the other institutional apparatus of decision-making. Succeeding in these socially foreign institutional spaces requires confidence, persistence, skills, and resources that many people simply lack. Often, they conclude that it is not possible for them to do anything about their situation.

In regional Australia, social distance compounds geographic and cultural marginalisation. Even educated and wealthy local elites generally struggle to have much of a say in the decisions that affect them. Each step further away from the mainstream makes it commensurately harder to be a part of the conversation. For people who are less educated, more remotely located, and who have fewer resources in time, money, energy, and transport, influence upon decision-making becomes progressively less feasible – and the imposition of external decisions into the centre of their lives, more likely. It is unsurprising that young people in a geographically remote Tasmanian town assessed that 'the way it is' was unlikely to change.

Regional communities: peripheral but grounded

> Sustainable regional development is not just an economic or social process, but a political and institutional one.[103]

Regional development theory posits that place-based communities and their own endogenous institutions can driving change from within. On the international stage, successful regions are not necessarily large and metropolitan. They include regions of different sizes that have developed the institutional conditions for success.[104] Yet these institutions are not mere technical arrangements, but social and cultural ways of working, set in political contexts. They must be understood up close.

This chapter has taken an up-close look at communities and institutions in regional Australia. It has revealed a wide 'institutional gap' between local and central institutions, and a clear absence of strong regional institutions. Most decisions come from central institutions based in capital cities, which necessarily have limited knowledge of local contexts. Most on-the-ground action is local in focus, with grounded knowledge, networks, and local legitimacy – but very little room to manoeuvre. Communities and their organisations remain on the periphery of significant decision-making.

This pattern is even more marked with culturally distinctive communities and socially marginalised groups. These communities and groups confront a wide gap between their ways of working and those of the institutions that propose to help them. Not only must these communities deal with the tendency for central institutions to standardise and control from afar, but dialogue with decision makers becomes doubly difficult owing to cultural difference and social distance. To work with mainstream institutions, these communities must learn a foreign language and a foreign way of working. Yet decisions and resources still cluster elsewhere.

This 'institutional gap' is clearly illustrated in the plight of regional development organisations. Strong regional institutions are elusive in Australia despite the large number of organisations that have been established to act at regional scale. The gap between grounded local organisations and powerful central organisations is visible in a wide range of other settings too, from branch offices, to community consultation efforts, to volunteers grappling with compliance requirements. This institutional gap persists as one of the key features of being regional in Australia. It serves to actively fragment and disarticulate the knowledges and networks that are needed for successful regional development.

Contemporary regional development theory proposes that place-based economic actors can leverage their multiple knowledges and networks to create innovative solutions: constructing new sources of competitive advantage from the ground up.[105] In Australia, however, being regional means being grounded but simultaneously peripheral; capable of driving change, yet structurally disarticulated from resources and decision-making centres.

Local communities in Australia have strong, grounded knowledge of local attributes and networks. Yet even when they are able to overcome their local differences and work together across cultural and social divides, it is not enough to spark real change. Communities and their organisations are always positioned on the periphery of significant decision-making. They have little voice, and limited room to manoeuvre. Decisions are still imposed from capital cities far away.

Meanwhile, regional organisations are weak, and regional institutions have failed to emerge. In theory, regional organisations could provide a stronger policy voice and a more diverse set of resources to construct regional-scale advantage. Yet in practice, these organisations are caught in the institutional gap, disarticulated from local institutions on the ground, yet unable to influence the central institutions that set the agenda and control the resources. As Andrew Beer and Alaric Maude observed a decade ago: 'More robust, powerful and coordinated agencies are needed if Australia's regions are to achieve their potential.'[106] Yet so long as the institutional environment in regional Australia remains polarised between local and central institutions, regional organisations will not have the institutional basis they need to drive change.

The current institutional environment in Australia does not, in short, allow regional development to happen. Decision-making continues to be dominated by standardised knowledge and central institutions. Even with the best of intentions, top-down knowledge and policy are incapable of driving endogenous development. By definition it must come from within. For true endogenous development to occur, resources and decision-making power need to be decentralised to the scale of real places: metropolitan and non-metropolitan alike.

Communities in regional Australia need to connect up their local organisations to create locally grounded regional institutions. Rather than weak, fragmented, elitist bodies designed to deliver resources and policies from the metropolitan centres, these new ways of working need to be inclusive, grounded in the social and cultural diversity of each region, and possess real decision-making power. By bringing their diverse knowledge-sets together across cultures and social divides, regional communities will be well placed to spark innovation.[107]

Notes

1 L&SR 2006.
2 The concept of development actors' 'room to manoeuvre' is borrowed from the anthropology of development (Olivier de Sardan 2005, p. 53).
3 Some of these were documented in Eversole *et al.* 2005.
4 See Eversole 2003.
5 The initial review of the 2007 Northern Territory Emergency Response (NTER) found that 'the Intervention diminished its own effectiveness through its failure to engage constructively with the Aboriginal people it was intended to help' (Yu *et al.* 2008, p. 10, quoted in Hunt 2013, p. 16). This was perhaps an extreme case of poor engagement but, as the review found, 'the single most valuable resource that the NTER has lacked from its inception is the positive, willing participation of the people it was intended to help' (ibid.). For recent media coverage of the threatened closure of remote Aboriginal communities, see for instance: https://www.youtube.com/watch?v=vsYSqcRjGUA (viewed 1 June 2015).
6 Eversole and Martin 2005, pp. 293–294.
7 Some were documented in Eversole 2011.
8 Gross 2015, p. 299.
9 Following North 1990. This definition includes organisations – the formal manifestations of how things are done – as well as the informal 'rules of the game' defining how things are done.

10 For a discussion of the centralisation of public services in Australia, see Gerritsen 2000.
11 Experiments with regional-scale governance arrangements in some form date back to the mid-nineteenth century; see Brown 2005.
12 Brown 2005, p. 28.
13 Some large Indigenous Land Councils, which administer Native Title claims and settlements, also operate at regional scale, such as the Central Land Council in the Northern Territory and the Cape York Land Council in Queensland.
14 Brown 2005, p. 19. Collits 2015, p. 29 has observed that: 'It is important to note that regional development interventions in Australia have been the province of all three levels of government, and the subject of ongoing political dispute and debate ... Interventions have been uneven in intensity and varying in purpose, with wild swings between periods of heightened policy interest and periods of negligible interest in regional matters.'
15 'There are numerous agencies and multiple programs operating unevenly across the nation ... a history of program initiatives and withdrawals has left a complex network of regional development programs and organisations.' (Beer 1999, pp. 187–188).
16 Beer 1999, p. 190 notes that most 'are engaged in a plethora of programs and projects, ranging from small business development, to lobbying governments or even managing projects aimed at improving urban aesthetics'. Beer *et al.* 2005, p. 55 observe that they have limited power to intervene in the economy, and unlike in the USA and the UK, are not involved in employment services, labour market training or property development.
17 Beer 1999, pp. 188–190.
18 Local and regional development organisations, compared with the formal apparatus of the state, 'are often relatively powerless bodies, with limited funding and few or no regulatory powers' (Beer and Maude 2005, p. 61). Brown 2005, p. 18 notes that 'while state and federal regional programs abound, the total resources allocated to them remain relatively small'. See also Beer 1999, 2000; Brown 2005, pp. 28–30; and Garlick 1999, p. 181.
19 See Gooding 2012. That report notes that 'The Australian Local Government Association defines ROCs as "partnerships" between groups of local government entities that agree to collaborate on matters of common interest'; it identifies 60 ROCs across Australia, the majority in New South Wales and Western Australia (p. 3).
20 By state governments via local government amalgamation; for ROCs, originally as a result of federal government policy in the 1970s; see Gooding 2012, p. 10.
21 See e.g. Gooding 2012.
22 A map is available at: http://nrmregionsaustralia.com.au/ (viewed 1 June 2015).
23 Head 2005 for instance, observed that these regional NRM bodies lack democratic legitimacy in the eyes of local stakeholders, while Moore 2005 makes the point that regional NRM groups do not meet the criteria for being democratic.
24 See e.g. Head 2005, p. 149: 'there is a risk that the pressures for vertical accountability to the federal government could undermine the participatory and horizontal dimension of regional decision-making.'
25 See Chapter 1.
26 A.J. Brown cites the 2003 Regional Business Development Analysis (RBDA) report findings which called for 'rationalisation of the current plethora of local and regional development bodies into a stronger, nationally coherent framework, with just one common agency for each "self-identified" region' (Brown 2005, p. 29). Beer *et al.* 2005, pp. 55–56 documented the 'lack of coordination and cooperation among regional development actors at the local level' and Eversole and McCall 2014, p. 259 observed 'limited communication or co-ordination of action' among organisations in a Tasmanian region. Recently, 'The need for a coordinated approach to policy, planning and investment across all levels of government' was the most common

governance issue identified by Regional Development Australia committees in 2013 (Faulkner *et al.* 2013, p. 21). This is further complicated by the fact that RDAs, as yet another example of quasi-governmental regional development agencies, often have responsibilities that parallel many of those of the formal tiers of government, but are not themselves a formal tier of government (see Beer 2015).

27 Scott 1995, pp. 22, 76.
28 Eversole and Scholfield 2006. See also Eversole *et al.* 2014 and Barraket *et al.* in press on the emergence of social enterprises and how they mobilise a range of resource types to meet needs at the local level.
29 Documented by Eversole 2005 for rural Victoria. Similar observations have been made in the Tasmanian context; one former student liked to observe that he could get more done with a slab of beer on the Coast than he could with money anywhere else.
30 Quote from Scott 1995, p. 309. Scott presents his critique of administrative forms of knowledge in the classic text *Seeing like a State.*
31 Brown 2005, p. 26 referring to top-down regional development programmes.
32 Tomaney 2014, p. 138.
33 Brown 2005, pp. 18, 27–30 refers to the issues facing regional organisations as simultaneously a lack of 'legitimacy' at the local level, and a lack of 'capacity' to deliver real policy change.
34 For example, Hogan *et al.* 2012, p. 14 note that: 'Within the current Australian model, the government promotes the ideals of localism but in practice it maintains close control over the budget and the investment program.'
35 See e.g. Head 2005 and Moore 2005 on democratic legitimacy in NRM bodies, and Beer and Maude 2005, p.62 on regional development agencies; they note that 'the practice of regional development is construed to be a concern of public and private sector "leaders" rather than elected representatives'. Grant and Rainnie 2005 also discuss elitism in regional development agencies with a focus on gender exclusion.
36 Beer *et al.* 2005, p. 55, writing on a survey of Australian regional development agencies. Susan Moore has observed for NRM groups in Australia, that: 'State government agencies are not only members of most regional groups, they have provided most of the data and technical expertise needed to prepare the regional plans' (Moore 2005, p. 131).
37 See Collits and Rowe 2015, p. 79 on 'regions seeking largesse from central governments'. Garlick 1999, p. 181 notes that: 'Most governments … over the years have seen regional development in "top down" structurist terms.'
38 Regional Business Development Analysis (RBDA) 2003, cited in Brown 2005, p. 29.
39 Grant and Rainnie 2005, p. 212.
40 Observed by Gaynor MacDonald 2008 in her work with the Wiradjuri people of New South Wales, cited in Hunt 2013, p. 8. Hunt notes that MacDonald's research 'showed that these Indigenous people want to engage with governments as Wiradjuri people, and have their cultural difference recognised'.
41 ABS 2012b. 'Indigenous Australian' comprises Aboriginal Australians and Torres Strait Islanders. Indigenous Australians live in both capital cities and regional Australia, and comprise about half of the population in very remote areas of Australia. Baxter *et al.* 2011 p. 2 note that: 'Although 2.4% of Australia's population are Indigenous, their geographic distribution across Australia is quite different. Indigenous people comprise 1% of the population in major cities, 3% in inner regional areas, 6% in outer regional areas, 15% in remote areas and 49% in very remote areas.'
42 See Hunt 2015, p. 115. Hunt 2013, p. 9 observes: 'Communities of people referring to themselves as "Bininj", "Noongar", "Yolngu" or "Yuin" have their own cultural boundaries, which generally bear no relationship to government administrative or jurisdictional boundaries.' A map of Indigenous Australian cultural groups has been developed by the Australian Institute of Aboriginal and Torres Strait Islander Studies

(AIATSIS) and is available at: http://aiatsis.gov.au/explore/culture/topic/language-map (viewed 1 June 2015).
43 Bauman *et al.* 2015 estimate there are around 8,000–9,000 Indigenous organisations in Australia. They note that these organisations 'have been progressively established since the 1970s partly in response to government requirements for Indigenous groups to incorporate in order to receive funding, services and infrastructure and to hold forms of land title. Another equally important driver of incorporation can be as a mechanism for the affirmation of the collective identities of Indigenous people' (Bauman *et al.* 2015, p. 3).
44 The concept of *terra nullius*, which was used to justify the colonisation or, as some Indigenous communities prefer to put it, the invasion of Australian lands. Hunt 2015, p. 118 observes that it remained the accepted wisdom in Australia until 1992, when the high court's Mabo decision formally 'overturned this legal fiction'.
45 Hunt 2013, p. 12; she refers to such organisations as 'intercultural'. Equally Altman 2008, p. 188 observes in his case study of Bawinanga Aboriginal Corporation (BAC) in Arnhem Land, Northern Territory, that: 'BAC is a distinctive form of organisation that is intercultural: its organisational governance has to accommodate both western legal requirements and Indigenous social norms and external and internal accountability.' The recent AIATSIS report on indigenous governance observes that the intercultural nature of indigenous governance can make people feel as though they are 'walking in two worlds' (Bauman *et al* 2015, p. 12).
46 A number of Indigenous Australian writers have written on the continued dominance of western or European institutions in Australia and the consequent marginalisation of Indigenous Australians; see e.g. Fredericks 2013, 2014; Lee in press; Moreton-Robinson 2005.
47 See e.g. Fredericks, 2013; on p. 2 she notes that: 'There seems to be a widespread myth that, when Aboriginal people and Torres Strait Islander people enter cities or regional centres, we somehow become less Indigenous.'
48 NE/ALGA 2014, p. 155 summarises: 'The 2011 Australian census shows that, at 55.8 per cent, the employment participation rate of Australia's Indigenous peoples (Aboriginal and Torres Strait islander) was 20.5 percentage points lower than that for Australia's non-Indigenous population. The Indigenous unemployment rate at the time was more than three times higher than for the non-Indigenous population. Indigenous people comprise around 1.5 per cent of the total working population.' Further, Hunt 2015, p. 116 notes that: 'Aboriginal people are more likely than other Australians living in regional areas to be unemployed or not in the labour force, to be on low incomes, and to have low levels of education. Their health is also likely to be considerably poorer.' A recent report by Amnesty International has documented that Indigenous young people are 26 times more likely to be detained or incarcerated than non-Indigenous young people (Amnesty International 2015).
49 In regional areas as elsewhere, Indigenous people are 'frequently problematized as the population most needing strengthening in order to address persistent disadvantage' (Saggers 2005, p. 196). The Council of Australian Governments (COAG, 2008) has set a number of targets to 'close the gap' in Indigenous disadvantage.
50 Hunt 2015 describes how protectionist-era policies encouraged the concentration of Aboriginal people onto missions and their training for casual and manual labour in domestic service and pastoral industries. Later, growing mechanisation and demands for equal wages in the 1960s led to many Indigenous people subsequently losing these positions and entering the ranks of the unemployed.
51 The Stolen Generation was the result of removing Indigenous children from their families and sending them to missions or into foster care with non-Indigenous families. See e.g. Commonwealth of Australia 1997 report on the Stolen Generation.
52 See e.g. FaHCSIA 2011, p. 9, quoted in Hunt 2013, p. 14: 'Engagement with Indigenous communities is essential to achieve measurable improvements in

economic, health and social indicators'. Also, Bauman *et al.* 2015, p. 118 observed that: 'Effective Indigenous governance requires cooperation and collaboration within and between Indigenous communities and organisations and their members, as well as governments and other stakeholders.'

53 See e.g. Hunt 2015. Pritchard 2000, p. 11 observes that: 'The emergence of Indigenous people as important stakeholders in many regional economies has encouraged consideration of the development of formal land and resource use agreements. These agreements would use the legal recognition of native title as a basis for broad regional strategies covering issues such as land access, employment, environmental management and the structures for public service provision.' He gives the example of the 1995 Economic Development Strategy for the Arnhem Region, Northern Territory, which 'looks to the construction of innovative joint ventures between Indigenous and non-Indigenous communities' (Pritchard 2000, p. 11).

54 Work by Bagshaw 1977 cited in Altman 2008, p. 197 observed 'cross-cultural incongruity' between 'European economic-based and Aboriginal kin-oriented governance' and that 'European political forms and objectives were imposed on Aboriginal social life and that this took away any discretionary power from Aboriginal councillors'.

55 Quote from Hunt 2015, p. 126.

56 Saggers concludes that 'the importance of such personal relationships to the formation of new governance structures deserves greater attention' (Saggers 2005, p. 206); she observes that the growth of local, personal relationships between Indigenous and non-Indigenous individuals over significant periods of time created the trust that ultimately enabled partnerships to succeed (Saggers 2005, p. 207).

57 Eversole *et al.* 2005.

58 Hunt 2013, p. 20.

59 Bauman *et al.* 2015, p. 11.

60 Moran 2004, p. 341 quotes research on participatory planning which 'raised questions of whether Aboriginal understandings of country and of management can be adequately conveyed through non-Aboriginal texts such as planning reports'. Smith 2003 has raised similar concerns about how Aboriginal land claims in Australia require Aboriginal knowledge about land and culture to be presented in certain formats which are 'detached' from contemporary Aboriginal practice. Lee (in press) has observed how the language of 'natural' and 'cultural' values in protected areas imposes a western binary which does not reflect Indigenous understandings of the connections between land and people.

61 Hunt 2013, p. 9 makes this observation: 'Concepts and terms that government staff use in everyday communications may be quite foreign to the Indigenous community. In all locations, translating "government speak" to enable community members to fully understand its meaning and implications is important to avoid confusion and misunderstanding and to ensure that communication is effective.'

62 Smith and Hunt 2008, p. 12.

63 Bauman *et al.* 2015, p. 2 cite research carried out by the Central Land Council (Chapman 2014) which found: 'Over a single year, this community (of only 240 adults) recorded 282 visits from public- and private-sector agencies, with the total number of official "visitor days" for the year (days stayed in the community) being 1959.'

64 Marika *et al.* 2009 cited in Hunt 2013, p. 8, based on work with the Yolngu of Arnhem Land, Northern Territory.

65 Smith and Hunt 2008, p. 11 observe that: '[T]he increased involvement of the private and voluntary sectors, and unilateral intervention by the public sector into Indigenous organisations and community life, highlights the potentially greater role of all these external players in either facilitating or undermining local governance arrangements.'

66 Altman 2008, p. 196 documents how the Bawinanga Aboriginal Corporation (BAC) as a 'significant regional development agency' was jeopardised by a series of government

policy decisions related to the Northern Territory Intervention and the abolition of the Community Development Employment Program (CDEP) scheme. Morphy 2008, similarly, documents challenges to survival faced by Laynhapuy Homelands Association Incorporated, in light of state policies, and highlights the significant differences between Indigenous and state understandings of good governance. The national Aboriginal and Torres Strait Islander Commission (ATSIC) was disbanded in 2005; Sanders 2004, p. 2 observes that ATSIC also faced tensions with mediating the gap between local communities and central institutions; noting that it had to distance itself from its government roots to gain legitimacy with Indigenous communities.

67 Taylor and Stanovic 2005, p. v.
68 See e.g. Hiruy 2014.
69 Refugees and other migrants tend to be highly engaged with social and economic life in Australia (see e.g. Commonwealth of Australia 2010, pp. 7–10; McDonald-Wilmsen *et al.* 2009, p. 102). McDonald-Wilmsen *et al.* further observe that: 'A range of rural and regional communities and economies have benefited from the employment of refugees' though 'the outcomes for refugees appear to be more mixed' (p. 102).
70 ABS 2014h.
71 Permanent migrants typically enter Australia under one of three visa types – family, skill, or humanitarian. Skilled and family migration are by far the largest categories of permanent migrants.
72 The humanitarian (refugee) stream provides a number of places – about 20,000 in 2012/13 up from around 14,000 in previous years (http://www.border.gov.au/about/corporate/information/fact-sheets/60refugee [viewed 27 August 2015]). Correa-Velez and Onsando 2013, p. 129 note that since 2000, about 160,000 people have entered Australia under the refugee and humanitarian resettlement programme. In 2007–08 the humanitarian programme represented about 6 per cent of total permanent migration to Australia (ABS 2009b).
73 Since the 1990s the Australian government has introduced a number of schemes – such as State Specific and Regional Migration (SSRM) visa categories and settlement of humanitarian visa-holders in regional areas – to encourage migrants to resettle in regional Australia. See e.g. Feist *et al.* 2014, p. 8; Hugo 2008; Taylor *et al.* 2014. Earlier examples of regional migration policy in Australia are documented in Townsend *et al.* 2014, p. 602 – for instance, European migrants were directed toward regional Victoria to work on major infrastructure projects such as the Snowy River hydroelectric scheme.
74 DIMIA's 2003 *Report of the Review of Settlement Services for Migrants and Humanitarian Entrants* (cited in McDonald-Wilmsen *et al.* 2009, p. 99) recommended that, 'where appropriate, unlinked refugees arriving in Australia be directed to parts of regional Australia in order to address the demand for less skilled labour in regional economies and to assist humanitarian entrants to achieve early employment'.
75 McDonald-Wilmsen *et al.* 2009, p. 103 note 'an increasing trend towards secondary migration of refugees from metropolitan to regional and rural areas'. For example, Feist *et al.* 2014, found that for both refugee-humanitarian and skilled migrants on the Limestone Coast of SA, just over half (n=28) of all migrants interviewed had family or friends already living in the town before moving there. Feist *et al.* 2014 also cite work by McDonald *et al.* 2008 and Boese 2013 who documented a similar pattern with migrants moving from Melbourne to regional Victoria.
76 AMES 2011 notes that Ballarat has a Togolese and Sudanese community, Bendigo has a Karen community from Burma/Myanmar, and Mildura and Swan Hill have Iraqi and Afghan communities. McDonald-Wilmsen *et al.* 2009, p. 100 observe that there are small but significant settlements of people from refugee backgrounds in Wonthaggi, Swan Hill, Shepparton, Mildura, the Latrobe Valley, Castlemaine, Colac, Ballarat, and Warrnambool. Taylor and Stanovic 2005, p. v give some background:

Iraqi settlement in the Shepparton area 'commenced in the 1990s and by 2004 the Iraqi community was estimated at 3000 people, including some on Temporary Protection Visas. Sudanese settlement commenced in Colac in 2002 and in Warrnambool in 2003, and by mid 2004 there were some 60 to 70 Sudanese refugees in each town, with the local meatworks their major employers.'

77 Feist *et al.* 2014, p. 15 note the presence of 'humanitarian migrants including people of Congolese and Burmese backgrounds in Mount Gambier, people of Afghan background in Naracoorte and people of Afghan, Sri Lankan and African backgrounds in Bordertown; and skilled migrants from a wide variety of backgrounds, including less developed countries such as the Philippines, Thailand and Vietnam but also people from developed countries such as South Africa, the UK, Argentina and the Netherlands'.

78 See e.g. McDonald-Wilmsen *et al.* 2009, p. 99 for a list of areas targeted for regional resettlement. Shepley's 2007 study of regional settlement of humanitarian entrants looked at Launceston, Tasmania; Toowoomba, Queensland; Wagga Wagga, New South Wales; and Warrnambool and Shepparton, Victoria – most of these migrants were from Sudan and other African countries. For a discussion of immigration experiences in Griffith, New South Wales and in Katanning, Western Australia see Jordan *et al.* 2010; for Afghan refugees in Young, New South Wales see Stilwell 2003.

79 Taylor and Stanovic 2005, p. 13 observe that: 'The first few Iraqis apparently came to the fruit and vegetable-producing Goulburn Valley in the early 1990s seeking employment. Larger numbers of Iraqi refugees arrived from 1997, having come from camps in Saudi Arabia and gone first to Sydney and Melbourne, then on to Kyabram, Cobram and Shepparton.' They also observe that in Colac in Victoria, Sudanese workers were recruited by an employment agency to work at the local meatworks (p. 43).

80 See e.g. Taylor *et al.* 2014 on skilled migrants in the Northern Territory.

81 A study by AMES 2011, p. 5 of new settlers in Ballarat, Bendigo, Mildura, and Swan Hill found that: 'The greatest challenge expressed by settlers in each location was access to secure employment. All settlers expressed a strong desire to have any job.' Shepley 2007, p. 58 identified the key elements for successful settlement as 'English language, employment, housing, education and health'. Taylor and Stanovic 2005, p. 3 note that: 'Key resources for refugees include employment, income, housing, education, and language.'

82 Townsend *et al.* 2014, p.604 observe that: 'CALD groups who enter Australia as skilled migrants have, on average, higher qualifications and are better educated than the native born population, yet continue to be over-represented in elementary services (retail, hospitality) and labouring work'. Correa-Velez and Onsando's 2013 study of South Sudanese men from refugee backgrounds in Queensland observed that the men living in regional areas were more likely that those in urban areas to be unemployed or to be working at a level below that of their qualification, and that few of the migrants had successfully received recognition of their existing qualifications and skills.

83 Shepley's 2007 study of regional settlement of humanitarian entrants found that: 'The majority of entrants felt it was "very difficult" to obtain employment' (p. 11). Taylor and Stanovic 2005 found that in Shepparton, lack of employment opportunities was a significant issue – as well as discrimination, and highly qualified people were unable to find work (see pp. 15–19). See also Feist *et al.* 2014, pp. 43–49; McDonald-Wilmsen *et al.* 2009, pp. 100–101; and Townsend *et al.* 2014, p. 604.

84 It has been observed that there is no agency charged with facilitating the recognition of overseas qualifications in Australia; see McDonald-Wilmsen *et al.* 2009, p. 101. See also Commonwealth of Australia 2010, p. 31 on difficulties migrants encounter in the recognition of their prior qualifications.

85 Taylor and Stanovic 2005, p. 45 observed that for the migrant communities they studied in regional Victoria: 'The type of work available was limited. It was mainly low skilled, seasonal or casual. For example, fruit picking in the Shepparton area was

only available for a couple of months a year, the jobs in the meatworks in Colac and Warrnambool were typically casual and the work available fluctuated and was influenced by factors such as drought.' Boese's 2013 study on South Sudanese migrants in regional Australia similarly observes the tendency for migrants to take low-skilled employment such as in meat processing, and their experiences of 'poor employment quality and lack of opportunities for career development' as well as unemployment and underemployment (p. 150).

86 Shepley 2007, p. 11 found that over half of the migrants studied 'stated that Job Network services did not meet their needs'. McDonald-Wilmsen *et al.* 2009, p. 101 noted that for Iraqi refugees in Shepparton, 'job placement agencies were inexperienced in catering for their employment demands and integration between relocation policies, human services, education systems and social support was lacking'.

87 See e.g. Feist *et al.* 2014, p. 21. AMES 2011 found that for the Victorian regional cities of Ballarat, Bendigo, Mildura, and Swan Hill most humanitarian entrants found their new cities welcoming and safe. This report also observed that: 'Across the locations strong connections with the host community were few but there was supportive contact with volunteers, council officers, Australian friends, church services and sporting clubs for young people. In Swan Hill and Mildura people acknowledged the strong support of the local council officers and church congregations who assisted them in many matters' (p. 35).

88 Feist *et al.* 2014, pp. 26–29 note a tendency for migrants to relate most regularly to their own group – participation in community groups tends to be predominantly in migrant, country-of-origin, church and sport groups (p. 29).

89 'English is a particular priority for entrants in regional centres as the often small numbers represented by each language group means there is a very limited network of people from their linguistic background to assist in communicating with service providers and the broader community' (Shepley 2007, p. 12). See also McDonald-Wilmsen *et al.* 2009, p. 101.

90 Jordan, *et al.* 2010, p. 261.

91 AMES 2011, p. 32 observed that: 'The majority of settlers considered that it was important to strengthen their ethnic communities and associations. These groups were important for providing social and emotional support for individuals and families, and also for maintaining aspects of culture and identity. Most of the communities had established community associations, although some with smaller numbers had not yet formed associations.' Migrant community organisations take a range of forms; with reference to African community organisations in Australia, Kiros Hiruy has suggested a typology of different kinds of migrant community organisations, and notes their roles include cultural support and service provision (Hiruy 2014).

92 See e.g. AMES 2011, p. 32, which documented 'the cost of venues for meeting and holding community events and festivals', and Taylor and Stanovic 2005, p. 24, who document 'an unsuccessful attempt to establish family day care in the Iraqi community. Council restrictions were seen as too difficult because of the level of the women's English required and the cost of fencing.' Similarly, breastfeeding mothers were unable to attend English classes at the TAFE (Technical and Further Education) centre because the TAFE policy did not allow children; in this case there was a local workaround and English classes were held at a local sports centre instead (Taylor and Stanovic 2005, p. 38).

93 See Hiruy 2014.

94 See Hiruy and Eversole 2015.

95 Feist *et al.* 2014, p. 73 note that: 'Settlement policy is predominantly a top down approach, driven by the federal government. Local governments and community organisations are often neglected when it comes to these policies and are largely left to their own (limited) devices.' Taylor and Stanovic 2005, p. 3 observe that from the perspective of migrant communities, central policy comprises 'selective and deliberate

policies of social exclusion in terms of the lack of rights to federally funded settlement support, family reunion, and employment for some categories of refugees, in
particular those with Temporary Protection Visas'.

96 Migration policy in Australia – particularly with reference to refugees – is highly
politicised. The arrival of many asylum seekers without visas – often, via 'irregular'
channels such as by boat – has been a persistent public issue in Australia. One
example of a central policy decision with strong impact on the ground in regional
communities are 'Temporary protection visas' (TPVs). TPVs limit work, study, and
permanent residency opportunities for certain classes of humanitarian entrants. In
2014, a temporary protection visa for refugees was reinstated, after being discontin-
ued in 2008 (see http://www.border.gov.au/Trav/Refu/Illegal-maritime-arrivals/temp
orary-protection-visas [viewed 27 August 2015]). This visa is only valid for three
years, limits the migrant's access to services, denies family reunification and travel
rights, and effectively blocks many refugees from applying for permanent residency,
even when their claims for refugee status are assessed as valid (Refugee Council of
Australia, 2014). The older version of TPVs enabled refugees to go on to apply for
permanent residency. This is no longer an option.

97 The lack of local consultation on settlement policy has frequently been noted. See e.g.
McDonald-Wilmsen *et al.* 2009, pp. 104–106, who note that participants in a roundtable emphasised the importance of strategies 'being driven by rural and regional
communities themselves (rather than through a "top-down" approach)'; Shepley
2007, p. 63 similarly documented that, 'a request was made by the entrants that there
be greater consultation with them on issues that concern them'.

98 Rural young person from the West Coast of Tasmania quoted in the title of Hawkins,
2011.

99 This was observed for instance, in a study of small towns in Victoria (Eversole 2007,
p. 126; Martin 2007, p. 68). On the movement of welfare-dependent families to
regional Australia, this has been documented in Alston 2002, p. 11 and Budge *et al*
1992, among others. Forth and Howell 2002, p. 8 observe the 'movement of so-called
"ferals" or disadvantaged families into declining small towns'. It is notable how often
garbage strewn along a rural road is diagnosed as a sign of 'blow-ins' who have taken
advantage of low-cost housing further along the road.

100 Some recent examples include Lê *et al.* 2015 on food security; Eyles *et al.* 2014b on
employment and training on the West Coast of Tasmania, and Eyles *et al.* 2014a on
older people's housing needs in Tasmania.

101 For instance, Eyles *et al.* 2014a, p. 10 noted that 'older Australians want the same
choice and independence as every other Australian' and therefore: 'There is no one-
size-fits-all model for retirement living' (p. 57).

102 See e.g. Hawkins 2014 on the cultural capital required for rural girls to access education, and Eversole 2013, pp. 17–20 on obstacles to job readiness for disadvantaged
young people.

103 Brown 2005, p. 35.

104 See e.g. OECD 2012; Tomaney 2014.

105 Cooke 2007; European Commission 2006; OECD 2009, 2012.

106 Beer and Maude 2005, p. 75.

107 For a discussion of the role of multiple knowledges in local development and innovation,
see Eversole, 2015.

5   Conclusion
Being regional

Being regional in Australia

> Anthropological enquiry attempts to understand how problems appear when seen
> from the viewpoint of those involved.[1]

This book has presented an up-close view of regional development in the
Australian context. The stories in each chapter have explored what it means to be
regional, in a nation that is institutionally and culturally dominated by its capital
cities. In Australia, being regional means being non-metropolitan, and regional
development is the development of non-metropolitan places.

Australian regions and capital cities are separated by a deep conceptual divide.
This is in many ways an imaginary chasm, yet it is recreated day after day, in
region after region, as Australians address regional issues and pursue regional
development. Whether the context is towns or industries, organisations or communities, regional issues are framed and understood in certain ways. This in turn
influences how regional development is done.

On the surface, regional development policy and practice in Australia look
similar to their equivalents elsewhere. Australian policy makers have taken on
board a number of ideas from the international context: ideas about endogenous
development, regional-scale governance, and the role of universities in regions.
Nevertheless, these ideas manifest very differently in Australia.

The way Australians think about and 'do' regional development is influenced by a number of unspoken development logics, which have their roots in
Australia's particular history, geography, and culture. These development logics
are based in the divide between the nation's capital cities and elsewhere. They
influence Australian regional development policy, practice – and ultimately, what
people believe to be possible in the regions.

This final chapter will sum up some of the key characteristics of regional development in Australia. First, it will describe what it means to be 'regional' – the
features of shared identity across Australia's diverse regions. Then, it will explain
how these ideas manifest in Australian regional development policy and practice.
Finally, it will explore how policy makers can respond to unleash the untapped
opportunities for more effective development in Australia's regions.

Regional identity in Australia has two aspects: identification with a particular region, and a shared identity as *regional*. All of Australia's diverse non-metropolitan regions share a common identity as regional – as places outside the nation's capital cities. Australia's regions are peripheral places: not a hinterland so much as a separate land, Australia's 'other nation' that defines itself, and is defined by others, as distant and different from the nation's centres of power and influence.

Peripherality is a key aspect of regional identity. Australia's regions are not only geographically peripheral – located outside the concentrations of population and resources in the metropolitan centres – but they are socially and politically peripheral, disconnected from the nation's dominant institutions. Peripherality is manifested over and over across Australia's regions, as local communities and their organisations grapple with the implications of decisions made in places far away, and try to create their own solutions distant from resources and support. It is driven home when local voices and innovations are rendered invisible beneath a dominant narrative of regional inadequacy and decline. Peripherality is part of the day-to-day experience of being regional in Australia.

People who live in Australia's regions directly experience peripherality in their dealings with powerful organisations elsewhere. At the same time, they themselves continually recreate their own peripherality. As they declare their disadvantage in competition to attract resources from the nation's centres, they reaffirm their position in the periphery. As they view outsiders with distrust, anticipating what they will take away this time, they magnify the distance between their place and other places.

Peripheral identity is self-reinforcing, a key part of being regional. It has become part of how regional Australians see themselves, and how others see them. Yet being regional is not just about being peripheral. There is another aspect to regional identity. Being regional is also about being grounded in a particular region – regardless of which one. It is about being present on the ground and conscious of the on-the-ground conditions.

Groundedness is a deep, yet difficult to articulate, aspect of being regional. Terms like *place*, *community*, and *the local* start to approximate it. Over and over across regional Australia, people and organisations emphasise the attributes of their particular region. They draw attention to the knowledge, experiences, and networks that are present at the local level. And they emphasise the connections among social, economic, and environmental processes on the ground.

A number of different terms can express this sense of groundedness. People may describe their approach as being *place-based*, *locally focused*, or *regionally focused* – with little precision as to geographic scale. Sometimes they describe themselves as *community-focused*, or use words like *community*, *regional*, or *sustainable*, often interchangeably. All of these are attempts to articulate that conditions and connections on the ground are important and need to be understood.

Being regional means being grounded – with an on-the-ground understanding of issues. In regional Australia, this deep sense of groundedness is expressed over and over: in appeals to local knowledge, to lived experience, and to the need to understand the linkages among communities, industries, and environments.

These linkages are clearly visible on the ground in Australia's regions, where communities and industries are closely reliant on each other and on the natural environment. Being grounded is contrasted to high-level decisions made elsewhere, work done in silos, and failures to understand the connections between this and that.

Across Australia's regions, people and organisations are conscious of on-the-ground conditions and connections. Yet they are simultaneously peripheral to the nation's decision-making centres. These two characteristics of peripherality and groundedness operate in continual tension. Peripheral identity brings a sense of disadvantage and disregard vis-à-vis the capital cities – ultimately, a sense of dependence. Groundedness, by contrast, brings a confident understanding of local places – an empowered, knowledgeable independence. In the tension between peripherality and groundedness lie the challenges – and the untapped opportunities – for regional development in Australia.

Regional development: place and peripherality

> The idea of devolving real power from central governments to regions has not been tried in Australia.[2]

The stories in this book have explored some of the lived experiences of towns, industries, organisations, and communities in Australia's regions. These stories illustrate how people in regional Australia regularly grapple with the gap between what they know and do on the ground, and what others believe and decide about them from afar. Being regional in Australia means being simultaneously grounded in real places, with in-depth knowledge of these places, and being peripheral to the nation's centres of decision-making. Regional development policy and practice in Australia directly reflect these themes of peripherality and groundedness.

Australian regional development approaches claim to be grounded in the specific attributes and lived experiences of Australia's regions. They claim to focus on endogenous development – development from within – and to take a place-based, regional focus to governance. Regional governance approaches connect policy across silos to create more sustainable place-based solutions, recognising that that the economy, communities, and the environment are not separate things, but interrelated. Endogenous development approaches aim to build the knowledge capabilities of regions and equip them to mobilise their own distinctive attributes to spark innovation.

Regional development policy and practice in Australia have taken on board these ideas from the international context. But in Australia, endogenous development and regional governance polices have been implemented according to a particular set of development logics. These logics are based on the understanding that *regions* are, by definition, non-metropolitan, and thus peripheral. Regardless of whether the context is regional towns responding to change or regional universities equipping people for the knowledge economy, regional development in Australia is always positioned as a peripheral activity. This manifests in particular ways.

First, Australian regional development focuses on the nation's non-metropolitan regions, ignoring the interconnections between regions and cities. Then, within non-metropolitan regions, Australian regional development further focuses on that which is peripheral and disadvantaged. Chapter 1, for instance, illustrated how Australian endogenous regional development efforts in the 1990s and early 2000s did not focus on regions at all, but on peripheral, disadvantaged small towns and community groups within them. Regional development became the province of small, under-resourced community committees, who were left to act in isolation from one another and their larger contexts.

Next, Australian regional development approaches do not significantly devolve resources or influence to non-metropolitan regions. Rather, they retain these firmly in the capital cities. Thus, regional Australia's organisations, institutions, and governance mechanisms remain structurally on the periphery. Chapter 4 discussed why the many attempts to establish regional-scale development organisations in Australia have had limited impact. These efforts have typically been multiple, uncoordinated, and driven from outside of regions themselves. They have had limited resourcing or authority, as well as limited local buy-in. Ultimately, they have remained caught in the gap between local and central ways of working.

In the end, regional development policy and practice in Australia are characterised by a wide gap between the rhetoric of place-based development and the reality of central control. Decision-making power is sharply divorced from on-the-ground knowledge. Regional actors are charged with identifying and exploiting place-based opportunities, yet the overarching decisions that determine their room to manoeuvre are not, in fact, place-based. Meanwhile, policies emanating from the centres focus on disadvantage and decline in the periphery, while overlooking the on-the-ground dynamism and innovation in Australia's regions.

Far from centres of power, diverse communities in diverse regions grapple with issues and mobilise their resources, yet they are disconnected from the ingredients they need to drive real change. More commonly, their insights are ignored and their place-based innovations curtailed or disallowed by head offices and central institutions. Decisions continue to be made in policy silos, far away in capital cities. Being grounded in real, interconnected settings yet peripheral to powerful institutions creates a particular dynamic for regional development in Australia.

Relationships, knowledge, and networks

> The region is increasingly the level at which innovation is produced. … Both local and distant networks are often needed for successful cooperative innovation projects.[3]

In Australia, the logics underpinning regional development policy and practice reflect, and continually recreate, the divide between the capital cities and the regions. Rather than strengthening networks and opportunities for knowledge exchange – broadly recognised, even in Australia, as central to effective regional development – Australian regional development logics fragment these networks: actively disconnecting capital cities from regions, regions from localities, and localities from each other.

Conceptually, Australia's non-metropolitan regions are disconnected from the nation's metropolitan cores. Despite many real economic and social linkages between capital cities and regions, these linkages are downplayed or ignored when discussions turn to regional Australia. *Regional Australia* excludes capital cities – and capital cities are not regional. While there are clear historical reasons for this divide, it has spread deep roots into how Australians see the world.

In the regions there is a deep suspicion of all things metropolitan. This is paralleled in metropolitan areas by an almost unconscious dismissiveness toward all things regional. Regions and capital cities portray themselves as having essentially different concerns. The issues facing regions – service equity, demographic decline, industry transition – are often framed in direct opposition to the situations in Australia's capital cities. Often, regions are losing or lacking what cities have.

As an example, one common regional issue is the loss of young people who move away from regions to the capital cities. Contrast this common framing of the issue to a different conceptualisation that sees regions and cities as linked in patterns of life-cycle migration: where young people from a region spend a few years studying or working in the city and then return to the regions. This alternate framing reveals the linkages and synergies between regions and capital cities. But these linkages, and the opportunities they imply, are hard to see across the divide.

Not only are regions conceptually disconnected from the capital cities, they are further homogenised into an undifferentiated category of 'regional Australia'. This creates a tendency to overlook the attributes of particular regions. Chapter 2, for instance, highlighted how the dominant image of regional industries in decline masks the diverse faces of industries that can be observed on the ground in different regions. While many regional firms have considerable competitive potential, they often struggle to connect with the knowledge, networks, and other resources that they need to take their work to the next level. Many of these are located in the capital cities.

The divide between Australia's capital cities and its regions not only disconnects regional organisations and communities from the resources they need to succeed. It also isolates capital cities from the benefits they could gain from a closer relationship with the regions. Despite their reputation as economic engines, capital cities do not exist in a vacuum. On their own, they possess little that is globally distinctive. Australia's real competitive opportunities at global scale lie in the regions, where natural resources meet grounded knowledge and know-how. Yet leveraging these opportunities effectively on the global stage requires stronger linkages between capital cities and regions.

Too often, those who are located in capital cities fail to recognise what is present in the regions and what benefits could be gained from working together. The logic that regions are peripheral and disadvantaged renders these opportunities invisible. Chapter 3, for instance, discussed regional campuses in the context of an Australian university sector that is centred in the capital cities. Regional campuses are grappling with some of the most compelling challenges facing universities in the twenty-first century. Nevertheless, few in the capital cities see regional campuses as anything more than peripheral service-delivery mechanisms. The benefits that could be gained from working with regional campuses are missed.

The divide between capital cities and regions also damages the ability of localities to join forces at regional scale. Over the years, regional-scale organisations have been imposed on localities, while local services have been 'regionalised' from the top down. These repeated experiences of forced regionalisation, driven from the capital cities, have undermined trust and confidence among localities, reinforcing a strong localism. Significant collaboration at regional scale thus remains a challenge across most of Australia. Nor is there much incentive to work regionally: even when local organisations work together, they struggle to have any real voice in the decisions that affect their region. These decisions come from the capital cities.

Rather than strengthening mutually beneficial relationships and linkages between capital cities and regions, regional development in Australia continues to cast the regions as essentially separate from the nation's centres. Capital-city people and organisations tend to relegate the regions to second-class status, while regional people and organisations in turn cast themselves as separate, peripheral fringe-dwellers – further isolating themselves from the networks and resources they need. These development logics serve to continually fragment the linkages that are needed for effective regional development.

From policy problems to opportunities

> But will Australia's regions ever be sustainable?[4]

The core logic of regional development in Australia is that regions are always disadvantaged, always struggling to achieve sustainability, and constitute a persisting policy problem for the nation. The stories in this book have described how the language and practices of regional development in Australia repeatedly focus on the negative: disappearing towns, declining industries, and disadvantaged regional populations. Yet on-the-ground observation in Australian regions demonstrates that alongside the oft-cited problems, there are abundant and untapped opportunities.

Typical policy approaches to 'regional Australia' render its diversity – and its opportunities – invisible. Specific regional attributes and networks are largely invisible to decision makers based in capital cities. As a result, regional development seen from afar becomes largely the art of grappling with decontextualised problems: propping up failing industries, delivering structural adjustment packages to counter decline, and exhorting local communities to take charge of change – while withholding many of the resources they need to do so.

This book has suggested a different approach to regional development in Australia: one that requires closer attention to what communities and organisations in Australia's regions know and do, what they see and understand, and what they experience on the ground in real, diverse regions. To date, much of this grounded knowledge has simply flown under the policy radar. Local firms and community groups simply 'get on with it', mobilising their local institutions and resources as best they can. Too often, they find themselves working in isolation, unable to access the information they need or influence the policy decisions that directly affect their work and their lives. They see themselves – and are seen – as peripheral. Much of what they do is invisible, unrecognised beyond their region.

Chapter 1 highlighted the incredible energy of local leaders and entrepreneurs as they mobilised local assets and sought solutions to complex sustainability problems in small towns, working on a shoestring. Though starved of external resources, networks, or influence in the nation's centres, these regional towns illustrated the real dynamism that is present on the ground in Australia's regions. Community groups and individual entrepreneurs were capable and willing to mobilise local attributes and local knowledge creatively to drive change. The tragic part of the story was that despite all this effort, many good ideas were never implemented. The necessary resources and support were out of reach.

Chapter 2 demonstrated that across regional Australia, the nation's 'old' resource-based industries are developing diverse new faces. Despite prevailing narratives of regional industry decline, the story on the ground is much more diverse and encouraging. Australia's future competitive advantages lie in its combination of rich natural resources and the ability to add value to these in new and clever ways. Regional firms can leverage these opportunities in ways that are grounded in the relationships among community, economy, and environment. Yet for success on a global stage, regional firms need to develop stronger relationships with Australia's capital-city-based resources and knowledge hubs – relationships that respect regional firms and their work.

Chapter 3 described the roles that regional university campuses play as key knowledge institutions in Australian regions. Regional campuses serve multiple policy agendas around educational participation, service equity, and regional development. They also face multiple expectations from both the university system and the regions where they work. Ultimately, in the Australian university system, regional campuses are peripheral actors with limited influence. Yet these peripheral campuses are regularly innovating new ways to mobilise knowledge – including non-academic knowledge – in ways that are directly relevant to diverse communities and industries on the ground.

Chapter 4 explored the diversity of regional communities and their institutions, unpacking the tensions between local and central ways of working. Once again, this chapter highlighted the existence of invisible and often untapped resources in Australia's regions. In particular, it drew attention to the on-the-ground knowledge of diverse communities, which often goes unrecognised. This chapter highlighted the need to overcome the 'institutional gap' between local and central institutions, in order to create more regional ways of working capable of connecting diverse local knowledges into decision-making processes.

These chapters confirm that Australia's regions have rich attributes and the capacity to drive positive change from within. Nevertheless, in region after region, in story after story, local people and organisations struggle to convert their on-the-ground resources, knowledge, and energy into positive change. In the end, Australian policy-making leaves grounded regional actors on the periphery of significant decision-making, rendering their knowledge and institutions invisible. Meanwhile, urban centres are portrayed as powerful yet conceptually placeless: top-down administrators rather than dynamic, knowledge-filled regions in their own right.

In the end, Australia's regional development issues can only be addressed by re-imagining what it means to be 'regional' – and re-thinking how Australian regional development policy is designed and implemented. There are some specific ways policy makers can respond.

First, it is necessary to re-think the artificial separation between capital cities and regions. There is a need to intentionally reconnect regions with capital cities, and small towns with their regional centres, strengthening networks and opportunities for knowledge flows. These connections are vital, but they have been actively frayed over time. Reconnecting regions and cities requires challenging the engrained logic of peripherality. Organisations based in the regions must cease to see themselves as peripheral, and those in the capitals must see them differently. They must become equal partners. In the end, Australia's regions are not peripheral, they are central to the national economy and way of life – and metropolitan areas are regions too.

Next, effective regional development approaches need to recognise that local knowledges and institutions are vital regional development resources. What local people know and how local people work have been repeatedly ignored – even actively suppressed – by highly centralised policy processes and institutions. Yet on the ground, local knowledge and local institutions have the potential to 'connect the dots' across entrenched policy silos to create more effective regional governance.[5] Furthermore, the multiple knowledges of Australia's socially and culturally diverse communities can offer new perspectives on old problems – and ultimately, new solutions. Regional universities have a particularly important role to play as regional knowledge institutions capable of bringing academic and non-academic knowledge together to catalyse innovation.

Finally, and following from the previous points, effective regional development policy must devolve real decision-making power to localities and regions. Endogenous development cannot be implemented from afar; regional actors themselves must have the resources and influence they need to put their ideas into practice. Dependence on decision makers far away stifles innovation and encourages a culture of seeking handouts rather than generating solutions. Decentralising decision-making and strengthening resource flows to local and regional levels would enable more effective regional development in Australia.

In Australia's regions, people and organisations are capable of driving change, yet often disconnected from the resources, networks, and influence they need to succeed. In region after region, in story after story, well-intentioned regional development efforts fail. Most are implemented from the top down. Many are poorly resourced. Nevertheless, it is perhaps in regional Australia that the potential of place-based development approaches has been most clearly articulated, and where their real potential can be observed.

The stories in the book suggest that people who live and work in regional Australia are adept at seeing connections and opportunities. Far from centres of power, diverse communities and organisations across diverse regions are grappling with complex sustainability issues. Despite their frequent isolation, they tackle problems, strategise new approaches, and regularly articulate their dissatisfaction with the institutions that do not allow them the room they need to manoeuvre. Their situation may well resonate with other peripheral regions around the world, in other places where on-the-ground knowledge and decision-making power do not go hand in hand.

Notes

1 Olivier de Sardan 2005, p. 204.
2 Collits 2011, p. 48.
3 European Commission 2006, p. 29.
4 Brett 2011, p. 56.
5 Kinnear and Charters 2014, p. 3 observe the need for regional policy 'to effectively "connect the dots" across a number of different portfolio areas (such as agriculture, water, energy, industry and social outcomes)'.

References

ABARES (2014a) *Australian Forest and Wood Products Statistics, March and June Quarters 2014*. Report (November). Australian Bureau of Agricultural and Resource Economics and Sciences. Canberra, Australian Government Department of Agriculture. Available online at: http://data.daff.gov.au/data/warehouse/9aaf/afwpsd9abfe/afwpsd 9abfe20141111/afwpsOverview20141111_1.0.0.pdf. Viewed 6 July 2015.

ABARES (2014b) *Australian Fisheries and Aquaculture Statistics 2013*. Report (November). Australian Bureau of Agricultural and Resource Economics and Sciences. Canberra: Australian Government Department of Agriculture. Available online at: http://data.daff.gov.au/data/warehouse/9aam/afstad9aamd003/2013/AustFishAquac Stats_2013_v1.2.0.pdf. Viewed 5 July 2015.

ABARES (2014c) *National Agricultural Statistics Review*. Australian Bureau of Agricultural and Resource Economics and Sciences. Canberra: Australian Government Department of Agriculture. Available online at: http://www.ausstats.abs.gov.au/ausstats/ subscriber.nsf/0/3702051BFED35F61CA257CA9000F4D52/$File/7105055003_201 314_nasr.pdf. Viewed 1 June 2015.

ABS (2007) *3218.0 – Regional Population Growth, Australia, 1996 to 2006*. Available online at: http://www.abs.gov.au/AUSSTATS/abs@.nsf/allprimarymainfeatures/3575E D18F54561ADCA25741A000E11D5?opendocument. Viewed 1 June 2015.

ABS (2009a) *4102.0 – Australian Social Trends, March 2009. 'Future Population Growth and Ageing'*. Available online at: http://www.abs.gov.au/AUSSTATS/abs@.nsf/Lookup /4102.0Main+Features10March%202009. Viewed 1 June 2015.

ABS (2009b) *3416.0 – Perspectives on Migrants, 2009. 'Permanent Migration to Australia – An Overview by Eligibility Category'*. Available online at: http://www.abs.gov.au/AUSS TATS/abs@.nsf/Lookup/3416.0Main+Features22009. Viewed 1 June 2015.

ABS (2011) *1270.0.55.003 – Australian Statistical Geography Standard (ASGS): Volume 3 – Non ABS Structures, July 2011*. Available online at: http://www.abs.gov.au/AUSSTATS/abs @.nsf/Previousproducts/FA98FE427F88B97FCA2578D40012D01C. Viewed 1 June 2015.

ABS (2012a) *4102.0 – Australian Social Trends, Dec 2012. 'Australian Farming and Farmers'*. Available online at: http://www.abs.gov.au/AUSSTATS/abs@.nsf/Lookup/41 02.0Main+Features10Dec+2012. Viewed 1 June 2015.

ABS (2012b) *2075.0 – Census of Population and Housing – Counts of Aboriginal and Torres Strait Islander Australians, 2011*. Available online at: http://www.abs.gov.au/ ausstats/abs@.nsf/lookup/2075.0main+features32011. Viewed 1 June 2015.

ABS (2013a) *2011 Census Quickstats – Burnie*. Available online at: http://www.census data.abs.gov.au/census_services/getproduct/census/2011/quickstat/LGA60610?opendo cument&navpos=220. Viewed 1 June 2015.

ABS (2013b) *4102.0 – Australian Social Trends, April 2013. 'Towns of the Mining Boom'.* Available online at: http://www.abs.gov.au/AUSSTATS/abs@.nsf/Lookup/4102.0Main +Features10April+2013. Viewed 1 June 2015.

ABS (2013c) *4102.0 – Australian Social Trends, July 2013. 'Hitting the Books: Characteristics of Higher Education Students'.* Available online at: http://www.abs. gov.au/AUSSTATS/abs@.nsf/Lookup/4102.0Main+Features20July+2013. Viewed 1 June 2015.

ABS (2013d) *1380.0.55.011 – Perspectives on Regional Australia: Non-School Qualifications in Regions, 2011.* Available online at: http://www.abs.gov.au/ausstats/ abs@.nsf/mf/1380.0.55.011. Viewed 1 June 2015.

ABS (2014a) *9503.0.55.001 – Tourism Region Maps and Allocation File, Australia, 2014.* Available online at: http://www.abs.gov.au/ausstats/abs@.nsf/mf/9503.0.55.001. Viewed 1 June 2015.

ABS (2014b) *1270.0.55.003 – Australian Statistical Geography Standard (ASGS): Volume 3 – Non ABS Structures, July 2014.* Available online at: http://www.abs.gov.au/ausstats/abs @.nsf/mf/1270.0.55.003. Viewed 1 June 2015.

ABS (2014c) *3218.0 – Regional Population Growth, Australia, 2012–13. 'Feature Article: Capital Cities: Past, Present and Future'.* Available online at: http://www.abs.gov.au/ ausstats/abs@.nsf/products/AC53A071B4B231A6CA257CAE000ECCE5?OpenDocu ment. Viewed 1 June 2015.

ABS (2014d) *3235.0 – Population by Age and Sex, Regions of Australia, 2013.* Available online at: http://www.abs.gov.au/AUSSTATS/abs@.nsf/mf/3235.0. Viewed 1 June 2015.

ABS (2014e) *3218.0 – Regional Population Growth, Australia, 2012–13.* Available online at: http://www.abs.gov.au/ausstats/abs@.nsf/Products/3218.0~2012–13~Main+Features ~Main+Features?OpenDocument. Viewed 1 June 2015.

ABS (2014f) *7503.0 – Value of Agricultural Commodities Produced, Australia, 2012–13.* Available online at: http://www.abs.gov.au/AUSSTATS/abs@.nsf/allprimarymainfeatur es/42A625A68572853CCA257E5300139593?opendocument. Viewed 1 June 2015.

ABS (2014g) *8155.0 – Australian Industry, 2012–13.* Available online at: http://www.abs. gov.au/AUSSTATS/abs@.nsf/Lookup/8155.0Main+Features12012–13? OpenDocument. Viewed 1 June 2015.

ABS (2014h) *6250.0 – Characteristics of Recent Migrants.* Available online at: http:// www.abs.gov.au/ausstats/abs@.nsf/mf/6250.0. Viewed 26 June 2015.

ABS (2015) *3218.0 – Regional Population Growth, Australia, 2013–14.* Available online at: http://www.abs.gov.au/ausstats/abs@.nsf/mf/3218.0. Viewed 1 June 2015.

Allison, J. and R. Eversole (2008) 'A New Direction for Regional University Campuses: Catalysing Innovation in Place', *Innovation: The European Journal of Social Science Research* 21(2): 95–109.

Allison, J., D. Broun and J. Lacey (2013) *The Rise of New Manufacturing: Implications of Game Changing Approaches for Productivity, Skills and Education and Training.* Report prepared for the Department of Regional Australia, Local Government, Arts and Sport. Burnie, Tasmania and Clayton, Victoria: University of Tasmania and CSIRO.

Alston, M. (1995) *Women on the Land: The Hidden Heart of Australia.* Sydney: UNSW Press.

Alston, M. (1996) 'Regional Development and Quality of Life', *Regional Policy and Practice* 5(2): 2–6.

Alston, M. (2002) 'Inland Rural Towns: Are They Sustainable?'. Paper presented at the Academy of the Social Sciences Session on Rural Communities, Outlook 2002 Conference, Canberra, 5–7 March.

Altman, J. (2008) 'Different Governance for Difference: The Bawinanga Aboriginal Corporation', in *Contested Governance: Culture, Power and Institutions in Indigenous Australia,* eds J. Hunt, D. Smith, S. Garling and W. Sanders, pp. 177–204. CAEPR Monograph No. 29. Canberra: Centre for Aboriginal Economic Policy Research.

AMES (2011) *Regional Settlement: An Analysis of Four Settlement Locations in Victoria.* Report (May). Melbourne: AMES Research and Policy Unit.

Amnesty International (2015) *A Brighter Tomorrow: Keeping Indigenous Kids in the Community and Out of Detention in Australia.* Report. Broadway, New South Wales: Amnesty International Australia.

Argent, N. and F. Rolley (2000) 'Lopping the Branches: Bank Branch Closure and Rural Australian Communities', in *Land of Discontent, The Dynamics of Change in Rural and Regional Australia,* eds B. Pritchard and P. McManus, pp. 140–168. Sydney: UNSW Press.

Argent, N., P. Smailes and T. Griffin (2007) 'The Amenity Complex: Towards a Framework for Analysing and Predicting the Emergence of a Multifunctional Countryside in Australia', *Geographical Research* 45: 217–232.

Argent, N., M. Tonts, R. Jones and J. Holmes (2010) 'Amenity-Led Migration in Rural Australia: A New Driver of Local Demographic and Environmental Change?', in *Demographic Change in Australia's Rural Landscapes: Implications for Society and the Environment,* eds G.W. Luck, D. Race and R. Black, pp. 23–44. Heidelberg: Springer.

Ausindustry (2013) *Australian Innovation System Report 2013, Industry Subsector Overview.* Canberra: Australian Government Department of Industry.

Baguley, M. (2009) 'Two Roads Diverged in a Wood and I – I Took the One Less Travelled By, and That Has Made All the Difference: An Early Career Researcher's Narrative Journey'. Paper presented at the Australian Association for Research in Education (AARE) Conference, Canberra.

Barr, N. (2009) *The House on the Hill: The Transformation of Australia's Farming Communities.* Canberra: Land and Water Australia, in association with Halstead Press.

Barr, N. (2014) *New Entrants to Australian Agricultural Industries – Where Are the Young Farmers?* Report. RIRDC Publication No. 14/003. Barton, ACT: Rural Industries Research and Development Corporation.

Barraket, J., R. Eversole, B. Luke and S. Barth (2015) 'Bricolage and its Effects on Innovation Amongst Locally-oriented Social Enterprises', *Entrepreneurship and Regional Development,* under review.

Bauman, T., D. Smith, R. Quiggin, C. Keller and L. Drieberg (2015) *Building Aboriginal and Torres Strait Islander Governance: Report of a Survey and Forum to Map Current and Future Research and Practical Resource Needs.* Report (May). Canberra: Australian Institute of Aboriginal and Torres Strait Islander Studies (AIATSIS).

Baxter, J., M. Gray and A. Hayes (2011) *Families in Rural, Regional and Remote Australia.* Report. Melbourne: Australian Institute of Family Studies (AIFS).

Beer, A. (1999) 'Regional Economic Arrangements in Australia', in *Sustainable Regional Development Final Report,* eds J. Dore and J. Woodhill, pp. 187–200. Canberra: Greening Australia.

Beer, A. (2000) 'Regional Policy and Development in Australia: Running Out of Solutions' in *Land of Discontent, The Dynamics of Change in Rural and Regional Australia,* eds B. Pritchard and P. McManus, pp. 167–194. Sydney: UNSW Press.

Beer, A. (2015) 'Structural Adjustment Programmes and Regional Development in Australia', *Local Economy* 30(1): 21–40.

Beer, A. and A. Maude (2005) 'Governance and the Performance of Regional Development Agencies in Australia', in *Participation and Governance in Regional Development,*

Global Trends in Australian Context, eds R. Eversole and J. Martin, pp. 61–78. Aldershot: Ashgate.

Beer, A., A. Maude and B. Pritchard (2003) *Developing Australia's Regions, Theory and Practice*. Sydney: UNSW Press.

Beer, A., T. Clower, G. Haughtow and A. Maude (2005) 'Neoliberalism and the Institutions for Regional Development in Australia', *Geographical Research* 43: 49–58.

BHERT (nd) 'The Role of Universities in the Regions'. Discussion Paper prepared for the Business Higher Education Round Table. Available online at: http://www.bhert.com/discussion-papers.html. Viewed 5 July 2015.

Birrell, B. (2001) 'Population Movement and Social Well-being in Gippsland', in *All Change! Gippsland Perspectives on Regional Australia in Transition*, eds J. Dibden, M. Fletcher and C. Cocklin, pp. 27–39. Monash Regional Australia Project Occasional Papers. Melbourne: Monash University.

Boese, M. (2013) 'At the Meatworks and Beyond, Southern Sudanese Employment Experiences in Regional Australia', in *South Sudanese Diaspora in Australia and New Zealand: Reconciling the Past with the Present*, eds J. Marlowe, A. Harris and T. Lyons, pp. 144–156. Newcastle-upon-Tyne: Cambridge Scholars Publishing.

Bohnet, I. C. and N. Moore (2010) 'Sea- and Tree-Change Phenomena in Far North Queensland, Australia: Impacts of Land Use Change and Mitigation Potential', in *Demographic Change in Australia's Rural Landscapes: Implications for Society and the Environment*, eds. G.W. Luck, D. Race and R. Black, pp. 45–70. Heidelberg: Springer.

Bonney, L., A. Castles, R. Eversole, M. Miles and M. Woods (2015) 'Accounting for Agriculture in Place-Based Frameworks for Regional Development: A Value Assessment and Development Framework, and Toolbox for Building Constructed Advantage in Agriculture Based Regions'. RIRDC Publication No 15/002 (April). Barton, ACT: Rural Industries Research and Development Corporation.

Bowman, M. (1981) 'Introduction', in *Beyond the City: Case Studies in Community Structure and Development*, ed. M. Bowman, pp. ix–xxvii. Melbourne: Longman Cheshire.

Braddon Business Centre (2012) *BRAD 2012 Annual Survey: North Western Tasmanian Businesses*. Report (December). Burnie, Tasmania: Braddon Business Centre.

Bradley, D. (2008) *Review of Australian Higher Education*. Final report (December). Canberra: Commonwealth of Australia.

Brett, J. (2011) *Fair Share: Country and City in Australia*. Quarterly Essay No. 42. Collingwood, Victoria: Black Inc.

Brown, A. J. (2005) 'Regional Governance and Regionalism in Australia', in *Participation and Governance in Regional Development, Global Trends in Australian Context*, eds R. Eversole and J. Martin, pp. 17–42. Aldershot: Ashgate.

Budge, T. (2006) 'Sponge Cities and Small Towns: A New Economic Partnership', in *The Changing Nature of Australia's Country Towns*, eds M. Rogers and D.R. Jones, pp. 38–52. Ballarat, Victoria: VURRN Press.

Budge, T., G. Hugo, J. D'Rozario & Associates (1992) *Housing and Services in Rural and Remote Australia*. Report. The National Housing Strategy, Social Justice Research Program into Locational Disadvantage (Australia). Canberra: Commonwealth of Australia.

Burnley, I. and P. Murphy (2004) *Sea Change, Movement from Metropolitan to Arcadian Australia*. Sydney: UNSW Press.

Butt, A. (2011) 'The Country Town and the City Network: The Expanding Commuter Field of Melbourne', in *The Sustainability of Australia's Country Towns: Renewal,*

Renaissance, Resilience, eds J. Martin and T. Budge, pp. 59–80. Ballarat, Victoria: VURRN Press.

Cameron, J. and K. Gibson (2001) 'Regional Communities Reinvent Economy', in *All Change! Gippsland Perspectives on Regional Australia in Transition*, eds J. Dibden, M. Fletcher and C. Cocklin, pp. 133–144. Monash Regional Australia Project Occasional Papers. Melbourne: Monash University.

Castles, A. (2014) *A New Identity for the Peri Urban*. PhD Thesis, Institute for Regional Development (IRD), University of Tasmania.

Charles, D. (2006) 'Universities as Key Knowledge Infrastructures in Regional Innovation Systems', *Innovation: The European Journal of Social Science Research* 19(1): 117–130.

Cheshire, L. (2006) *Governing Rural Development: Discourses and Practices of Self-Help in Australian Rural Policy*. Aldershot: Ashgate.

COAG (2008) *Closing the Gap in Indigenous Disadvantage*. National Indigenous Reform Agreement (Intergovernmental Agreement). Council of Australian Governments. Available online at: http://www.federalfinancialrelations.gov.au/content/national_agree ments.aspx. Viewed 1 July 2015.

Coates, L. (2014) *Can Contemporary Regional Development Identify a Future for Islands? King Island: A Case Study*. PhD Thesis, Institute for Regional Development (IRD), University of Tasmania.

Cocklin, C. and M. Alston (2003) (eds) *Community Sustainability in Rural Australia: A Question of Capital?* Wagga Wagga, New South Wales: Charles Sturt University, Centre for Rural Social Research.

Collits, P. (2011) 'Country Towns in a Big Australia: The Decentralisation Debate Revisited', in *The Sustainability of Australia's Country Towns: Renewal, Renaissance, Resilience*, eds J. Martin and T. Budge, pp. 23–58. Ballarat, Victoria: VURRN Press.

Collits, P. (2015) 'Regional Policy in Post-War Australia: Much Ado About Nothing?', in *Rural and Regional Futures*, eds A. Hogan and M. Young, pp. 19–37. New York: Routledge.

Collits, P. and B. Gastin (1997) 'Big Town, Small Town: The Centralisation of Services and Economic Activity, the Decline of Small Towns and the Policy Response in New South Wales', *Regional Policy and Practice* 6(2): 9–21.

Collits, P. and J. Rowe (2015) 'Reimagining the Region', *Local Economy* 30(1): 78–97.

Commonwealth of Australia (1997) *Bringing them Home, Report of the National Inquiry into the Separation of Aboriginal and Torres Strait Islander Children from Their Families*. Commonwealth of Australia. Available online at: https://www.humanrights. gov.au/sites/default/files/content/pdf/social_justice/bringing_them_home_report.pdf. Viewed 1 July 2015.

Commonwealth of Australia (2010) *Economic, Civic and Social Contributions of Refugees and Humanitarian Entrants – A Literature Review. Prepared by the Refugee Council of Australia for the Department of Immigration and Citizenship*. Report (February). Barton, ACT: Commonwealth of Australia.

Commonwealth of Australia (2012) *Smarter Manufacturing for a Smarter Australia, Prime Minister's Manufacturing Taskforce, Report of the Non-Government Members*. Report (August). Canberra: Commonwealth of Australia.

Commonwealth of Australia (2014a) *Progress in Australia's Regions Yearbook 2014*. Canberra: Department of Infrastructure and Regional Development.

Commonwealth of Australia (2014b) *Manufacturing Workforce Study*. Report (April). Australian Workforce and Productivity Agency. Canberra: Commonwealth of Australia.

Cooke, P. (2007) 'To Construct Regional Advantage from Innovation Systems First Build Policy Platforms', *European Planning Studies* 15: 124–146.

Correa-Velez, I. and G. Onsando (2013) 'Longitudinal Evidence on Educational and Occupational Outcomes amongst South Sudanese Men from Refugee Backgrounds Living in Urban and Regional Southeast Queensland', in *South Sudanese Diaspora in Australia and New Zealand Reconciling the Past with the* Present, eds J. Marlowe, A. Harris and T. Lyons, pp. 129–143. Newcastle-upon-Tyne: Cambridge Scholars Publishing.

Craig, A. and F. Vanclay (2005) 'Questioning the Potential of Deliberativeness to Achieve "Acceptable" Natural Resource Management Decisions', in *Participation and Governance in Regional Development, Global Trends in Australian Context*, eds R. Eversole and J. Martin, pp. 155–172. Aldershot: Ashgate.

CSU (2009) *Inquiry into Rural and Regional Access to Secondary and Tertiary Education Opportunities, Submission by Charles Sturt University*. August. Bathurst, New South Wales: Charles Sturt University.

DAFF (2010) *Submission to Productivity Commission inquiry into the Australian Government Rural Research and Development Corporations Model*. (August). Canberra: Australian Government Department of Agriculture, Fisheries and Forestry.

Daley, J. and A. Lancy (2011) *Investing in Regions: Making a Difference*. Melbourne: The Grattan Institute.

Dalziel, P., C. Saunders and W. Kaye-Blake (2009) 'The Role of Universities in Theories of Regional Development', in *Theories of Local Economic Development*, ed. J. Rowe, pp. 193–212. Farnham: Ashgate.

DEEWR (2010) *Regional Participation: The Role of Socioeconomic Status and Access*. Canberra: Australian Government Department of Education, Employment and Workplace Relations.

Deloitte Access Economics (2011) *The Connected Continent – How the Internet is Changing the Australian Economy*. Report (August) Sydney: Deloitte Access Economics.

Deloitte Access Economics (2014) *Positioning for prosperity? Catching the Next Wave*. Available online at: http://www.deloitte.com/view/en_AU/au/news-research/lucky country/index.htm. Viewed 1 June 2015.

Dibden, J. (2001) 'Regional Australia in Transition', in *All Change! Gippsland Perspectives on Regional Australia in Transition*, eds J. Dibden, M. Fletcher and C. Cocklin, pp. 1–17. Monash Regional Australia Project Occasional Papers. Melbourne: Monash University.

Dibden, J. and L. Cheshire (2005) 'Community Development', in *Sustainability and Change in Rural Australia*, eds C. Cocklin and J. Dibden, pp. 212–229. Sydney: UNSW Press.

Dibden, J. and C. Cocklin (2005) 'Introduction', in *Sustainability and Change in Rural Australia*, eds C. Cocklin and J. Dibden, pp. 1–18. Sydney: UNSW Press.

Dibden, J., M. Fletcher and C. Cocklin (eds) (2001) *All Change! Gippsland Perspectives on Regional Australia in Transition*. Monash Regional Australia Project Occasional Papers. Melbourne: Monash University.

DIUS (2008) *A New 'University Challenge': Unlocking Britain's Talent*. London: Department of Innovation, Universities and Skills.

Dodgson, M. and J. Steen (2010) 'New Innovation Models and Australia's Old Economy', in *Creating Wealth from Knowledge: Meeting the Innovation Challenge*, eds J. R. Bessant and T. Venables, pp. 105–124. Cheltenham: Edward Elgar.

Drucker, J. and H. Goldstein (2007) 'Assessing the Regional Economic Development Impacts of Universities: A Review of Current Approaches', *International Regional Science Review* 30(1): 20–46.

EBC, RMCG, Marsden Jacob Associates, EconSearch, G. McLeod, T. Cummins, G. Roth and D. Cornish (2011) *Community Impacts of the Guide to the Proposed Murray–Darling Basin Plan. Volume 3: Community Impacts*. Report to the Murray–Darling Basin Authority (May). Canberra: Commonwealth of Australia.

The Economist (2000) 'Something Old, Something New: A High Tech Economy is a Matter of Definition'. Special report Australia. Available online at: http://www.econo mist.com/node/359651. Viewed 5 July 2015.

Enterprise Connect (2013) *Mapping the Connections: Engineering and the Engineering Services Sector, North West Tasmania*. Report by Enterprise Connect Innovative Regions Centre in association with the University of Tasmania Cradle Coast (March). Burnie, Tasmania: Enterprise Connect.

European Commission (2006) *Constructing Regional Advantage – Principles, Perspectives, Policies*. Report. Brussels: European Commission.

Eversole, R. (2000) *Warren–Blackwood CoFHE Project, Training Needs Survey Final Report*. Report (September/October). Bunbury, Western Australia: Edith Cowan University.

Eversole, R. (2001) 'Keeping Youth in Communities: Education and Out-Migration in the South West', *Rural Society* 11(2): 85–98.

Eversole, R. (2003) 'Value Adding Community? Community Economic Development in Theory and Practice', *Rural Society* 13(1): 72–86.

Eversole, R. (2005) 'The Competitive Advantage of Towns: Transaction Costs and Innovation in a Rural Service Town'. In 2nd National Conference on the Future of Australia's Country Towns Refereed Papers, Centre for Sustainable Regional Communities, La Trobe University, Bendigo, Victoria.

Eversole, R. (2007) 'Ouyen', in *Towns in Time 2001 Analysis: Population Change in Victoria's Towns and Rural Areas, 1981–2001, Incorporating the Study of Small Towns in Victoria Revisited*, pp. 121–136. Melbourne: Victorian Government Department of Sustainability and Environment.

Eversole, R. (2011) 'Community Agency and Community Engagement: Re-theorising Participation in Governance', *Journal of Public Policy* 31(1): 51–71.

Eversole, R. (2013) *Jobs4Life Evaluation Report*. In Partnership with Whitelion, JLD Restorative Practices, and Tasmanian Department of Economic Development, Tourism, and the Arts (DEDTA). Report (October). Burnie, Tasmania: Institute for Regional Development (IRD), University of Tasmania.

Eversole, R. (2015) *Knowledge Partnering for Community Development*. New York: Routledge.

Eversole, R. and T. McCall (2014) 'Constructing Advantage in the Cradle Coast Region, Tasmania: Knowledge Partnering as a Regional Development Platform Approach', *Regional Science Policy and Practice* 6(3): 251–264.

Eversole, R. and J. Martin (2005) *Participation and Governance in Regional Development*, Aldershot: Ashgate.

Eversole, R. and J. Martin (2006) 'Jobs in the Bush: Global Industries and Inclusive Rural Development', *Social Policy and Administration* 40(6): 692–704.

Eversole, R. and K. Scholfield (2006) 'Governance in the Gaps: Inter-Agency Action in a Rural Town', *Rural Society* Special Edition on Governance 16(3): 320–328.

Eversole, R., L. Ridgeway and D. Mercer (2005) 'Indigenous Anti-Poverty Strategies in an Australian Town', in *Indigenous Peoples and Poverty in International Perspective*, eds R. Eversole, J.A. McNeish and A. Cimadamore, pp. 260–273. CROP International Studies in Poverty Research. London: Zed Books.

Eversole, R., J. Barraket and B. Luke (2014) 'Social Enterprises in Rural Community Development' in *Community Development Journal* 49(2): 245–261.

Eversole, R., L. Coates and D. Wells (2015) 'Rural Development from the Ground Up: Agro-food Initiatives in Tasmania', *Development in Practice* 25(5): 703–714.

Eyles, K., A. Wild and R. Eversole (2014a) *Retirement Living in Tasmania: Expanding Choices, Informing Decisions*. Report (May). Burnie, Tasmania: Institute for Regional Development (IRD), University of Tasmania.

Eyles, K., R. Eversole and D. Broun (2014b) *West Coast: Place Based Workforce Planning Project*. Report commissioned by the Department of Education Employment and Workplace Relations and the Cradle Coast Authority. Burnie, Tasmania: Institute for Regional Development (IRD), University of Tasmania.

Faulkner, C., C. Robinson and H. Sparrow (2013) *Review of Regional Development Australia Committee 2010–11 Regional Plans: Issues Identified by Regions*. ABS Catalogue No. 1381.0. Belconnen, ACT: Commonwealth of Australia.

Feist, H., G. Tan, K. McDougall and G. Hugo (2014) *Enabling Rural Migrant Settlement: A Case Study of the Limestone Coast*. Report (September). Adelaide: Australian Population and Migration Research Centre (APMRC), University of Adelaide.

Fletcher, M. (2001) 'Reading a Postwar Industrial Landscape', in *All Change! Gippsland Perspectives on Regional Australia in Transition*, eds J. Dibden, M. Fletcher and C. Cocklin, pp. 19–23. Monash Regional Australia Project Occasional Papers. Melbourne: Monash University.

Forth, G. (2000) 'Shooting the Messenger: The Future of Australia's Declining Country Towns', *Regional Policy and Practice* 9(2): 3–10.

Forth, G. and K. Howell (2002) 'Don't Cry for Me Upper Wombat: The Realities of Regional/Small Town Decline in Non Coastal Australia', *Sustaining Regions* 2(2): 4–11.

Foster, M. (2014) *Emerging Animal and Plant Industries: Their Value to Australia*. RIRDC Publication No 14/069 (September). Barton, ACT: Rural Industries Research and Development Corporation.

Fredericks, B. L. (2013) '"We don't leave our identities at the city limits": Aboriginal and Torres Strait Islander People Living in Urban Localities', *Australian Aboriginal Studies* 1: 4–16.

Fredericks, B. L. (2014) '"There is nothing that identifies me to that place": Indigenous Women's Perceptions of Health Spaces and Places', in *History, Power, Text: Cultural Studies and Indigenous Studies*, eds T. Neale, C. McKinnon and E. Vincent, pp. 291–309. Sydney: UTS E-Press, University of Technology Sydney.

Garlick, S. (1999) 'The Australian History of Government Intervention in Regional Development', in *Sustainable Regional Development Final Report*, eds J. Dore and J. Woodhill, pp. 177–186. Canberra: Greening Australia.

Garlick, S. (2000) *Engaging Universities and Regions: Knowledge Contribution to Regional Economic Development in Australia*. Report: Evaluations and Investigations Programme (00/15). Canberra: Department of Education, Training and Youth Affairs, Commonwealth of Australia.

Garlick, S. and G. Pryor (2002) *Universities and Their Communities: Creating Regional Development Through Knowledge-based Engagement*. Report (August). Canberra: Department of Transport and Regional Services.

Gerritsen, R. (2000) 'The Management of Government and its Consequences for Service Delivery in Regional Australia', in *Land of Discontent, The Dynamics of Change in Rural and Regional Australia*, eds B. Pritchard and P. McManus, pp. 123–139. Sydney: UNSW Press.

Goddard, J. and L. Kempton (2011) *Connecting Universities to Regional Growth: A Practical Guide*. Report (September), prepared for European Union, Regional Policy. Brussels: European Commission.

Goddard, J., and P. Vallance (2013) *The University and the City*. New York: Routledge.

Gooding, A. (2012) *A Comparative Analysis of Regional Organisations of Councils in NSW and Western Australia*. Report (January). Broadway, New South Wales: Australian Centre of Excellence for Local Government.

Government of Western Australia (2013) *Living in the Regions 2013*. Report (December). West Perth: Western Australian Department of Regional Development.

Gralton, A. and F. Vanclay (2006) 'Quality Food Production, Diversity and Sustainability: Opportunities for Small Towns', in *The Changing Nature of Australia's Country Towns*, eds M. Rogers and D. R. Jones, pp. 126–138. Ballarat, Victoria: VURRN Press.

Grant, J. and A. Rainnie (2005) 'The Hidden Role of Gender Exclusion in Regional Development Agencies', in *Participation and Governance in Regional Development, Global Trends in Australian Context*, eds R. Eversole and J. Martin, pp. 211–228. Aldershot: Ashgate.

Gray, I. and G. Lawrence (2001) *A Future for Regional Australia: Escaping Global Misfortune*. Cambridge: Cambridge University Press.

Gray, I. and P. Sinclair (2005) 'Local Leaders in a Global Setting: Dependency and Resistance in Regional New South Wales and Newfoundland', *Sociologia Ruralis* 45(1/2): 37–52.

Gross, C. (2007) 'Community Perspectives of Wind Energy in Australia: The Application of a Justice and Community Fairness Framework to Increase Social Acceptance', *Energy Policy* 35: 2727–2736.

Gross, C. (2015) 'Understanding the Aspirations of People Living in Rural and Regional Australia', in *Rural and Regional Futures*, eds A. Hogan and M. Young, pp. 299–318. New York: Routledge.

Growcom (2012) *Submission on Queensland's Agricultural Strategy*. December. Fortitude Valley, Queensland: Growcom. Available online at: http://www.growcom.com.au/_uploads/Submisson%20on%20Qld%20Ag%20Strategy.PDF. Viewed 5 July 2015.

Gunasekara, C. (2006) 'Leading the Horses to Water: The Dilemmas of Academics and University Managers in Regional Engagement', *Journal of Sociology* 42(2): 145–163.

Hamper, D. (2012) 'Regional Economies and the Place of Tourism', *Geography Bulletin* 44(1): 48–52.

Harcourt, T. (2007) 'Innovation Not a Question of Old or New Economies', *The Age* Business Day, June 1. Available online at: http://www.theage.com.au/news/business/innovation-not-a-question-of-old-or-new-economies/2007/05/31/1180205426789.html. Viewed 5 July 2015.

Harding, S. (2007) 'Pastoral Care Gives Regionals the Edge', *The Australian*, Higher Education Supplement, 24 November.

Hawkins, C. (2011) *'This is the way it is and is gonna be'. The Rural Reality for Young People Living on the West Coast of Tasmania*. Report (June). Wynyard, Tasmania: TigerHawk Consulting.

Hawkins, C.L. (2014) *Young, Female, and Looking to the Future: Exploring the Aspirations of Adolescent Girls in Regional Tasmania*. PhD Thesis. Institute for Regional Development (IRD), University of Tasmania.

Head, B. (2005) 'Participation or Co-Governance? Challenges for Regional Natural Resource Management', in *Participation and Governance in Regional Development,*

Global Trends in Australian Context, eds R. Eversole and J. Martin, pp. 137–154. Aldershot: Ashgate.

Henshall Hansen Associates (1988) *Study of Small Towns in Victoria*. Prepared for Victorian Government Department of Agriculture and Rural Affairs. Fitzroy, Victoria: Henshall Hansen Associates.

Hillman, K. and S. Rothman (2007) *Movement of Non-metropolitan Youth towards the Cities*. Research Report Number 50. Longitudinal Surveys of Australian Youth. Camberwell, Victoria: Australian Council for Educational Research.

Hindmarsh, R. (2010) 'Wind Farms and Community Engagement in Australia: A Critical Analysis for Policy Learning', *East Asian Science, Technology and Society* 4: 541–563.

Hiruy, K. (2014) *Bottom-Up Driven Community Empowerment: The Case of African Communities in Australia*. PhD Thesis. Institute for Regional Development (IRD), University of Tasmania.

Hiruy, K. and R. Eversole (2015) 'NGOs and African Grassroots Community Organisations in Australia', *Third Sector Review* 21(1): 143–159.

Hogan, A. and M. Young (2015) 'The Making of Rural and Regional Australia: An Introduction', in *Rural and Regional Futures*, eds A. Hogan and M. Young, pp. 1–16. New York: Routledge.

Hogan, A., J. Cleary, S. Lockie, M. Young, K. Daniell and M. Hickman (2012) 'Localism and the Socio-Economic Viability of Rural and Regional Australia', in *Scoping a Vision for the Future of Rural and Regional Australia*, Collection of Papers presented at the Sustaining Rural Communities Conference 2012. Canberra: National Institute for Rural and Regional Australia.

HRSCRA (House of Representatives Standing Committee on Regional Australia) (2013) *Cancer of the Bush or Salvation for our Cities?* Canberra: Commonwealth of Australia.

Huggins, R., A. Johnston and C. Stride (2012) 'Knowledge Networks and Universities: Locational and Organisational Aspects of Knowledge Transfer Interactions', *Entrepreneurship & Regional Development* 24(7–8): 475–502.

Hugo, G. (2002) 'Changing Patterns of Population Distribution in Australia', Joint Special Issue, *Journal of Population Research* and *NZ Population Review* (September): 1–21.

Hugo, G. (2008) 'Australia's State-Specific and Regional Migration Scheme: An Assessment of its Impacts in South Australia', *Journal of International Migration and Integration/Revue de Integration et de la migration internationale* 9(2): 125–145.

Hugo, G., H. Feist, and G. Tan (2013) *Population Change in Regional Australia, 2006–11*. Australian Population & Migration Research Centre Policy Brief, Vol. 1 No 3. Adelaide, South Australia: The University of Adelaide. Available online at: http://www.adelaide. edu.au/apmrc/pubs/policy-briefs/APMRC_Policy_Brief_Vol_1_3_2013.pdf. Viewed 1 June 2015.

Hunt, J. (2013) *Engaging with Indigenous Australia – Exploring the Conditions for Effective Relationships with Aboriginal and Torres Strait Islander Communities*. Issues paper no. 5 produced for the Closing the Gap Clearinghouse (October). Canberra: Australian Government. Available online at: http://www.aihw.gov.au/uploadedFiles/ ClosingTheGap/Content/Publications/2013/ctgc-ip5.pdf. Viewed 1 June 2015.

Hunt, J. (2015) 'The Commonwealth's Policies and Aboriginal people in Rural & Regional Australia', in *Rural and Regional Futures*, eds A. Hogan and M. Young, pp. 115–128. New York: Routledge.

IRD (2007) *Knowing our Place: North West Tasmania Regional Profile*. Burnie, Tasmania: Institute for Regional Development, University of Tasmania.

Jericho, G. (2013) 'Australia in Transition: The Truth behind this Latest Economic Buzzword'. *The Guardian*, 16 December. Available online at: http://www.theguardian. com/business/grogonomics/2013/dec/16/australia-transition-truth-behind-buzzword. Viewed 5 July 2015.

Johns, S., N. Crawford, M. Harris, C. L. Hawkins, L. Jarvis and D. McCormack (2014) *'A Turning Point': Impact of Participation in the University Preparation Program (UPP) on Cradle Coast Students*. Report (March). Burnie, Tasmania: The University of Tasmania.

Jordan, K., B. Krivokapic-Skoko and J. Collins (2010) 'Immigration and Multicultural Place-Making in Rural and Regional Australia', in *Demographic Change in Australia's Rural Landscapes: Implications for Society and the Environment*, eds G.W. Luck, D. Race and R. Black, pp. 259–280. Heidelberg: Springer.

Kelly, J. F. and P. Donegan (2014) *Mapping Australia's Economy*. Melbourne: The Grattan Institute.

Kennedy, M. (2011) 'Binding a Sustainable Future: Book Towns, Themed Place-Branding and Rural Renewal: A Case Study of Clunes "Back to Booktown"', in *The Sustainability of Australia's Country Towns: Renewal, Renaissance, Resilience*, eds J. Martin and T. Budge, pp. 207–226. Ballarat, Victoria: VURRN Press.

Kenyon, P. and A. Black (2001) *Small Town Renewal: Overview and Case Studies*. Report (June). RIRDC Publication No 01/043. Barton, ACT: Rural Industries Research and Development Corporation.

Kinnear, S. and K. Charters (2014) 'JESP Special Edition: Research and Policy in Regional Australia', *Journal of Economic and Social Policy* 16(1): 1–3.

KPMG (2013) *Analysis of the Changing Resident Demographic Profile of Australia's Mining Communities*. Report for the Minerals Council of Australia (February).

L&SR (Landscape and Social Research) (2006) *A Review of 'Care' Group Support*. Report. Burnie, Tasmania: Cradle Coast NRM.

Lê, Q., S. Auckland, H. B. Nguyen, S. Murray, G. Long, and D. R. Terry (2015) 'The Socio-Economic and Physical Contributors to Food Insecurity in a Rural Community', *Sage Open* (January–March): 1–21.

Lee, E. (2015) 'Protected Areas, Country and Value: The Nature–Culture Tyranny of the IUCN's Protected Area Guidelines for Indigenous Australians', *Antipode*. DOI: 10.1111/ anti.12180.

LGAT (2011) *The Future of Tasmanian Forests, Socio-economic Implications at the Community Level*. Submission to the Kelty Round Table. Local Government Association of Tasmania, June. Available online at: http://www.lgat.tas.gov.au/webdata/resources/ files/Submission_to_Kelty_Round_Table.pdf. Viewed 5 July 2015.

Lockie, S. (2000) 'Crisis and Conflict: Shifting Discourses of Rural and Regional Australia', in *Land of Discontent, The Dynamics of Change in Rural and Regional Australia*, eds B. Pritchard and P. McManus, pp. 14–32. Sydney: UNSW Press.

Mcdonald-Wilmsen, B., S. M. Gifford, K. Webster, J. Wiseman and S. Casey (2009) 'Resettling Refugees in Rural and Regional Australia: Learning from Recent Policy and Program Initiatives', *Australian Journal of Public Administration* 68(1): 97–111.

McKinsey Global Institute (2013) *Disruptive Technologies: Advances That Will Transform Life, Business, and the Global Economy*. Report (May). Available online at: http://www. mckinsey.com/insights/business_technology/disruptive_technologies, Viewed 5 July 2015.

McManus, P. and B. Pritchard (2000) 'Concluding Thoughts', in *Land of Discontent: The Dynamics of Change in Rural and Regional Australia*, eds B. Pritchard and P. McManus, pp. 218–222. Sydney: UNSW Press.

MAMR (Ministère des Affaires Municipales et des Régions, Québec) (2006). *The Québec Rural Policy: An Approach Supporting Local Dynamism*. Presentation to Investment Priorities for Rural Development, October 19–20, Edinburgh, Scotland. Available online at: http://www.oecd.org/rural/krasnoyarsk/37620078.pdf. Viewed 5 July 2015.

Martin, J. (2007) 'The Study of Small Towns in Victoria Revisited: Summary of Findings and Conclusions', in *Towns in Time 2001 Analysis: Population Change in Victoria's Towns and Rural Areas, 1981–2001, Incorporating the Study of Small Towns in Victoria Revisited*, pp. 62–70. Melbourne: Victorian Government Department of Sustainability and Environment.

Martin, J., T. Budge and A. Butt (2011) 'Introduction', in *The Sustainability of Australia's Country Towns: Renewal, Renaissance, Resilience*, eds J. Martin and T. Budge, pp. 1–10. Ballarat, Victoria: VURRN Press.

Measham, T. G., F. H. McKenzie, K. Moffat and D. M. Franks (2013) 'An Expanded Role for the Mining Sector in Australian Society?', *Rural Society* 22(2): 184–194.

Miller, E. and L. Buys (2014) '"Not a Local Win": Rural Australian Perceptions of the Sustainable Impacts of Forest Plantations', *Rural Society* 23(2): 161–174.

Mitchell, W. and R. Stimson (2010) *Creating a New Geography of Functional Economic Regions to Analyse Aspects of Labour Market Performance in Australia*, Centre of Full Employment and Equity Working Paper No. 10–09, November. Callaghan, New South Wales: The University of Newcastle.

Moore, S. (2005) 'Regional Delivery of Natural Resource Management in Australia: Is it Democratic and Does it Matter?', in *Participation and Governance in Regional Development, Global Trends in Australian Context*, eds R. Eversole and J. Martin, pp. 121–136. Aldershot: Ashgate.

Moran, M. (2004) 'The Practice of Participatory Planning at Mapoon Aboriginal Settlement: Towards Community Control, Ownership and Autonomy', *Australian Geographical Studies* 42(3): 339–355.

Moreton-Robinson, A. (2005) 'Patriarchal Whiteness, Self-Determination and Indigenous Women: The Invisibility of Structural Privilege and the Visibility of Oppression', in *Unfinished Constitutional Business: Rethinking Indigenous Self-Determination*, ed. B.A. Hocking, pp. 61–73. Canberra: Aboriginal Studies Press.

Morphy, F. (2008) 'Whose Governance, for Whose Good? The Laynhapuy Homelands Association and the Neo-Assimilationist Turn in Indigenous Policy', in *Contested Governance: Culture, Power and Institutions in Indigenous Australia*, eds J. Hunt, D. Smith, S. Garling and W. Sanders, pp. 113–152. CAEPR Monograph No. 29. Canberra: Centre for Aboriginal Economic Policy Research.

MPIGA (Montreal Process Implementation Group for Australia and National Forest Inventory Steering Committee) (2013) *Australia's State of the Forests Report 2013*. Report (December). Canberra: ABARES. Available online at: http://www. agriculture.gov.au/abares/forestsaustralia/Pages/SOFR/sofr-2013.aspx. Viewed 5 July 2015.

Murphy, P. (2006) 'Seachange to Hillchange: A New Equilibrium?', in *The Changing Nature of Australia's Country Towns*, eds M. Rogers and D. R. Jones, pp. 26–37. Ballarat, Victoria: VURRN Press.

The Nationals (2013) 'Our Plan for Regional Australia', Policy Platform 2013 Document. Barton, ACT.

NE/ALGA (2011) *State of the Regions 2011–2012, Beyond the Mining Boom*. Report (19 June). Canberra: National Economics and Australian Local Government Association.

NE/ALGA (2014) *State of the Regions 2014–2015, Regional Development in a Globalised Economy*. Report (15 June). Canberra: National Economics and Australian Local Government Association.

NFF (2012) *NFF Farm Facts: 2012*. Barton, ACT: National Farmers Federation.

NFF (2013) *Blueprint for Australian Agriculture 2013–2020*. Kingston, ACT: National Farmers' Federation.

North, D. (1990) *Institutions, Institutional Change and Economic Performance*. Cambridge: Cambridge University Press.

Norton, A. and I. Cherastidtham (2014) *Mapping Australian Higher Education 2014–15*. Report (October). Melbourne: The Grattan Institute.

OECD(2007a) *Globalisation and Regional Economies: Can OECD Regions Compete in Global Industries?* Paris: Organization for Economic Cooperation and Development.

OECD (2007b) *Higher Education in Regions: Globally Competitive, Locally Engaged*. Paris: Organization for Economic Cooperation and Development.

OECD (2009) *Regions Matter: Economic Recovery, Innovation and Sustainable Growth*. Paris: Organization for Economic Cooperation and Development.

OECD (2012) *Promoting Growth in All Regions*. Paris: Organization for Economic Cooperation and Development.

OECD (2014) *OECD Economic Surveys Australia*. Paris: Organization for Economic Cooperation and Development.

Olivier de Sardan, J. P. (2005) *Anthropology and Development: Understanding Contemporary Social Change*. London: Zed Books.

O'Toole, K. and N. Burdess (2004) 'New Community Governance in Small Rural Towns: The Australian Experience', *Journal of Rural Studies* 20: 433–443.

Oxley, H.G. (1981) 'The Two Towns: A Semi-Industrial Community in the NSW Tablelands', in *Beyond the City: Case Studies in Community Structure and Development*, ed. M. Bowman, pp. 1–22. Melbourne: Longman Cheshire.

Parliament of Victoria (2009) *Inquiry into Geographical Differences in the Rate in which Victorian Students Participate in Higher Education*. Report (July), Education and Training Committee. East Melbourne: Parliament of Victoria.

Perry, M. and J. E. Rowe (2015) 'Fly-in, Fly-out, Drive-in, Drive-out: The Australian Mining Boom and Its Impacts on the Local Economy', *Local Economy* 30(1): 139–148.

Pew Partnership (2003) *University + Community Research Partnerships: A New Approach*. Report. Charlottesville, Virginia: Pew Partnership for Civic Change. Available online at: http://www.compact.org/wp-content/uploads/media/UCRP_report.pdf. Viewed 5 July 2015.

Plowman, I., N. M. Ashkanasy, J. Gardner and M. Letts (2003) *Innovation in Rural Queensland: Why Some Towns Prosper While Others Languish*. Report (December). St Lucia, Queensland: University of Queensland Business School and Queensland Department of Primary Industries.

Pritchard, B. (2000) 'Indigenous Issues in Regional Australia', *Regional Policy and Practice* 9(1): 9–12.

Pritchard, B. and P. McManus (eds) (2000) *Land of Discontent, The Dynamics of Change in Rural and Regional Australia*. Sydney: UNSW Press.

Pritchard, B., N. Argent, S. Baum, L. Bourke, J. Martin, P. McManus, A. Sorensen and J. Walmsley (2012) 'Local – If Possible: How the Spatial Networking of Economic Relations Amongst Farm Enterprises Aids Small Town Survival in Rural Australia', *Regional Studies* 46(4): 539–557.

PWC (2014) *Australia Uncovered: A New Lens for Understanding Our Evolving Economy*. PricewaterhouseCoopers Report (March). Available online at: http://www.

pwc.com.au/consulting/assets/publications/Australia-uncovered-Mar14.pdf. Viewed 5 July 2015.

Race, D., G. W. Luck and R. Black (2010) 'Patterns, Drivers and Implications of Demographic Change in Rural Landscapes', in *Demographic Change in Australia's Rural Landscapes: Implications for Society and the Environment*, eds G. W. Luck, D. Race and R. Black, pp. 1–22. Heidelberg: Springer.

Ragusa, A. T. (2010) 'Seeking Trees or Escaping Traffic? Socio-Cultural Factors and "Tree-Change" Migration in Australia', in *Demographic Change in Australia's Rural Landscapes: Implications for Society and the Environment*, eds G. W. Luck, D. Race and R. Black, pp. 71–100. Heidelberg: Springer.

RAI (2015) *Login or Logout? Online Work in Regional Western Australia*. Report (February). Barton, ACT: Regional Australia Institute.

Refugee Council of Australia (2014) Temporary Protection Visas. Information Sheet. Surry Hills, New South Wales: Refugee Council of Australia. Available online at: http://www.refugeecouncil.org.au/n/mr/1409_TPVs.pdf. Viewed 5 July 2015.

Richardson, S. and T. Friedman (2010) *Australian Regional Higher Education: Student Characteristics and Experiences*. Report (July). Australian Council for Educational Research. Summary available online at: http://research.acer.edu.au/higher_education/22/. Viewed 5 July 2015.

RIRDC (2014) *Annual Report 2013–2014*. Barton, ACT: Rural Industries Research and Development Corporation.

Rogers, M. and J. Barker (2001) 'Community Leadership Programs and the Government: A Partnership for Building Learning Communities', *Regional Policy and Practice* 10(1): 3–8.

Rogers, M. and D. R. Jones (eds) (2006) *The Changing Nature of Australia's Country Towns*. Ballarat, Victoria: VURRN Press.

RUN (2013) *Regional Universities Network (RUN) – Regional Development Policy Position*. 28 June. Lismore, New South Wales: Regional Universities Network. Available online at: http://www.run.edu.au/resources/RUN%20Regional%20Development%20Policy%20Position.pdf. Viewed 5 July 2015.

RUN (2014) *Submission to the Senate Education and Employment Legislation Committee on the Higher Education and Research Reform Amendment Bill*. 22 September. Lismore, New South Wales: Regional Universities Network. Available online at: http://www.run.edu.au/resources/RUN%20HERRA%20submission%20Sept%202014.pdf. Viewed 5 July 2015.

RUN (2015a) 'About Us'. Regional Universities Network Webpage: http://www.run.edu.au/cb_pages/about_us.php. Viewed 5 July 2015.

RUN (2015b) *Submission to the Senate Education and Employment Legislation Committee Inquiry into the Higher Education and Research Reform Bill*. 20 February. Lismore, New South Wales: Regional Universities Network. Available online at: http://www.run.edu.au/resources/Senate%20Ed%20and%20Employ%20Leg%20Committee%20-Feb%202015.pdf. Viewed 5 July 2015.

Saggers, S. (2005) 'Negotiating Definitions of Indigenous Participation in Community Development', in *Participation and Governance in Regional Development, Global Trends in Australian Context*, eds R. Eversole and J. Martin, pp. 195–210. Aldershot: Ashgate.

Sanders, W. (2004) *ATSIC's Achievements and Strengths: Implications for Institutional Reform*. Paper, CAEPR. Canberra: Centre for Aboriginal Economic Policy Research. Available online at: www.anu.edu.au/caepr/. Viewed 5 July 2015.

Schirmer, J. and H. Berry (2014) *People and Place in Australia. The 2013 Regional Wellbeing Survey – Summary Report*. Canberra: University of Canberra.

Scholfield, K. (2005) 'Keeping the Romance Alive – The Four R's of Relationship Building'. Proceedings of the AUCEA conference 2005: Earning and Engaging through Sustainable Partnership. Australian Universities' Community Engagement Alliance.

Scott, J. C. (1995) *Seeing like a State, How Certain Schemes to Improve the Human Condition Have Failed*. New Haven, CT: Yale University Press.

SGS (2014a) 'What's Driving Regional Australia'. *Urbecon*, Volume 1. Available online at http://www.sgsep.com.au/insights/urbecon/whats-driving-regional-australia/. Viewed 13 March 2015

SGS (2014b) 'The Rise of Urban Manufacturing? *Urbecon*, Volume 2. Available online at: http://www.sgsep.com.au/insights/urbecon/the-rise-of-urban-manufacturing/. Viewed 13 March 2015.

Shepley C. (2007) *Regional Settlement in Australia: Research into the Settlement Experience of Humanitarian Entrants in Regional Australia 2006–07*. Canberra: Department of Immigration and Citizenship. Available online at: https://www.dss.gov.au/sites/default/files/documents/12_2013/evaluation-regional-settlement-australia_access.pdf. Viewed 5 July 2015.

Sher, J. P. and K. R. Sher (1994) 'Beyond the Conventional Wisdom: Rural Development as if Australia's Rural People and Communities Really Mattered', *Journal of Research in Rural Education* 10(1): 2–43.

Skills Tasmania (2008) *Industry Skills Analysis: Agriculture (Vegetable Sector)*. Report (June). Hobart, Tasmania: Skills Tasmania.

Smailes, P. J, T. L. C. Griffin and N. M. Argent (2012) 'The Future of Australian Rural Communities: How Powerful are the Forces of Change?', *South Australian Geographical Journal* 111: 18–42.

Smith, B.R. (2003) '"All has been washed away now": Tradition, Change and Indigenous Knowledge in a Queensland Aboriginal Land Claim', in *Negotiating Local Knowledge: Power and Identity in Development*, eds J. Pottier, A. Bicker and P. Sillitoe, pp. 121–154. London: Pluto Press.

Smith, D. and J. Hunt (2008) 'Understanding Indigenous Australian Governance – Research, Theory and Representations', in *Contested Governance: Culture, Power and Institutions in Indigenous Australia*, eds J. Hunt, D. Smith, S. Garling and W. Sanders, pp. 1–26. CAEPR Monograph No. 29. Canberra: Centre for Aboriginal Economic Policy Research.

Smith, E. F. and B. Pritchard (2015) 'Australian Agricultural Policy: The Pursuit of Agricultural Efficiency', in *Rural and Regional Futures*, eds A. Hogan and M. Young, pp. 58–70. New York: Routledge.

Sorensen, T. (2015) 'Regional Development in an Age of Accelerating Complexity and Uncertainty: Towards Survival Strategies for a Sparsely Settled Continent', *Local Economy* 30(1): 41–52.

State Government of Victoria (nd) *Internal Migration in Victoria*. Report: Department of Planning and Community Development. Available online at: http://www.dtpli.vic.gov.au/data-and-research/regional-victoria/internal-migration-in-victoria. Viewed 5 July 2015.

State of Tasmania (2012) *Regional Economic Development Plan: North West Tasmania*. Hobart, Tasmania: Department of Economic Development.

Stilwell, F. (2003) 'Refugees in a Region: Afghans in Young, NSW', *Urban Policy and Research* 21(3): 235–248.

Sweeney Research (2009) *Youth Migration Study Report*. Prepared for the Victorian State Government Department of Planning and Community Development. Reference No. 18129 (April). Albert Park, Victoria: Sweeney Research.

TA (2012) *2020: New Research to Help Australia's Tourism Reach its Potential.* Summary Document. Sydney: Tourism Australia. Available online at: http://www.tourism.australia.com/documents/Statistics/Research_130624_CDP6pagesummary.pdf. Viewed 5 July 2015.

Taylor, A. J., L. Bell and R. Gerritsen (2014) 'Benefits of Skilled Migration Programs for Regional Australia: Perspectives from the Northern Territory', *Journal of Economic and Social Policy* 16(1): Article 3.

Taylor, J. and D. Stanovic (2005) *Refugees and Regional Settlement: Balancing Priorities.* Fitzroy, Victoria: Brotherhood of St Laurence.

Tomaney, J. (2014) 'Region and Place I: Institutions', *Progress in Human Geography* 38(1): 131–140.

Tonts, M. (2000) 'The Restructuring of Australia's Rural Communities', in *Land of Discontent, The Dynamics of Change in Rural and Regional Australia*, eds B. Pritchard and P. McManus, pp. 52–72. Sydney: UNSW Press.

Townsend, R. J. Pascal and M. Delves (2014) 'South East Asian Migrant Experiences in Regional Victoria: Exploring Well-Being', *Journal of Sociology* 50(4): 601–615.

TRA (2011) *The Economic Importance of Tourism in Australia's Regions.* Forrest, ACT: Tourism Research Australia.

TRA (2014) *Tourism Update: Updated Results to 'State of the Industry 2014',* September *Quarter.* Report. Forrest, ACT: Tourism Research Australia.

TRA (2015) *Tourism Businesses in Australia June 2010 to June 2013.* Report (January). Forrest, ACT: Tourism Research Australia.

UA (2009) *Submission to Inquiry into Rural and Regional Access to Educational Opportunities.* 8 October. Deakin, ACT: Universities Australia.

Uyarra, E. (2010) 'Conceptualizing the Regional Roles of Universities, Implications and Contradictions', *European Planning Studies* 18(8): 1227–1246.

Wainer, J. (2001) 'Some Insights into Economic Rationalism, Health and the Bush', in *All Change! Gippsland Perspectives on Regional Australia in Transition*, eds J. Dibden, M. Fletcher and C. Cocklin, pp. 41–50. Monash Regional Australia Project Occasional Papers. Melbourne: Monash University,

Wilkinson, R., N. Barr and C. Hollier (2011) *Segmenting Victoria's Farmers.* Rutherglen, Victoria: Department of Primary Industries.

Winter, A., J. Wiseman and B. Muirhead (2006) 'University–Community Engagement in Australia: Practice, Policy and Public Good', *Education, Citizenship and Social Justice* 1: 211–230.

Woodburn, J. (2015) 'Farmers Warn Murray Darling Basin Plan Needs to End, but Scientists Say Signs of River System Recovery on Display'. ABC News, 8 February. Available online at: http://www.abc.net.au/news/2015-02-08/murray-darling-basin-plan-needs-to-end-farmers-say/6076946. Viewed 5 July 2015.

Woolley, K. and R. Eversole (2013) *Manufacturing Industry Innovation: Future Directions for North West Tasmania.* Report (May). Burnie, Tasmania: Institute for Regional Development (IRD), University of Tasmania.

Index

Note: references to notes are indicated by an 'n' after the page number, and references to tables are in **bold** type.

Taylor & Francis eBooks

Helping you to choose the right eBooks for your Library

Add Routledge titles to your library's digital collection today. Taylor and Francis ebooks contains over 50,000 titles in the Humanities, Social Sciences, Behavioural Sciences, Built Environment and Law.

Choose from a range of subject packages or create your own!

Benefits for you

» Free MARC records
» COUNTER-compliant usage statistics
» Flexible purchase and pricing options
» All titles DRM-free.

REQUEST YOUR FREE INSTITUTIONAL TRIAL TODAY

Free Trials Available
We offer free trials to qualifying academic, corporate and government customers.

Benefits for your user

» Off-site, anytime access via Athens or referring URL
» Print or copy pages or chapters
» Full content search
» Bookmark, highlight and annotate text
» Access to thousands of pages of quality research at the click of a button.

eCollections – Choose from over 30 subject eCollections, including:

Archaeology	Language Learning
Architecture	Law
Asian Studies	Literature
Business & Management	Media & Communication
Classical Studies	Middle East Studies
Construction	Music
Creative & Media Arts	Philosophy
Criminology & Criminal Justice	Planning
Economics	Politics
Education	Psychology & Mental Health
Energy	Religion
Engineering	Security
English Language & Linguistics	Social Work
Environment & Sustainability	Sociology
Geography	Sport
Health Studies	Theatre & Performance
History	Tourism, Hospitality & Events

For more information, pricing enquiries or to order a free trial, please contact your local sales team:
www.tandfebooks.com/page/sales

 **Routledge**
Taylor & Francis Group

The home of
Routledge books

www.tandfebooks.com

For Product Safety Concerns and Information please contact our EU
representative GPSR@taylorandfrancis.com
Taylor & Francis Verlag GmbH, Kaufingerstraße 24, 80331 München, Germany